Picture of the birthplace of Bishop E. R. Hendrix, Fayette, Mo. The Hendrix home, the one with door ajar.

Eugene Russell Hendrix

Servant of the Kingdom

By
BISHOP IVAN LEE HOLT

PARTHENON PRESS
Nashville, Tennessee

Preface

Many years have passed since the death of Bishop Hendrix and for twenty years I have been working on this biography. Since there had to be a subsidy for its publication it was impossible to get the money in the depression of the thirties. Then during the war period it was impossible to secure the paper and to arrange for the printing.

The book is being published after many of the bishop's associates have died, but his great service to the church should be known to those of a later generation. In carrying out this task and labor of love I was aided by the children of Bishop Hendrix resident in Kansas City, Mrs. Mastin Simpson, Mrs. Paul Mohr, and Mr. Nathan Hendrix. While Mr. Hendrix has died since I began to write the biography I visited often in the home of Mr. and Mrs. Nathan Hendrix because for some years after the death of the bishop they lived in his old home. Here was his library and here were his papers, and I could not have undertaken the writing without the valuable help and encouragement of Mr. and Mrs. Hendrix. So often was I with them and their children Peggy, Patty and Eugene that they seem like members of my own family.

To friends who assisted me in reading the proof as well as to members of my own family I am indebted, as well as to my secretary, Mrs. A. G. Vieth, for the typing of the manuscript. The work is being finished as I cross the Atlantic for my thirty-first time, and it seems appropriate that the last words about a world citizen should be written as I go to arrange for the next Methodist World Conference at Oxford in 1951. It is my earnest hope that the bishop's friends may keep company with him as they read these pages and that younger Methodists, preachers and laymen, may find inspiration in the life and achievements of one of the ablest leaders Methodism has ever produced.

Ivan Lee Holt

May 9, 1950

Table of Contents

Chapter I

The Background of a Life

THE GREATEST forces known to the world are clear thought, intense feeling and determined will. They found embodiment in Eugene Russell Hendrix, who was born in the town of Fayette, Missouri, May 17, 1847. The background of his life is the settlement of the West by the heroic pioneers who crossed mountains and plains as they journeyed from their homes on the Atlantic Seaboard. No more inspiring story has ever been written than that of the explorers for whom "something was lost behind the hedges," something which they must find.

The American ancestry of Eugene Russell Hendrix goes back to the last quarter of the seventeenth century. Four brothers, of Huguenot extraction, came to Pennsylvania from Holland between 1683 and 1700, and settled at a spot now within the limits of Germantown. Their names were Wilhelm, Hendrick, Lorenz and Gerhart Hendricks. The names of their descendants are found in the records of Pennsylvania, West Virginia, Virginia, Maryland, North Carolina, Tennessee, Ohio, Minnesota, Indiana, Iowa, and Missouri. A son of one of these brothers laid out the town of York, Pennsylvania; a son of another was tax collector of Cumberland County, Pennsylvania, and his descendants moved to Ohio about 1790, later going west to Indiana; from the Indiana family came Thomas R. Hendricks, Vice-President of the United States under Grover Cleveland. The name of Hendrick Hendricks is found in the records of Pennsylvania and Maryland. He came to Pennsylvania about 1685 and his name appears in one record as Hendrick Hendrickson. He aided in the establishment of community life in the early years of white settlements along the eastern shores of America; only two generations had passed since the first settlers had come from European shores to the new world, and he belongs to the group of pioneers. A hundred years later the movement to the Middle West began, and a descendant of Hendrick Hendricks, be-

7

longing to the second generation in the West, aided largely in the building of Brazil, Indiana. The family is associated with the settlement of the Atlantic Seaboard, and the building of the West. One descendant of Hendrick Hendricks, probably a grandson, was Adam Hendricks, who was born in York County, Pennsylvania, January 26, 1757, and who died November 7, 1836. A son of Adam Hendricks was Joseph M., who was born in York County, Pennsylvania, and died there August 4, 1867. He married Agnes McDaniells and there were born of that marriage five sons and two daughters. One of the five sons was Adam Hendrix (the name is now spelled with an x), who was born in York County, Pennsylvania, August 25, 1813, and died May 31, 1876.

The name of Hendrix is identified with the building of community life in the East, the South, and the Middle West through seven generations; it is found also in the lists of those who fought with Washington for American independence, with Jackson at New Orleans, with Taylor in the Mexican War, with the armies of the North and the South in the War between the States, with the American Expeditionary Forces in World War I. Through the years of sacrifice and devotion there is a keen interest in political affairs, and each generation of the Hendrix family has helped to shape the policies of county, state, and nation. All of the fine traditions of service were brought to Missouri by Adam Hendrix when he came to Fayette with his bride in 1844.

As early as 1837 Adam was contemplating a move to the West. At the time he was teaching school at Middletown, Maryland. Under the date of April 3, 1837, he writes to his mother at the home in Shrewsbury, York County, Pennsylvania, "I expect to leave Middletown this summer sometime and perhaps go to the West. If John has a notion of going to the West perhaps he and I had better go together, as I am determined to get at some other business before long. . . . I will now give you some idea of the reason of my leaving this place. On the 25th ult. I received a notice from the secretary of the Board of Trustees intimating a wish that I should resign, stating no cause whatever for such a course of conduct. This notice I showed to a very respectable patron of mine; he immediately sat down and wrote a letter signed by 10 or 15 of the patrons, asking them why such a communication was sent without assigning some reason. And for the high opinion they entertained for my moral character together with my intellectual qualifications and business habits they deemed it necessary and due to Mr. H . . . to inquire into the cause of such a course of conduct. . . . Now I can lead you into the secret of the conduct of the Trustees. *I will not deal in the store of the Secretary of the Board, and vote the Whig ticket and put on a long face when I go to church.* He is opposed to me . . . and has succeeded in getting a majority against me. . . . The people here are indignant . . . they will call a meeting . . . and moreover, publish the proceedings in the papers. They say I must not leave them, but I think I shall." The reasons given for opposition to him need to be remembered in following the career of Adam's son.

Adam carried out his purpose of going to the West, and his brother John went with him. Adam remained in the West, but John returned to the Pennsylvania home in 1839. A letter written by Adam to John, under date of November 17, 1841, tells something of their experiences together in the West. "I can scarcely realize that you are married; it seems but yesterday since you and I were traversing the prairies of Illinois and Missouri together. In reading your letter in reference to the road leading from Palmyra to Mr. Richmond's, it recalled to my mind the tinkling of the ox's bell very forcibly. . . . The cause of democracy seems to be going on finely; the ball is certainly in motion. . . . I did expect that when we parted in Franklin in May, 1839, we should have seen each other ere this."

At first Adam Hendrix taught school in the Missouri community. Becoming interested in the economic development of the new section he left the school room for the bank. For almost forty years he was the banker of his town and county. Many letters went back to the old home in Pennsylvania and they carried messages like this one dated March 25, 1863: "A letter has come from Fremont (his oldest son) at the Naval Academy. He still stands ahead of his class of 77 members in mathematics. Money is very abundant here now

9

and loans freely at 6 per cent. I take deeds of trust or mortgages generally when I loan. . . . I sold seven slaves the second of February belonging to the estate of Judge Hill. . . . the planters here are making great efforts to plant large crops of tobacco this coming season."

The bride Adam Hendrix brought to Fayette in 1844 was Isabelle Jane Murray, the daughter of John E. Murray, at one time sheriff of Baltimore County in Maryland. Her grandfather had come to the United States from Scotland when he was twelve years old; her mother was of Welsh descent and bore to her husband eleven girls and three boys. Isabelle Jane was born December 18, 1820, and died in Fayette on Easter Sunday, April 11, 1909. She has left an interesting account of her life: "I was born in Hampstead, Maryland, in Baltimore County, now Carroll County. I joined the Methodist Church as a Sabbath School scholar when a small child. I cannot recollect the time when I did not love the Methodist Church. My father's home was the home for all ministers. I never moved my membership but once, from my old home to Fayette, Missouri. When I was 19 years old I made my first trip west (1840), came over the Allegheny Mountains with my friends in a spring wagon. I enjoyed walking up the side of the mountains to get the flowers in bloom, the laurel and wild honeysuckle. . . . I returned in 1842, went to Cincinnati and took boat to Pittsburgh. I did not get quite to Wheeling, West Virginia, as the river was so low the boat got on a sandbar. I had to be taken ashore in a skiff, then to Wheeling in a wagon; from there to Hagerstown in the overland stage. We then took cars to Baltimore; the steam cars were not allowed to run in through the city, and they were taken in by horses with bells on them. In 1844 I was married to Mr. Adam Hendrix and came to Missouri. We came on the cars then to Cumberland, Maryland, and from there took stage to Wheeling, then boat to St. Louis, and then change to Missouri River for Boonville. We crossed the Missouri River in a skiff to reach the Howard County side, and then took stage to Fayette. . . . It took us two weeks for our trip from Baltimore. . . . The Lord has been very

10

good to me in all the years passed, and He will still take care of me if I trust him."

It would be impossible to overrate the influence of Adam and Isabelle Hendrix in the little college town. Dr. W. A. Webb, President of Central College at the time of the death of Mrs. Hendrix, wrote of that influence: "Adam Hendrix, who brought his bride from Maryland to Howard County in 1844, was a splendid type of the men who laid the foundation of education and religion in the West. Himself a school teacher before he became a banker, he was one of the organizers and early benefactors of Central College, and for many years its treasurer and curator. Mrs. Hendrix retained her grasp upon living issues of the present and though her life encompassed eight of the most marvelous decades of history she was never content with the past but was always planning for the future. Her conversation was a constant surprise to the distinguished visitor from a distance who might pay his respects to her as it was a continual delight to the neighbor who dropped in for a friendly chat."

Of the marriage of Adam Hendrix and Isabelle Jane Murray the following children were born: Fremont Murray, September 13, 1845; Eugene Russell, May 17, 1847; Joseph Clifford, May 25, 1853; Mary Belle, September 2, 1855; Wilbur Fisk, August 31, 1861. Fremont Murray Hendrix became an ensign in the United States navy and was brilliant as a mathematician. He married Mary Himes, of New Oxford, Pennsylvania, and died at the early age of 35 in Fayette, Missouri. His funeral service was conducted by Rev. J. R. A. Vaughan. Between him and his brother, Eugene, there was a very strong attachment, and their feeling for one another is revealed in the correspondence of student days. Fremont attended the United States Naval Academy. A letter written to Eugene, then a student at Wesleyan University, is dated August 13, 1865, on board the United States Ship Winnipec: "Your recent letter was to me a great surprise. I have for a long time thought that you intended to follow the calling of a minister, but was uncertain as to the truth of my conjectures. I had no idea that you would commence so soon, but since you feel it to be your duty I can only bid

you Godspeed and wish for you many souls in your crown of rejoicing. My dear brother, I must ask you to remember me every
time you bow before the throne of prayer. I have felt for a long
time as if I were no longer identified with the people of God, and I
know that I have been very lukewarm in the discharge of my
duties as a member of the church; but my desire as well as my resolve is to become an inheritor of a priceless reward above. The
many deaths of my friends have provoked serious thoughts and
now that I have a loved brother whose life is to be devoted to saving
souls I have resolved tonight to live more closely to my Heavenly
Father, and endeavor by His grace to share Heaven with my
brother. Oh! happy thought of a family united in Heaven. Eugene,
my life is one of more than usual temptation to a young Christian
and you well know that seafaring men are rather Godless than
God-fearing, and it is on this account that I need your prayers for
I believe you to be a truly righteous man and the Bible says that
'the prayer of the righteous availeth much.' I am glad to learn that
you have begun your work of usefulness and reiterate my best
wishes. I would like to spend some weeks with you at grandpa's
but it is impossible, considering that I cannot leave the Academy
until October 15th. I will be very happy to see you in New London.
I shall be here frequently, in fact almost every day, until after the
first of September, and should you determine to visit me, stop at
the 'Metropolitan,' writing a note to Captain Greer, asking for
permission for me to come ashore, telling him at the same time how
long it has been since we met. I shall be most happy to see you."

Joseph Clifford Hendrix died in Brooklyn, New York, November
9, 1904, and is buried in Greenwich, Connecticut. His wife was
Alice Rathbone, of Norwich, Connecticut. At the time of his death
he was one of the leading bankers of the United States, having
served as President of the National Bank of Commerce in New
York, and as President of the American Bankers' Association. During his life of usefulness and public service he was Postmaster of
Brooklyn under appointment of Grover Cleveland, and a member
of Congress from the Brooklyn District. A letter to his mother, written at Christmas time in 1901, reveals both his own soul and the

influence of his Fayette home: "I am so glad that you had such a happy birthday party, and I know that your friends are always very happy to have an occasion to show you their affection and gratitude. All of your life you have been doing little deeds of kindness for Fayette people, and I am sure that you will be long remembered for your goodness. . . . Spring will come soon with you, and then your old love for flowers can have its way. It was always good medicine to you to get your flowers to grow. I have always felt that you marked me with the same love. . . . I always keep the image of my dear father and mother before me, and bless them for what they have done. Your evening of life should be very peaceful in the feeling that your duty has been well done in this world."

Mary Belle Hendrix married Mr. Arthur F. Davis in Fayette, Missouri, June 22, 1875. Mr. Davis became a banker, and succeeded to the leadership in the community his wife's father had so long held.

Wilbur Fisk Hendrix married Mary Stafford of Sedalia, Missouri, and has been a banker of Rye, New York. The Dutch, Scotch and Welsh strains were blended in these five children who came to such positions of honor and influence in the service of community, state and nation.

In the home of his grandfather in Pennsylvania Eugene spent most of his vacations during his college days at Wesleyan. Here he found an atmosphere of religion, with family prayers every day, and a regular attendance at the services of the camp meetings held in that section. The family life was normal and natural; there were opportunities for recreation, and especially for long walks through the country; reading and conversation about great themes were encouraged. The religious life was deep and earnest, but it had little of that fanaticism into which the religion of many of the country folk of that day deteriorated. The grandfather wrote to Eugene as he was beginning his ministry: "Eugene, as you are about to enter upon a high and holy calling may you be blest with the holy spirit, and your heart burn within you, as did those of the apostles when Christ talked with them in the way. May you be the means of converting many from the error of their way and may they be stars in your crown in a better world."

More influential in the life of Eugene Russell Hendrix than New Oxford, Pennsylvania, or even the college town of Fayette, Missouri, is Kansas City. Here he lived for forty years, and here he knew the influence of the wife whom he married as Ann Eliza Scarritt, June 20, 1872. The family of Ann Eliza Scarritt was one of the pioneer families of the Middle West; she was the daughter of Nathan Scarritt and Martha Matilda Chick Scarritt.

The father and mother of Nathan Scarritt came to Scarritt's Prairie, near Godfrey, Illinois, from New Hampshire. There are records of that migration and they testify to the character of Nathan Scarritt, Sr., and Lotty Olds Scarritt. The elder Nathan Scarritt was born October 15, 1788, and died December 12, 1847; his wife, Lotty Olds Scarritt, was born December 6, 1793, and died December 7, 1875. They came to Illinois in 1820, and the schedule of the overland trip follows:

New Hampshire to Albany	200 miles
Albany to Buffalo	300 miles
Along Lake Erie to Cleveland	200 miles
Cleveland to Columbus	150 miles
Columbus to Cincinnati	150 miles
Cincinnati to Vincennes on the Wabash	200 miles
Vincennes to Edwardsville	150 miles

The schedule is in the original handwriting and at the close of it is this comment: "There were thirty miles of bad road west of Buffalo, but most of the way the road is good." From the new home in the West to the old home in New Hampshire went this letter under date of June 30, 1821: "I will first inform you of the goodness of God to us. . . . The prairies are generally rich, dry, beautiful. . . . Our religious privileges are good. We have a small meeting house. We meet twice a week for worship. The gospel is gaining ground in this country. May we live so here as to meet in heaven!" It is not necessary to say that the elder Nathan Scarritt was a deeply religious man; his wife was just as earnest and devout. The children often recalled the fact that he was seen kneeling in prayer in the furrow while the team rested. The family endured all the labors, trials, hardships and privations of pioneer life. They not only endured them without murmur but songs of rejoicing arose every morning and evening from the family altar for all the great blessings which the Father had vouchsafed unto them and which in their humbleness of spirit they felt entirely unworthy to receive. God was to them an ever present help in time of need: "He helpeth those who help themselves" was also a part of their creed. They put their shoulders to the wheel and then called on God to help. They fenced the land, provided a shelter for the stock and built a cheap clapboard house. This house contained two rooms, one downstairs and one upstairs. The downstairs room was parlor, dining room, sitting room and kitchen combined. The upstairs was divided by curtains into sleeping apartments. These two rooms accommodated "decently and in order" a family of eleven persons, the parents and nine children, and there was always room to spare for neighbors and friends, or for the circuit preacher on his rounds, or for the presiding elder when he came to hold the Quarterly Conference. Out of such a home came Nathan Scarritt, Missionary to the Indians, Methodist minister and founder of Methodism in Kansas City, successful businessman and philanthropist. Wherever he went he carried the moral convictions and the religious faith of the home on the Illinois prairie. His wife was Martha Matilda Chick, the daughter of Col. W. M Chick, whose ancestors came to America from Scotland in 1666. In this marriage they were the parents of:

Ann Eliza, born at the Shawnee Mission, May 23, 1851;
Edward Lucky, born in Jackson County, August 30, 1853;
Mary Lotty, born in Westport, January 15, 1856;
Nathan, born in Fayette, August 12, 1858;
William Chick, born in Westport, March 21, 1861;
Juliet Virginia, born in Kansas City, August 7, 1863;
Joseph Olds, born in Jackson County, March 14, 1866;
Charles Wesley, born in Jackson County, July 20, 1869;
Martha Matilda, born in Jackson County, February 17, 1872.

Of these children, Joseph Olds and Juliet Virginia died in early childhood, and Mary Lotty died in her nineteenth year. Martha Matilda married Elliott H. Jones and lives in Kansas City. The sons were among the leading citizens of Kansas City, except Nathan, who died years ago.

Eugene Russell Hendrix married Ann Eliza Scarritt! What traditions meet in that union! Each of the families runs back through the great periods in the nation's life—the development of the Middle West, the settling of the early colonies, and the prompting to leave the shores of Europe and seek homes in the new world! Each of the families carries through generations deep religious and moral convictions. Each of the families is interested in the building up of the entire life in its economic, cultural and religious aspects!

To Eugene Russell Hendrix and Ann Eliza Scarritt Hendrix were born four children:

Evangeline Isabelle, who married George Houston Waring and lives in Grand Rapids, Michigan;
Mary Matilda, who married Mastin Simpson, and lives in Kansas City;
Nathan Scarritt, who married Marguerite Krueger, lived and died in Kansas City;
Helen Chick, who married Paul Miller Mohr, and lives in Kansas City.

The Kansas City home was one of comfort, culture, and Christian considerateness. The wife and children were ever in the mind and heart of Eugene Russell Hendrix. Three letters of Mrs. Hendrix to her husband create the atmosphere of the home, and reveal a source of strength as he carried the heavy responsibilities of his life. Each letter was written at a crisis in her husband's life. The first reached him at Richmond, Virginia, just after his election as bishop, and is dated May 18, 1886: "The telegram bearing the sad tidings of your election to the office of a bishop reached me about an hour ago. How can I give you up, my husband? I hope I appreciate the honor the church has bestowed upon you but what a lonely life my future will be. Helen said with tears in her eyes, 'There are plenty of other men they could have made bishop. I want Papa to come home.' After the children fell asleep I sat down to read, through my tears, the ninety-first Psalm, the comforter of other days. I need it all. Do come home as soon as possible. When will you be ordained? Others may have the sacred privilege of seeing my husband ordained, but none can ever have the love for you that fills this sorrowing heart tonight."

The second letter was written at the time of the death of Mrs. Adam Hendrix, her husband's mother: "I am so disappointed, my precious husband, that I can't be with you in this great sorrow of yours. I had expected to be, but on account of the heavy rain, and extreme dampness, the children will not consent to my going.

"Oh! isn't it beautiful that Grandma could go on Easter Day? Her going is so much like she would like to have it—no long suffering, and in the early dawn, just as our blessed Savior was rising from the tomb. How good God is, and she was so ready to go. . . . You were such a comfort to me when my mother went away, I wish I could be with you. You have so much to comfort you. I love you so."

The third letter was written just before his sixty-seventh birthday and is dated, "Home, May 15, 1914: I have been thinking so much of you this morning, and of the approaching anniversary of your birth, which this year comes on Sunday—at which time I shall be with you in spirit, if not in person.

"O these happy, happy years—42 of them—surely goodness and mercy have followed us. We have lacked no good thing. God has been so loving and forgiving, despite our mistakes. . . . O, I wish I could have done more for Him who has done so much for me.

"O how thankful I am for such a patient, loving Heavenly Father, and that He can be touched with a feeling of our infirmities. May this be the very best Sabbath you have ever had and one of great usefulness, my dear precious husband."

The Bishop is in New York to deliver some very important addresses as President of the Federal Council of the Churches of Christ in America. The eyes of the religious world are on him. What is he doing the morning of his arrival? Let him answer in a letter addressed to his wife: "Now the first thing I did yesterday

17

morning was to buy me a bouquet of sweet peas for my room, such as my invisible wife would enjoy."

In the life of Eugene Russell Hendrix there are many inspiring services, but they seem to be the outgrowth of experiences in the family life of New Oxford, Pennsylvania, Fayette, Missouri, and Kansas City, Missouri. On revisiting Tintern Abbey Wordsworth looked on scenes that had become a part of his life, that had been translated into "nameless, unremembered acts of kindness and of love." What scenes come to view as one examines the influences on the life of Eugene Russell Hendrix!

His father as a country school teacher in Maryland refuses to trade at the store of the Secretary of the Board of Trustees, will not vote the Whig ticket, cannot wear a long face as he goes to church! The urge to go West drives him on to Missouri, and changes him from a teacher to a developer of the economic resources of the new community. He never loses his interest in education, aids in the founding of Central College, and sends his own children to the best schools he can find in the nation. The honesty, the lack of cant, the constructive ability, the thirst for knowledge of that father find a full expression in the life of the son.

His mother has the pioneer spirit, is willing to endure the hardships of the long trip from Maryland to Missouri, enters into the life of the primitive community, shares the fortunes of her neighbors, trusts God to guide her, and prays always for her husband and children. Her courage, her sympathy, her religious convictions, her lack of fear as she faced the future in God's world are reflected in the career of her son.

His wife came from a family of equally courageous pioneers, who were most grateful for the privileges of religion in their new home in the West, whose father carried on the family tradition of interest in the economic, educational and religious improvement of every community he touched. Knowing the privilege of making a home for her family, she surrounded them with an atmosphere of love, and sacrifice, and unselfishness. That atmosphere she kept about her husband when he was absent in distant places, and on important missions, by a series of letters, remarkable for their devotion and consecration to life's more serious responsibilities. Her husband was a lovely guest in any home because he had learned the meaning of a home from a wife who knew, and more than one manifestation of love for others in his human world was a passing on of an influence in his own home. One who knew him from the days of her girlhood was impressed with his love for children and recalled that as his hand rested on the head of any child tears were always in his eyes. "Now the first thing I did yesterday morning was to buy me a bouquet of sweet peas for my room, such as my invisible wife would enjoy."

Inheritance and environment combined in an effective way to influence a life of remarkable service. In one of the most beautiful of the old Hebrew traditions is a story of the love of Joseph for his brethren. The father, Jacob, has died; his beloved son, Joseph, is in a position of power in Egypt; the other sons are afraid that Joseph will punish them for the evil way they have treated him. "And they sent a messenger unto Joseph, saying, Thy father did command before he died, saying,

"So shall ye say unto Joseph, Forgive, I pray thee now the trespass of thy brethren, and their sin; for they did unto thee evil; and now, we pray thee, forgive the trespass of the servants of the God of thy father. And Joseph wept when they spake unto him.

"And his brethren also wept and fell down before his face; and they said, Behold we be thy servants. And Joseph said unto them, Fear not. . . . I will nourish you and your little ones. And he comforted them and spake kindly unto them."

Whatever may be the explanation of the brothers' attitude, Joseph passed on to his brethren a love that he had received of his father. So marvelously are human beings the carriers of intangible values. A gift, whether of inheritance or environment, is passed on to others, and the test of any man's greatness is his ability to hand down the gift untarnished. Fortunate is the world if his hands have given it a polish it did not have.

Chapter II

The Student

THE HISTORY of the United States can be written in the story of its colleges. When the first colonists erected their homes and meeting houses they planned their schools. When the settlers of the Middle West cleared their land they began to think of the education of their children. The commercial empire of the Far West has created great universities. Throughout New England are colleges which can trace their ancestry through many generations. Wesleyan University at Middletown, Connecticut, is not one of the oldest but it claims more than one hundred years of history. In 1825 Captain Alden Partridge, first Superintendent of the United States Military Academy at West Point, opened in Middletown the American Literary, Scientific and Military Academy. A history of Wesleyan University records the passing of this institution into the hands of the Methodist Episcopal Church. Through the liberality of the citizens of Middletown two substantial stone buildings had been erected for the school; and it was for a time very prosperous, drawing cadets from almost every state in the Union. Its prosperity, however, soon waned; and failing to obtain a charter from the Legislature, it was removed, early in 1829, to Norwich, Vermont, leaving vacant the buildings it had occupied. The Rev. Laban Clark, D.D., then Presiding Elder of the New Haven District, happened shortly after to be in Middletown; and being informed that one of the trustees of these buildings had casually suggested selling them to the Methodists, for the sum of five thousand dollars, he at once notified them that he would be one of ten to purchase the property, and would promptly secure the other nine. After discussion by the New York Conference and the New England Conference a plan was worked out with the citizens of Middletown. The trustees of the property offered it to the conferences on two conditions; first, that it should be perpetually used for a college or university, and second, that a fund of forty thousand dollars should be raised for an endowment fund of the college. The fund was soon subscribed and the college was organized in 1830 under the name of Wesleyan University; in May, 1831, a charter was granted to the institution and in September of that year it opened its doors to students. The Rev. Wilbur Fisk, D.D., was elected the first President. In view of a reorganization plan recently announced by the University of Chicago it is interesting to note that Dr. Fisk advocated a system of education in which a student would receive his diploma of graduation when he showed a certain proficiency in his subjects of study, without regard to the length of time he spent at the college. In another respect Wesleyan University was far in advance of its day because it established a scientific course to meet the wants of those who sought scientific training, and who were not interested in a regular classical course, such as all colleges of that day provided. Wesleyan University has maintained its interest in the sciences, its professors sometimes facing criticism in periods of warfare between science and religion. While Dr. Fisk was forced to abandon his scheme of graduation for attainment of a certain standard, irrespective of the length of residence of a student at the University, he anticipated by one hundred years a part of the policy of the new education at the University of Chicago.

At the death of Dr. Fisk in 1839, Dr. Stephen Olin was elected President. Because of the feebleness of health of Dr. Olin, Dr. Nathan Bangs served as President from February, 1841, until July, 1842. Dr. Fisk was an administrator, a man of culture and winning manner; Dr. Olin was a pulpit orator, whose noble character was an inspiration to every student. No institution was ever more fortunate in its first presidents. When Dr. Olin died in 1851, Dr. Augustus W. Smith was elected President; he gave himself to the raising of an endowment fund, and secured about eighty thousand dollars in the six years between 1851 and 1857. On the resignation of Dr. Smith in 1857 the Rev. Joseph Cummings, D.D., President of Genesee College, was elected President. During his presidency several buildings were erected, and at the commencement of 1868 a new library building was finished, and one donor, Mr. Isaac Rich, completed his gift of one hundred thousand dollars to the endowment fund, at the same time providing for the cost of the library. Under the guidance of Drs. Foss, Beach, Van Vleck, Raymond, Rice, Shanklin, Wesleyan University increased its influence and multiplied its services to New England and the nation. Our present interest in Wesleyan University centers in the years 1864 to 1867, because in that period Eugene Russell Hendrix was a student, graduating in the class of 1867. As a boy of seventeen he was sent by his father to the most progressive of the Methodist institutions of learning; there was no southern college to which he could go. Fortunately he kept a diary of those student days and we have a full record of his experiences there. His reflections, written at the close of each day, give us glimpses of happenings at Wesleyan and in the nation, and reveal the ambitions, attitudes and aspirations of a growing student in those days of the War Between the States.

Saturday, March 25, 1865—Arose at 6:30 A.M. Spent the morning in exercise and reading. In the afternoon was engaged in study and conversation, likewise the evening. Felt anxious to hear from home but did not. Can commit absent ones to a Father's care and prepare myself for the Sabbath. Retiring at 10 P.M.

Monday, April 3, 1865—Arose at 6:30 A.M. Spent the morning in reading Irving's Works, and study. At 12 the bells announced the capture of Richmond. The cannons' roar confirms the dispatches.

Saturday, April 15, 1865—Dr. Cummings announced with great effect the assassination of President Lincoln. The confirmation of the report caused a number of flags to appear at half mast and the bells to toll for two hours.

Monday, April 24, 1865—Arose at 5:30 A.M. Tolerable recitation in Greek and perfect one in mathematics. Received letter from Pa in afternoon expressing his view about my entering the ministry: Favorably inclined. Gives me the advice of an affectionate parent. Hope to go forth into the world to do good. Strive for preparation here in college.

Then came the usual experiences of a college student. On May 1 he was criticised for a failure in Latin scansion—"not much but felt it very sensitively. Must expect something of the kind in this great world." On May 3 he received a letter from his mother with a

photograph—"much affected to see those features again I left under
such scenes of peril. May I be granted the happy privilege of seeing
face to face." On May 7 he writes, "Arose at 5:30 A.M. Usual prayer
meeting, partook of the sacrament and reconsecrated myself to God.
Felt more like it after reading the life of Dr. Fisk in the afternoon.
Resolved to strive to emulate the virtues of this great and good
man."

The first vacation after entering college was spent with relatives
in Pennsylvania and in a visit to Washington. Phrases from the
diary of those summer days are these: "Assisted in unloading oats."
"Family prayer in the morning." "Played with twelve pound cannon ball." "Met Rev. Mr. Stevens of Hanover, also Presiding Elder
McMurray." "Took part in interesting prayer meeting at camp-
meeting." "Preached, not attended with so much liberty in the
morning as in the evening." "Engaged in noticing Kane's Arctic
explorations."

On returning to college in the fall there is manifested the same
interest in things religious, and the same eagerness to keep in touch
with life.

Sunday, October 8, 1865—Arose at 6 A.M. Deeply impressed with
gratitude for great change in situation from October 8, '64. Impressed too during day with differences in religious feelings.

Thursday, October 12, 1865—Arose at 5:15 A.M. Usual gymnastics.
Made tolerable recitation in Homer. Good in Hebrew. Seniors gone
to Mt. Holyoke. Practiced on melodeon at noon. Read letter from
Mary Kelly. Talk with North about Mary Manning. Read some in
"The Model Preacher."

Tuesday, October 31, 1865—Had Rowe and Fremont (brother)
go with me to chapel exercises. . . . Thought much of Fremont's
unfortunate condition religiously. May God help him!

Friday, December 15, 1865—Arose at 7:15 A.M. Studied and wrote
my sermon in the morning. Text: "What is the Almighty that we
should love Him? and what profit should we have if we pray unto
Him?" Took walk after dinner for elocutionary purposes. Too
cold. Talk with Mr. Dickinson about John Brown. Was furnished

a copy of "Uncle Tom's Cabin." Attended prayer meeting. Felt want of more religion for myself!

Sunday, December 31, 1865—Read in recent weeks Hawthorne's "Marble Faun" and Cooper's "Last of the Mohicans." Conducted College prayer meeting and was somewhat refreshed. . . . Read over my diary for the year. See all through its pages an aching void which full salvation alone can fill. Oh! for a sanctified heart! . . . Attended watch-night services at the Methodist Episcopal Church. Most gracious meeting of prayers and testimony after sermon. Dear and heavenly testimonies of the converts—Oh! that everyone might say, "Heaven's my home." Had my own soul gloriously blessed. Consecrated myself with an earnest heart to God's services. Feel still the Holy Fire. Glory to God!

Wednesday, January 24, 1866—Met for the purpose of a "band" organization. Solemn consecration. United in love and for Christian labor (Twelve were in this band.) Memorable night!

Sunday, January 28, 1866—The entire "Praying Band" left for Weathersfield. Began the day's labors with an earnest prayer meeting.

Thursday, February 1, 1866—Studied Addison's style much during the day. Glad tidings received from Weathersfield of the Band's labors on Sunday. The cry still "Come over and help us."

Sunday, February 4, 1866—Preached. Church awakened. God crowned our labors. Some seven penitents at the altar. Richest of blessings!

Saturday, February 10, 1866—Attended Quarterly Conference in evening, passed my examination, and obtained license of a local preacher.

Monday, February 12, 1866—Wrote home my views in reference to Union Theological Seminary, New York.

Tuesday, March 13, 1866—This day marks seven years since my conversion to God, March 13, 1859. Tribute to my pious parents for early guidance. Grateful for the rich and glowing experience of the entire term. Amen!

Sunday, April 15, 1866—(Recently read "Oliver Twist" and "Vanity Fair.") Enjoyed preaching very much because of God's help. Much feeling in congregation. No doubt about call to ministry.

Wednesday, May 9, 1866—Burns leads class in Hebrew. Stand second. Completed "Othello." Heard Mr. Hudson deliver a very fine lecture on it in the evening.

Thursday, May 17, 1866—My nineteenth birthday! The year greatly blessed of God in study and in Christian labor! . . . Propose more systematic preparation for the ministry.

Tuesday, June 26, 1866—Fine now after tea down the river. My health very good for gymnasium exercise.

In the summer of 1866 there was a visit to Yale and the Delta Kappa Epsilon fraternity there. A chapter of this fraternity was afterwards established at Wesleyan and Eugene Hendrix became an active member. He took the first degree in the Masonic Order that summer. But the event of greatest importance was a visit to the Missouri home in Fayette. He journeyed by steamer to New York, by train from New York to Baltimore, and by train from Baltimore west. There are interesting comments on that journey: "Trip enlivened by acquaintance with young lady enroute from Cumberland. Passed by Harper's Ferry. Grand scenery. Tried a sleeping car with tolerable success. Fine road between Columbus and Cincinnati. Travel like the New York and Boston Express. Met J. Taylor, Centre College, Danville, Kentucky, on cars. Comparison of Southern and New England Colleges. Former impressions unchanged. 'East St. Louis' very pleasant when sung out by the conductor. Glad to stand on Missouri soil once more. Stopped at Mr. Dines, 209 North Fourth Street (in St. Louis). Could never realize Centralia Massacre until I saw the graves. Home! People much discouraged from the war. C. W. Pritchett preached in the morning on 'Forgiveness of Sin.' Fayette in some respects too natural."

It was the twenty-first of July, 1866, when Eugene reached home. His experiences of the summer were varied.

Tuesday, July 24, 1866—Walked through the building of Central College. Neat edifice but sadly defaced during the war.

Thursday, July 26, 1866—Called on Rev. Carr W. Pritchett, a strange man but of considerable depth, about to establish an original school at Glasgow. Called on Rev. B. F. Johnson.

Sunday, July 29, 1866—Preached in Fayete, home, on "Christianity the Light of the World." Large congregation and hope much good. Some fine sacred music in our parlor in the evening. Bless God for the day!

Monday, August 20, 1866—Missouri the place for future labor! Large congregation for funeral service of Mr. Lewis Crigler. Service by Fristoe and Pritchett. Many "Good-byes" and "God bless you's!"

The return trip to college was made by Chicago, Niagara Falls and Albany. In the city of Albany Eugene saw President Andrew Johnson, Secretary Seward, Secretary Welles, General Grant and Admiral Farragut, and he was much impressed by the sight of these national leaders. Returning for his senior year he is more and more convinced of the need of adequate preparation for his life's work.

Friday September 28, 1866—Blessed with system of reading the scriptures in the original each morning!

Thursday, November 1, 1866—Interesting private talk with Dr. Johnston on Geologic Ages. His ideas beautiful and clear. Faith not troubled by discrepancies.

Wednesday, November 21, 1866—Beautiful theory of some astronomers comparing relation of heavenly bodies to the arrangement of the leaves of some plants. Think much benefit to be derived from study of character as portrayed by Dickens.

Friday, November 23, 1866—In evening heard George William Curtis lecture on "Conservatism." Delighted with his easy style of speaking. Lecture well written!

Sunday, December 2, 1866—Preached morning and afternoon. Not very lively to me. Too much pride.

Monday, December 31, 1866—Look back upon the closing year as one of peculiar profit mentally and spiritually. Believe by God's assistance that I have grown much in grace, and have received the witness of the spirit of full salvation.

Saturday, January 19, 1867—Heard a Second Adventist. Strange to hear men proclaiming from the sacred desk the immediate or at least speedy coming of our Lord!

Sunday, February 10, 1867—See by examination of my heart that much of my doubts largely have been suggested for the trial of my faith because I had ceased to grow in grace.

Wednesday, March 27, 1867—Wrote to Rev. James Oswald Swinney. Caught some of his enthusiasm relative to the itinerant labor of my future.

Thursday, April 18, 1867—Hope to make my religious life one tested by head work and faith as well as feeling.

Tuesday, April 30, 1867—See a great growth since fall term but not the devotedness to be wished.

Tuesday, May 14, 1867—Jefferson Davis released on bail of $100,000.

Friday, June 14, 1867—Very interesting talk in "Evidences" on "Inspiration of the Scriptures." How much of the very words is inspired? Which of the evangelists were apostles?

Monday, June 17, 1867—Much interested in reviewing my experiences. Fear I have lost ground but am determined by God's grace to regain it.

Sunday, June 30, 1867—Last college prayer meeting of my course. . . . My heart more mellowed of late but not humble and consecrated enough.

Monday, July 15, 1867—I was awarded the Rich prize for excellence in oratory. Glad for my parents' sake.

On July 18, 1867, the class of '67 graduated and the student days at Wesleyan ended. Eugene was twenty years old, having entered at the early age of seventeen. He seems more mature than his years as one reads the pages of his diary. The college student of today would feel little kinship with him. His experiences lie beyond the life of modern youth, but there are some attitudes of mind and soul easily comprehensible and worthy of emulation.

Early in his college course Eugene learned the value of system. He arose at about the same hour each morning, outlined carefully his day, completed his task, and retired for a good night's sleep. He was interested in the world about him and through his study window one has glimpses of the great events of his day, hears the bells announce the fall of Richmond and toll for the death of President Lincoln.

Consecrated as he was to his life's work and interested in courses that would prepare him for it he turned again and again to general literature, history and science. He wanted a mind well furnished. As he went on with his work some of the emotionalism of his adolescent days disappeared and his ardor cooled. Some might call that the effect of too much education. But not he. He knew his heart was still mellow in the days of his mental growth, and he was ever planning larger things for the kingdom.

He was interested in the Delta Kappa Epsilon fraternity and also in his Praying Band. He met his fellow students on the plane of human exchange and intercourse, and had one of the happiest days of his student life when his fraternity was recognized at Wesleyan. One night he could laugh and play with the members of his fraternity, but he did not fail to throw himself the following night into the labors of the Band as they prayed, and preached and exhorted. He knew homesickness, and felt keenly the criticisms of his teachers and the laughter of the students when he declaimed Poe's Raven with its mournful "Nevermore." He knew also the joy of accomplishment with a lesson well recited, and a prize taken. Perhaps the greatest joy he knew was the happiness of those who found the way to God under the ministry of his preaching. Whether in a neighboring town, or at the camp meeting near his grandfather's farm in Pennsylvania, or in the old home church in Fayette he loved to preach. Was he too serious for one of his years? He was serious but not morbid. He was too human, with too many human contacts, to become as morbid as some youths with his religious background and experience. He came from pioneer stock where men struggled with great difficulties and needed strength of character and faith in God. He entered college just as the War Between the States was coming to an end, a period in which tragedy was everywhere. Men could not face the present or the future without making available for themselves all the resources in themselves and in their world. Among these resources Eugene had been taught from his childhood to seek God. Him he found as real as his fathers had found Him, and in forming the purpose of his life he decided to serve Him with all the power of his life and soul. Wesleyan was dear to his heart as the place where his faith was tested, as the school of his preparation for his life's service.

Youth of today is interested in its newly won freedom. It is impatient of too much guidance or too much emphasis on religion. It needs to learn that throwing off restraint is not necessarily acquiring freedom. The people of France would be rid of Louis, and found they had Robespierre in his place. Russia overthrew the Czar and then enthroned Lenin. If one thing is apparent it is that youth must have moral autonomy or face disaster. When one hears a young man say that he can no longer believe what his father believes, one is justified in asking him what he does believe. When one hears a young lady say that she can no longer accept her mother's standards one ought to ask her what her standards are. One must think; one must have standards; one must have some purpose. Granting that the age is different, and that the background for most young people is not the same as that of Eugene Russell Hendrix, yet there is surely something challenging to the youth of today in that youth of the Sixties who entered Wesleyan to think, and plan and serve. We can go further and say that there is something inspiring in the courage and consecration of a religious faith which desires to be intelligent and adventurous, but which purposes in a shifting world to be stubborn. "If it be so, our God whom we serve is able to deliver us from the burning fiery furnace; and he will deliver us out of thy hand, O King. But if not, be it known unto thee, O King, that we will not serve thy gods nor worship the golden image which thou hast set up."

The summer of 1867 was spent with relatives in Pennsylvania. Happy days there were in family gatherings and in human companionship. Under date of August 21 there is this entry: "Met a couple of merry girls on the coach. Female character an object of study as for the past two weeks." But the chief interest of the summer centers again in the Shrewsbury Camp Meeting. On August 23 the opening sermon was preached: "Powerful exhortation of the

Elder following the sermon. Holiness the secret of the power and longed to have my own soul baptized. Willing to work anywhere for Christ, in the 'school houses' of Missouri or city church."

When Tuesday, September 3, came, he said "Good-bye" to his aged grandmother and left for New York City. He entered Union Theological Seminary to spend two years in further preparation for the ministry. Very few men of those days had the privilege of seminary training and it is doubtful whether any other from his church had the educational opportunity of Eugene Hendrix. Union Theological Seminary has been regarded for years as one of the really inspiring "schools of the prophets" and its faculty has always been scholarly and able. Wednesday, September 11, was the day when Eugene Hendrix entered the Middle Class of the Seminary. His experiences of readjustment in the autumn of 1867 form the theme for his reflections.

Sunday, September 29, 1867—Went to hear Henry Ward Beecher at Plymouth Church, Brooklyn. Fine gospel sermon on love. Surprised with his wonderful ability and oratory, and the singing of his people. Heard Dr. Deems preach in the chapel of New York University in the evening.

Monday, September 30, 1867—Witnessed General Phil Sheridan's reception at Union Square. "Little Phil" no speechmaker.

Tuesday, October 8, 1867—Heard John B. Gough at Cooper Institute on "Fact and Fiction." Wonderful acting and some eloquent passages.

Wednesday, October 9, 1867—Attended the Jewish Synagogue and heard the Jews chant Hebrew. A very discordant sound.

Friday, October 11, 1867—Doctrine of original sin a topic for investigation and study during the day. Not wholly satisfied with the results. Anxious for clearness. This my position as regards sanctification at present—believe in a complete consecration and want to know more fully as to what is done to inbred sin by holiness; want to know where to stand.

Thursday, October 17, 1867—Heard Horace Greeley at Cooper Institute on "Railroads." Clear, forcible, full of information.

Wednesday, October 23, 1867—Heard Hon. Schuyler Colfax in

Cooper Institute on "The Political Situation." Delighted with noble bearing and manly eloquence. Intense enthusiasm.

Sunday, October 26, 1867—Found much comfort in assuring a sick woman of the Savior's love and care. My own heart grows larger in working for others.

Tuesday, November 5, 1867—Impressed more deeply with the efficiency of simple fervid oratory as seen in Newman Hall. Strong Saxon language used by him to be sought for.

Sunday, November 17, 1867—Heard Beecher in the evening. The tenor of his preaching right but minor faults of introducing improper things into the pulpit.

Tuesday, November 19, 1867—Heard Hon. Charles Sumner of Massachusetts on "Are We a Nation?" Much pleased with it on the whole. Deep-toned voice, impassioned style, elegant and chaste language. Quite radical.

Wednesday, December 4, 1867—Heard Ward Beecher lecture on "Hands and Brains." Very fine. Becoming an ardent admirer of Beecher as an orator though not as a Christian minister.

December 31, 1867—The old year left me as it found me a year ago on my knees reconsecrating myself to God. Fear that it was more formal the last time than the first. Bless God for the precious blessings and privileges I now enjoy; for the friends on every hand and for the opportunities for preaching His gospel. "67," an old familiar friend thou art, but now "Good-bye" forever—thy name familiar through all my college course.

The city of New York was a new world to the young minister. Eagerly he went to hear the great leaders of the nation, irrespective of subject. He was interested in temperance and railroads and political situations as they were discussed on the platform. At the same time he was thinking more deeply about theological problems, and found himself disturbed over some issues he had once thought settled. He was not so sure as formerly whether holiness could eliminate "inbred sin"; he felt that his kneeling for prayer on the last night of the year was formal. But with the widening of his horizons and the challenge of new interpretations he goes on with his preaching and reconsecrates himself to his task. The two years at Union Seminary were influential in shaping his ministry and life. Reflections of the last few months of his seminary course show his development and his spirit as he is about to take up his work in the ministry.

Tuesday, January 12, 1869—How largely and strangely I have been brought in touch with distinguished men! How I should condemn myself in later life if I had failed to improve that acquaintance. Let me never sacrifice right to personal advantage!

Wednesday, January 13, 1869—During day read Dr. William A. Smith's address on "Representative Character of Bishop Soule," setting forth the southern view of the separation of 1844. My heart still set on removing the fierce opposition of the churches along the border.

Friday, January 15, 1869—Was examined in evening by Presiding Elder Faris and Washington Square Quarterly Conference and recommended "to travel."

Monday, January 25, 1869—Heard a very sharp and able speech on "The Bible and Total Abstinence" before the New York Preachers' Meeting. Showed that the use of wine was countenanced in the Bible. Was a total abstinence man but did not believe in perverting the scriptures. . . . A remarkable debater, very self-possessed and ready, J. M. Buckley would make his mark were he in Congress.

Wednesday, January 27, 1869—My first great work is to preach but when demanded and imperative I may have to teach a while as well. . . . Still reading French on the "Study of Words." Thinking favorably of belles-lettres as my department should I ever feel it my duty to hear the voice of the church saying, "Accept this proposed professorship and prepare others to preach."

Sunday, January 31, 1869—Preached on "What Lack I Yet?" at my mission. Had a good time. Enjoy extemporizing after good preparation.

Tuesday, February 2, 1869—Are intelligence, piety and health to be found combined in a high degree in a lady? Given the first two is there not more hope of the last than, given the last, of them? Am considering this important matter as one of duty and I hope in the case under consideration or some other I may be so guided as to glorify God. . . . Impressed with the variety of experiences to be had in New York in a single day—after seminary duties heard a lecture on "Constitutional Law" and went to a prayer meeting on Bedford Street.

Friday, February 12, 1869—Upon looking over my diaries I find that during the 65 Sabbaths I have been in the city since September 3, 1867, I have preached 68 times—4 times in '67, 55 times in '68, and 9 times in '69. . . . My opportunities for labor have been hardly less frequent in that time than were I in charge of a church regularly. What has been my improvement? What the result of my sowing? Believe I have tried in each case to do my duty and God must give the increase.

Saturday, March 13, 1869—A memorable anniversary as it is ten years ago today since I a lad of 11 years 10 months started on the journey of Bunyan's pilgrim to the Heavenly City. With a child's faith I grasped the promises of the Savior and the grace that has brought me safe thus far surely will lead me home. . . . Want a spiritual power to clothe me for a successful future and consecrate myself, God being my helper, to the work of the holy ministry as my life work and shall try to make it my only work.

Friday, March 26, 1869—"Good Friday" but so engaged as not to attend the services at St. Albans. My Easter Sunday will also be occupied as last year and I shall not be able to attend my ritualistic observance of it.

Wednesday, April 7, 1869—Brother Rush writes me again about going to Leavenworth City. Have not yet decided what reply to make. Am willing to enter at once upon the work of the ministry but sure of late, more than ever before, how illy prepared I am for it. I have toiled to faithfuly improve my remarkable privileges of nearly five years past . . . but fear that while I have good habit of systematic reading my habits of study and thought are yet quite imperfect and as long as they remain so my efficiency must be impaired.

Tuesday, April 27, 1869—Memoriter preaching or that which borders on it as my own style as unsuccessful as extemporaneous, and if I were to drill myself so thoroughly in the latter as in the former what hinders success? I need the sympathy of a congregation whether I know all that I am going to say or not.

Monday, May 10, 1869—Finis! . . . Upon leaving college I put my seminary course between me and the ministry. Now I stand face to face with my all important work. Who is sufficient for these things!

Thursday, May 13, 1869—(His brother, Fremont, had arrived in New York, and he is happy over seeing his brother.) A letter from home suggests Glasgow as my possible future field of labor which is more organized to my mind than Fayette.

So ends the record of the seminary days. Eugene went with his brother to his home in Fayette to be with his family and to rest before taking up the active work of the ministry. The seminary experience and the life in New York furnished the young minister with a wealth of knowledge and human contacts. Constantly he was preaching and testing on Sunday his technique of sermon preparation as well as his knowledge and convictions. It is so easy in a college or theological seminary to be theoretical; one's ideas and views need to face up to life's realities as they must in the pulpit and in the ministry to human need. It might be a good thing if theological professors were permitted to teach only a few years and then required to take pastorates for a few years before resuming their teaching. At any rate Eugene Russell Hendrix knew wholesome and friendly associations every day, faced human need and sorrow every Sunday as he preached, and these were as vital a part of his seminary training as the lectures to which he listened in the classroom. A sane, broad-minded, consecrated, well-prepared young minister returned from the East to his home in the South, and was ready for service.

E. R. Hendrix class picture 1867. Wesleyan University, Conn.
Age 20 years.

CHAPTER III

The Pastor

NO INTRODUCTION to the ministry of Eugene Russell
Hendrix can compare with that recorded in his diary of
December 31, 1868. It is the last Watch Night Service of his student
days, and he is consecrating himself to his task. Here are his reflections:

"Encouraged as to the prospects of more or less success in my en-
deavors to promote a better feeling between Northern and Southern
Methodists. Much has already been gained in the approval of the
distinguished gentlemen I have conversed with on the subject. They
have without exception shown the most friendly and Christian spirit
in the whole matter. Would that the whole South could see the real
heart of Dr. Curry, the most radical of men in this matter. Believe
this work of showing the one body to the other to be the peculiar
feature of my ministry for a few years at least. Were all things to
move so well as in the past week the whole matter might be settled
in months rather than a wait of years upon the sentiment and prejudices of the people. I have no past course with which I should
shape my present one as in Dr. Curry's case or the case of many
leading men in the Southern Church. I stand on present right and
shall be governed by present views of present duty. I shall bring
the matter to some test, be the result to myself what it may. Surely
the South is ready for it if the Extremists in the North are. I think
I see the finger of providence in my past five years preparing to act
a part of this important matter. Especially does this appear in the
events of the present year. In April and May I felt like leaving the
border when the opposition was most violent. I went home with
that expectation at least for a year or two. The very violence of the
opposition awoke my sympathies while fearing that one so young
could do but little toward accomplishing a result so desirable. Mr.
Pritchett's suggestion inspired confidence in my own influence. Peculiar circumstances showed how great that influence might be-

35

come by growing up among the people, until finally I concluded that if it were God's will I should no longer rebel. . . . Am grateful to God. . . . and shall recall with supreme satisfaction among the memories of 1868 my labors in the Pacific Street Church, Brooklyn. . . . and I do hope some good done by my labors there. 'Give me souls for my hire' I want ever to be my prayer. . . . We repeated together upon our knees the first two verses of the Covenant Hymn and then after a few minutes of silent prayer during which the old year took its departure we consecrated ourselves to God for another year."

The ministry of Eugene Russell Hendrix was ever a ministry of reconciliation. He began his first pastorate in Leavenworth, Kansas, by preaching Sunday morning, June 27, 1869, from a text in Galatians 6:14, "Let God forbid that I should glory save in the cross of our Lord Jesus Christ." There had been bitter feeling between the southern sympathizers in Missouri and the abolitionists of Kansas long before the days of the War Between the States. During the days of the war the border states knew the strife of neighbor against neighbor, and the consecration of Eugene Russell Hendrix to his ministry of reconciliation is shown in his taking the pastorate of a Southern Methodist Church in Leavenworth, Kansas. He served there from June, 1869, until the session of the Missouri Conference in the month of September, 1870. At that Conference he was assigned to Macon, Missouri, as pastor.

A careful record of that year in Leavenworth is preserved. At the close of the year the pastor reports 111 members and 59 probationers. His salary was $508.85 for the fourteen months, and he records two marriage ceremonies. He remarks after the first ceremony: "My first marriage ceremony—$10—to be given to the Delta Kappa Epsilon Fraternity as promised in 1867." After the second wedding the record reads: "Provoked into kissing the bride whose tears became laughter—Paid $5." During the year he secured 11 subscriptions to the St. Louis *Christian Advocate* and baptized 54 children and adults. He entered on his work in Macon with $35 in cash.

As he started for Leavenworth from his Fayette home he carried with him the memory of "a very memorable prayer by Pa at the family altar"; on the Saturday before his first Sunday he sees his church. "I visit my church, and some of its members. The building is about all that we have, but with God's help I am determined to fill it with converted men and women, and then build larger." The first Sunday did not bring much encouragement: "A rainy morning and only about 35 present, but the Holy Spirit so touched my heart that it was as though I preached to hundreds. . . . (in the evening) the attendance numbered about fifty. . . . and one joined by letter."

The diary of that year bears witness to the zeal and earnestness of the young minister, as it records his successes and failures.

Monday, June 28, 1869—I call on Rev. Mr. Sheppard of the Sixth Street M. E. Church. . . . and on Rev. Mr. Marshall of the First M. E. Church. . . . Selfishness is the besetting sin of both pew and pulpit in this whole western country. Men come to make money and make it.

Wednesday, June 30, 1869—Took in my own hands the business interests of our church, and fixed up the gas fixtures, window fastenings, etc.

Thursday, July 1, 1869—Engaged in preparing a number of articles for the four daily papers of Leavenworth on the Methodist Episcopal Church, South. They were designed to disabuse some minds of the idea that the term South had a political significance. This may drive some away from us who are with us in sympathy because of our Southern name but we had better rid ourselves of all such political allies.

Saturday, July 10, 1869—Believe that one of my greatest needs is a logical turn of mind. I reason out for myself and to some extent for others but still my style would not be called logical.

Wednesday, July 14, 1869—Would not be deprived of my favorite walk to the river where I love to stroll thinking of nature and her God.

Thursday, July 22, 1869—Shall I remain here with much to interrupt my studies or go to such a place as Glasgow where they will be more unbroken?

Saturday, July 24, 1869—At the Quarterly Conference in the afternoon I was examined and recommended to the Traveling Connection.

Monday, August 2, 1869—As usual much worried after the Sabbath's labors. Was better satisfied with my extemporized than with my written sermon of yesterday.

Saturday, August 7, 1869—Busily engaged in preparing my two sermons for tomorrow. Two a week used to seem an impossibility but still they have to be prepared. Time passes very quickly while thus so busily engaged. The present week seems hardly twenty-four hours long.

Monday, August 30, 1869—Felt prostrated as usual on Monday morning after my usual loss of sleep on Sunday night.

Sunday, September 19, 1869—Was ordained deacon by Bishop Pierce.

Monday, October 4, 1869—Engaged in preparing for the evening when we organized our "Ladies' and Pastor's Christian Union." A number of ladies out and after an explanation and presentation of the plans we proceeded to organize by the election of officers and the appointment of necessary committees.

Saturday, October 16, 1869—Relieved somewhat this week by anticipated exchange tomorrow with Brother Shepard of the Second Methodist Church. Am glad that I am so soon realizing one object of my frontier and border life, the bringing about a better understanding between the two great branches of Southern and Northern American Methodism.

Saturday, October 23, 1869—Mapped out a course of study for the future which I shall try strictly to follow unless I can amend it for the better. This will enable me to accomplish far more.

Saturday, December 4, 1869—Preparing for a children's sermon tomorrow. Early piety has become a delightful theme with me because I believe that it is often realized. If children do not understand, it is not a want of capacity but a want of proper instruction.

Sunday, January 2, 1870—A mass meeting of all the evangelical churches met for a Union Service to inaugurate a "Week of Prayer." An overwhelming attendance and a good spirit. Unless I have a larger share of the Holy Spirit I shall accomplish but little during this year.

February 3, 1870—Returned home today after 11 days of labor with the Francis Street Church in St. Joseph. Preached nightly the blessed Gospel and some men fully and many more almost persuaded to be Christians. . . . Bless God for having so moved me in the preaching of His gospel!

February 13, 1870—A precious Sabbath after a precious week wherein the Lord has graciously poured out the Spirit and saved souls in our own congregation. Nine have united with the church since last Sabbath and as many more have been converted.

February 19, 1870—Our services have been continued through the week. Brother Joseph W. Lewis of Kansas City has preached nightly to large congregations.

March 13, 1870—Baptized eleven and received thirteen into the church. . . . Judge David J. Brewer present representing a kindly feeling on the part of the Congregational Church.

April 4, 1870—Our District Conference adjourned today. . . . Bishop Marvin preached at our church to large congregations morning and night. . . . Impressed with him as an able and eloquent divine with simplicity, philosophical analysis, vivid imagination and earnest piety as elements of his power.

March 27, 1870—I returned at 3 o'clock this morning from Memphis, Tennessee, where I have been attending the General Conference of our church. Formed the acquaintance of many of its most prominent members. . . . A growing interest in the conference on behalf of a longer and unlimited pastoral term, of higher theological training and, but for legal issues involved, for a change of name. Nebraska and Kansas formed into a new conference which settles the question of my future as I will probably transfer to the Missouri Conference this fall.

September 4, 1870—Preached perhaps for the last time to my dear flock in Leavenworth. The following reasons urge me to ask for a transfer: (1) An older man is needed for the work here. (2) If I remain in this conference I shall hold myself in readiness to be sent to any part of it—this would too far remove me from my parents in their feeble health and declining years to be near whom was one of my objects in coming to the Missouri Conference from New York. (3) My health will not improve in such work. (4) The work here is so largely pastoral as to keep one out of his study more than I ought to be. . . . Another with more pulpit experience can do both kinds of work better than I. (5) Our finances are so limited that in one year there are no plans for a new church. . . . and I am not willing to labor to no purpose. (6) I believe our work in Kansas is mostly of a tentative character until we change the name of the church. (7) I prefer to identify myself with a conference, and live, labor and die in it.

September 12, 1870—The past week full of interesting, pleasant memories. The Western Conference met at 9 A.M. Thursday, September 8, in my church here. Bishop McTyeire presided and some fifty or sixty ministers were present. . . . Charles A. King from Alabama is my successor, my request for a transfer to the Missouri Conference having been granted. . . . The appointees are mostly young men who know but little of what awaits them not only in the opposition to religion but to themselves as representatives of the M. E. Church, South.

Thus ended the first pastorate of Eugene Russell Hendrix! At the session of his conference he was ordained Elder, by Bishop McTyeire and transferred to the Missouri Conference. He was urged to go to St. Louis, but declined to transfer there and the Bishop appointed him to Macon. He began his work there on October 7, 1870, after preaching the opening sermon at Central College in Fayette on September 26.

One cannot turn away from that ministry at Leavenworth without commenting on three references in the record. One Sunday the presence of Judge David J. Brewer in the congregation is noted, and reference is made to it in the diary. The friendship of those days at Leavenworth continued through the years when the Kansas judge became one of the ablest Justices ever to sit on the Supreme Court of the United States. Few church leaders of his day knew as friends so many able and distinguished financial and political leaders of his own and other countries as Eugene Russell Hendrix. He was always meeting them, and they were happy to become his friends.

Long before others he organized a Ladies' Aid Society or rather a Missionary Society. One of his first contacts in Leavenworth was that with the ministers of the Methodist Episcopal Church. He went to call on them as soon as he arrived; he did not wait for them to call on him. He was not satisfied until he had arranged an exchange of pulpits with one of them. He would not recognize divisions and discords, and it required more courage and consecration to do what he did in Leavenworth than to lead a movement later in life for unification.

He was convinced also that his denomination had no future in the state of Kansas. He showed thus early that wisdom which caused men to refer to him often as an ecclesiastical statesman. There was much of sentiment for a Southern church for Southerners in Kansas, but he did not favor the adoption of a policy for any merely sentimental considerations.

Thus early are shaping themselves those purposes which made him the great leader of after days.

There is no daily record of the ministry in Macon. The diary is a record of Sundays only, and it is a part of a pastor's record book. Here are the names of the trustees, the names of the stewards, the list of subscribers to the *Christian Advocate,* the record of baptisms, marriages and deaths, the lists of probationers, members of the church, and friends of the church in the community. In the pocket of that record book is one of the cards used by the young minister in his calls. It reveals both his zeal in the church's program and the spirit of his ministry. Across each end of the card, and across the top, are quotations from the Scriptures. Beginning with the quotation at the top and reading from left to right the verses quoted are these:

"I was glad when they said unto me, Let us go into the house of the Lord."
"For the Lord hath spoken good concerning Israel."
"Come thou with us and we will do thee good."

In the center of the card are the words

"Methodist Episcopal Church, South,
Pearl Street, Macon, Missouri
Rev. Eugene R. Hendrix, Pastor,"

followed by the list of services:

Young Men's Prayer Meeting at 3 P.M. on Sabbath
Class Meeting on Tuesday Evening
Prayer Meeting and S. S. Teachers' Meeting on Wednesday Evening
Rehearsal on Friday Evening
Social Gathering Every Monday Evening

That card would indicate also that this young minister was anticipating the religious education and recreation programs in a modern church. His conception of the church's function in the community was doubtless looked upon by some of his elder brethren as a radical departure from accepted ideas and programs. Let us turn now to some quotations from the record of those days:

October 9, 1870—My first Sabbath with my new charge. Small Sunday School owing to previous irregularities but hope to have a very superior one in a few months. Good congregations at both services. Intelligent, attentive, but apparently not spiritual. Need first a baptism from on high for pastor and people for which I humbly and earnestly pray.

October 16, 1870—During the past week have visited nearly every member of my church. Prayer meeting attendance greatly increased.

November 13, 1870—Christ very precious to me today. His incarnation more real than ever before.

January 15, 1871—A memorable Sabbath. . . . Rev. C. I. Vandeventer from St. Joseph with me all week and preached today. Nineteen baptized and twenty-five received into the church.

April 2, 1871—Endeavored to meet and check the evil of talebearing in my flock in evening service.

May 14, 1871—Can but wish for a high grade of intelligence in my people but must cultivate it.

July 1, 1871—Returned last evening from a two weeks' visit to

Fayette where I delivered the annual address before Howard Female College and attended the Commencement of Central College. Declined the presidency of St. Charles College to devote myself wholly to the work of the ministry.

September 3, 1871—Returned on the 30th ult. after a very pleasant visit to the St. Louis Camp Meeting where I heard profitable discourses from Bishops Kavanaugh and Marvin, Doctors McAnnally and McFerrin. Made a large number of acquaintances and hope I did some good. Preached with deep emotion today my last sermon for this Conference year. Tried to get rid of some thorns in the flesh.

September 22, 1871—Returned last evening from the most pleasant and lengthy session of the Missouri Conference at Palmyra. Bishop Doggett presided. Bishop Marvin and Dr. Redford in attendance. Received into full connection and made my maiden speech on Central Female College. Restationed in Macon.

October 5, 1871—Returned last night from a most pleasant visit among old friends in Kansas City and Leavenworth. A memorable Sabbath with my former flock! . . . Especially enjoyed my visit to Brother N. T. Scarritt's beautiful country residence.

December 17, 1871—Greatly interested in a murder case during the week and listened to arguments of counsel. . . . Interested in Col. Thomas L. Anderson's speech.

January 17, 1872—Returned today from over a week's labor in St. Joseph. Much blessed in my work and hope blessed others. Sunday night sermon to an immense crowd of young men. Some seed of last winter just bearing fruit. Not disposed to encourage advances for the future but leave all to the Bishop and Council.

February 29, 1872—Returned at midnight from Gallatin *via Kansas City*. Profitable services at Gallatin, resulting in 187 accessions and continued interest. Rested a few days in Kansas City mostly at Brother Scarritt's. . . . Wholly satisfied with the prospective life awaiting me with one of the finest of mortals. Am deeply grateful to God for so signal a providence. (The reason for the resting at Brother Scarritt's is quite apparent—Miss Ann Eliza Scarritt.)

March 12, 1872—Just returned from a memorable visit to Fayette after lecturing in Salisbury on the 4th and seeing old friends in Glasgow. Gracious revival in progress at Fayette and many seeking Jesus. Tried to preach the Gospel of a Savior doubly precious to me. . . . Knelt with unspeakable pleasure on the spot of my first espousal to Christ 13 years ago.

April 7, 1872—Leave on the morrow to spend a few days with "gentle Annie" at Minnehaha, and rest.

April 17, 1872—Reached home at midnight from delightful visit with one esteemed above all others of earth. Intimate acquaintance only increases my desire to enter for life into the holiest of relations with one so pure and noble. My health much improved by the trip.

May 5, 1872—Accepted D K E invitation for oration on 15th of July at Middletown, Connecticut. Heard Blind Tom again to my great delight.

May 17, 1872—Twenty-five years ago today God gave me my being and for twenty-five years he has preserved and prospered me. One third of my life has doubtless passed and by His grace not in vain. May the summer and fall of my life abound in harvests and fruit. Wrote to my dear mother and to my precious friend at Minnehaha.

June 16, 1872—Pleasant Sabbath's labor and my last but one before I will have a precious helpmate to pray for and sympathize with me in my great work. Delivered the annual address before Pritchett Institute on Thursday. Bishop Marvin present and complimentary.

June 24, 1872—The past week has been a most eventful one as on the 20th inst. my marriage with Miss Annie E. Scarritt was celebrated at Minnehaha in the presence of a large circle of friends. "A provident wife is of the Lord" and am deeply grateful for the superior one I have from Him. Believe that I can now better than ever do the Lord's work and hope to be greatly useful.

July 25, 1872—Returned on the 19th after an extensive bridal trip east. . . . Spent three days at old Wesleyan where I delivered the oration at the Quadrennial of the D K E Fraternity. . . . A cordial greeting awaited us at our reception in Macon on Saturday night.

September 8, 1872—My last Sabbath probably in Macon. Have spent two very pleasant and profitable years here and am willing to return but probably can do more good elsewhere. . . . Do not know my probable future home. St. Joseph, Carrollton and Richmond all striving to determine it. Will try to do my duty anywhere.

September 19, 1872—Tonight's prayer meeting closed our ministry at Macon, a memorable hour. By appointment of Bishop Pierce I go to Francis Street Church, St. Joseph, a very responsible charge, and truly I "must live very near to God," as Bishop Pierce told me. . . . A delightful conference. . . . Especially memorable occasion to me as ripening the friendship between Dr. Haygood and myself as we were inseparable chums. . . . Endeavored to prepare the way for Brother Harris, my successor, by getting the people to praying for him. May God bless his future and mine, and may the seed sown here during two years past in God's own time produce the full corn at length.

So closes the ministry at Macon. There are some experiences which leave their lasting impression on life. The young minister had to direct the work of a church in an established community and that required ability and consecration. He was very much concerned because some of his best men signed petitions for saloon licenses. He was worried because the community was not greatly desirous of changes in its way of living. But he labored, and preached and prayed, giving attention to every detail of his work. The record shows many absences and in his second year several of them were visits to his future wife in Kansas City. But the others are all journeys in the interest of the Kingdom. He was holding special meetings at St. Joseph, and Moberly, and Mexico and Palmyra. He was delivering addresses at Salisbury, Pritchett Institute, Howard College. He was attending conference sessions. His zeal was such that he could never seem to do enough for the church and her Lord.

Nothing in his Macon experience so influenced his life as his marriage with Annie E. Scarritt. There are some delightful touches in the diary as he visits that young lady. At first we read that he went to Brother Nathan Scarritt's to rest. Then comes that other visit when he reports that he returned from Kansas City greatly improved in health. Love is ever the same and the scholarly young minister is as human as any other man as he praises his sweetheart. He was correct and did not exaggerate when he said that his own work would be better with the aid of such a woman as he married. She became a part of all his hopes, his trials, and his triumphs.

To St. Joseph Eugene R. Hendrix went in the fall of 1872, and he found himself pastor of one of the best churches in his denomination. He began his ministry on Sunday, September 29, 1872, by preaching from the text in Galatians 6:14, "God forbid that I should glory save in the cross of our Lord, Jesus Christ." The closing sermon of this pastorate was preached on September 10, 1876, from the text in John 6:35, "I am the bread of life." After that last Sunday is this comment in the pastor's record book: "Four years of pleasant ministry with as noble a people as a pastor ever served. Thank God the ministry was not a fruitless one."

The record at the Francis Street Church, for the four years, shows forty-nine marriages, seventy-eight funerals, additions to the church 223, adults baptized sixty-two, children baptized sixty. There were church improvements that cost $4,000 and the sum of $1,988 was raised for missions; the salary for the four-year period was $6,100 and the minister had saved $600 out of that. The membership of the church is given at 339 and the enrollment of the Sunday School at 447. Friendships were formed which enriched life, and Francis Street Church was related through those friendships to the advancement of Methodism in the state of Missouri.

In the autumn of 1877 Eugene Russell Hendrix became pastor of the Methodist Church in Glasgow. The town was one of the oldest in the state and the people of the community were cultured and widely influential. The Bishops of the Methodist Episcopal Church, South, in that year were Robert Paine, George F. Pierce, H. H. Kavanaugh, W. M. Wightman, Enoch M. Marvin, D. S. Doggett, Holland N. McTyeire and John C. Keener. Doctors D. D. Mc Annally and A. G. Haygood were editors of the St. Louis *Christian Advocate,* and E. R. Hendrix served as corresponding editor, in addition to his work as pastor at Glasgow. For one year the pastorate at Glasgow continued, until the election of the pastor to the presidency of Central College at Fayette. The last sermon of the Glasgow pastorate was preached September 8, 1878, from the text in John

12:32: "And I, if I be lifted up from the earth, will draw all men unto myself." The record of the pastor, at the close of that last service, reads: "Thus closed a very pleasant ministry at Glasgow, resulting in thirty-seven accessions, a net increase of thirty-five, a missionary collection of $525.68 and increased home religion."

The pastoral service of Eugene R. Hendrix was two years in Leavenworth, Kansas, two years in Macon, four years in Francis Street Church in St. Joseph, and one year in Glasgow. The nine years' period reveals no unusual or startling statistics of gains; no new churches were built and there were not more than 500 additions to the churches. But there was this evidence of faithfulness, consecration and success—not an interest of the church was overlooked. There was progress in every department. There were increased contributions to benevolences. There was a busy program for each group in the church. There was a deepening of interest in home religion and a building up of individuals in Christ. The administration of the church was so able as to be an inspiration to any modern minister who studies the record. Two tasks were supreme, the ministry of the pulpit on Sunday and pastoral ministry in the homes during the week. Both were influential because the pastor found time always for his own devotions and study. First things came first and there was no crowding of them by a multiplicity of details. He was the prophet and seer on Sunday; he was a shepherd of souls every day. He did a great amount of work and yet found time for each task that was worth his effort. Because of the fellowship with God, real and vital to him, he never forgot the "blooming almond tree," and preaching never lost its romance.

In these modern days pastors often preach out and move on to other pastorates, or wear themselves out in attention to petty details of administration, or forget their great responsibilities as spiritual leaders in the community. While they are busy here and there their strength slips away. They arise to shake themselves against the enemies of the souls of their people and realize that the Lord has departed from them. A way must be found to renew strength. Is the way of Eugene Russell Hendrix any less productive of results than in former days? He kept close to people, and studied constantly, and

47

went often to his place of prayer. Sympathy, earnestness, devotion, were the watchwords of his pastorate. In the farewell sermon at Francis Street in St. Joseph, he said: "It has been, in the providence of God, my duty and pleasure to labor with this people for the last four years. If at any time you have asked for bread and I have given you a stone, I pray God to forgive me. I have certainly tried faithfully and with a singleness of purpose and sincerity of heart to feed you with living bread. If I have failed my heart goes out to God for forgiveness for so sad a neglect of pastoral duty." The daily paper in St. Joseph closes its account of the service in these words: "The Apostolic benediction by the pastor closed the exercises, but for a long time the people lingered behind and the leavetakings were very affecting."

Chapter IV

The College President

IN THE town of Fayette, in Howard County, Missouri, is Central College. This institution is one of the strong colleges of the Middle West with equipment and endowment valued at more than three million dollars. The college has had a history of seventy-five years of service, and numbers among its alumni some of the most distinguished men and women of the state of Missouri. Founded before the Civil War it has been a potent factor in the development of the state. Its presidents have been men of ability with far more than local reputation as educators. The list is imposing: Nathan Scarritt, A. A. Morrison, W. H. Anderson, W. A. Smith, J. C. Wills, E. R. Hendrix, J. D. Hammond, Tyson S. Dines, E. B. Craighead, C. W. Pritchett, O. H. P. Corprew, T. Berry Smith, J. C. Morris, W. A. Webb, Paul H. Linn, E. P. Puckett, W. F. McMurry, Robert H. Ruff, Harry S. Devore. Among these executives no one rendered a finer service than President Hendrix, for it was he who raised the money to pay the debt incurred in opening the college after the war, and it was he who initiated a building program to increase the equipment and an endowment campaign to give greater stability.

Central College was chartered by an enactment of the Missouri General Assembly March 1, 1855, and it was formally opened in 1857 under the leadership of Rev. Nathan Scarritt. During the War Between the States the college was closed, and the Board of Curators did not open it until 1867. When President Hendrix took charge of the college in 1878 there was one building, the debt was $12,000 and there was an endowment of $45,000. The debt was paid, the campus was enlarged, three buildings were erected and the endowment increased to $110,000 as a result of the leadership of President Hendrix. In the years since there have been three periods of definite expansion when President Paul H. Linn led in two campaigns to increase the endowment and insure the future of the college, and when

49

President W. F. McMurry led the movement to unite all Methodist schools in the state in Central College and to transform the campus as by a miracle in a building program and when Harry S. Devore ably led to great development on the campus. The college property includes fifteen modern buildings, and a campus of forty-two acres. The enrollment is seven hundred, and the college takes high rank among the educational institutions of the North Central Association. When Eugene Russell Hendrix assumed the presidency in 1878, at the age of thirty-one he made this statement to the Board of Curators:

"Since my election to the office of President of the College in April last, I have addressed myself to making whatever preparation I could for the wisest and most successful performance of my new and responsible duties. By a visit to Vanderbilt University, Nashville, and to Emory College, Oxford, Georgia, and by personal conversation with many of the most eminent educators in our church, I have sought to acquaint myself with the best methods of instruction pursued elsewhere as well as those so long and successfully pursued at Central College. I hope to be able to utilize this information during the next year, especially in the Department of Biblical Literature.

"I have carefully read the entire history of the College as recorded in the Book of the Secretary of the Board, and trust that I shall be able to profit, as the Board itself is beginning to do, by its past mistakes. The errors were those natural to inexperience in educational matters, and not due to any lack of ordinary business sagacity. Some of the mistakes appear to have been the result of the unanimous actions of the Board even when such men as A. Leonard, John A. Talbot, Wm. D. Swinney, Judge Hill, Gov. Polk, A. Hendrix and others of like stamp were members. Even when they might have rallied after they saw the unwisdom of the scholarship plan, and some other features of the system adopted, the war threatened to destroy all that they had done and utterly thwart their entire educational plans. More is to be laid to the charge of inexperience, however, than to all other causes.

"Since the war through the voice of its able President Dr. Smith the College made a profound impression in behalf of higher education on the Methodist public in Missouri, and Dr. Wills has nobly built on that foundation in training the large numbers of young men, who were turned to the College. The Church has already received back in a quickened religious life and a brightened future far more than she has ever given to the College. If the annoyance occasioned by old debts was out of the way, and the Board could go before the Church with records of what the College has already done, despite its financial weakness, I believe that there would be liberal response, such as would greatly increase the efficiency of the College. It must be expected that members of the Board most familiar with its debts, most interested in their payment, will give, and whatever contributions they can give to the College will perhaps be wisely devoted toward removing the difficulties which stand in the way of large liberality from the rest of the Church. I would suggest that a prime matter with the Board, is to address themselves toward the payment of these debts. A liberal spirit on our part will doubtless be met by a liberal spirit on the part of the claimants, and they can be adjusted speedily to the great relief of the College. Especially is it important to make provision for the payment of the Professors' claims which fall due next June.

"With these debts paid the outlook for increased endowment and an increased number of students is good. The officers of the College will be able to travel more in its interest and with hope of its prosperity. I am glad to report the receipt of many letters of inquiry and other things which betoken a deepened interest in the College, within our own and adjoining states."

In his report to the Board of Curators on June 21, 1880, President Hendrix records this progress:

"The club house arrangement proposed more than a year ago has been in successful operation during the year. As many as thirty-six students at a time have availed themselves of these facilities for cheaper board, while during the year nearly fifty have been members of the association. We invite the Board to inspect the building known as Wills Hall which has been erected for this purpose. It accommodates some twenty-four students with rooms, while many others take their meals there. The cost of table board has averaged $1.45 per week while the room rent of fifty cents has still left the cost of board at not over $2.00 per week. Some most valuable apparatus has been added during the year while the minerological collection has also been increased. . . . The library has received some choice additions from the alumni." The professors received salaries of $1,000 each and the total expenditure for instruction was $8,700.

In the report to the Board of Curators on June 20, 1881, the President recorded further progress: "I am to call the attention of the Board to the relief of the College from its burden of debt. A gymnasium 30x50 has been erected at a cost of $1,400. The next great need is for a new chapel that we may have more room for recitations in the main building."

In the report of the President presented June 13, 1882, mention is made of a large gift. "The magnificent gift of Robert A. Barnes of St. Louis, amounting to $25,000 for a professorship endowment demands some suitable recognition by the Board."

Further gifts are announced in the report of June 12, 1883: "I have to report some generous donations to the college since the Board last met. First of these was the gift of $20,000 in November last by Mr. Robert A. Barnes of St. Louis to endow the Mary Evans Barnes Chair of English and Modern Languages. This, like Mr. Barnes' other gifts, was unsolicited and is as creditable to his head as to his heart, the gift being in honor of his mother whose name that chair hereafter bears.

"A most timely gift was made in January last by the faithful treasurer of your Board, whose valuable services as counsellor have not been surpassed even by the generous gift of $5,000 to establish the 'Arthur Davis Students' Loan Fund.'

"During the year the local members of the Executive Committee took steps looking to the material enlargement of our campus by the purchase of six large double lots at a cost of $4,000. The whole campus as thus enlarged will cover over eleven acres.

"The generous response to the Chapel subscription led your committee to reconsider the original plan for a $15,000 chapel and to adopt one for a $20,000 chapel. . . . Moreover with the great prosperity of the college they were justly afraid to build on a scale so small as to be beyond remedy but not beyond reproach. They preferred to show their faith in the church and in the future of the college within the limits of a thoughtful prudence.

"There are several very urgent needs to which I would call the attention of the Board. . . . One is a library fund of not less than $25,000, the income from which shall go to replenishing our library. . . . A thing to be kept constantly in mind is increased endowment. We need $250,000 at the earliest possible date."

The completion of Centenary Chapel is announced in the report of June 10, 1884: "By the favor of God and the liberal aid of our friends Centenary Chapel has been completed and at a cost, including furniture, of $26,000. A balance of $6,000 on the building remains unpaid. Of the whole cost some $11,000 has been contributed by the people of Fayette and vicinity."

On June 8, 1886, the President made his last report to the Board of Curators of Central College:

"In presenting you my last annual report as President of Central College it will be fitting to review the history of the college during the eight years since you called me to the responsible office which I must resign this day, at the call of the church. During that period 1,233 students have been in attendance—an average of 154 each year, as against 861, or an average of 107 a year, for the eight years previous since the college was reorganized in 1870. The debt of $12,000 which then oppressed us has long since been paid. The Endowment of $45,000 has grown to nearly $110,000. The campus has been doubled, and the Gymnasium, Wills Hall and Centenary Chapel have been erected at a total cost of $37,400.

"The addition of the Scientific Hall at once completes our campus and gives the needed room for our growing scientific department. These improvements and additions have all been paid for save a balance of $3,500 on Centenary Chapel. This includes the furnace and gas fixtures, not originally provided for, and a balance caused by some unpaid subscriptions which we failed to collect. This paid, we have no liabilities, and we have assets to the amount of $200,000— $90,000 in realty and $110,000 in Endowment as against assets of scarcely $100,000 eight years ago and an indebtedness of $12,000, or more than one tenth of the whole. While the showing of the financial condition and of the attendance of the students is thus encouraging, as to the standard of scholarship the record is even more satisfactory. Perhaps, fully a third more work, and that of a very high order, is necessary to graduation now than was the case eight years ago. Still we have 44 graduates during the period as against 16 for the first eight years. The showing proves the substantial basis upon which the college rests and the esteem in which it is held, alike by its students and the public at large. Rev. Wm. M. Rush has handed the president his obligation for $1,000 to establish two scholarships of $500 each to be known as the Wm. M. Rush Scholarships for the benefit of ministerial students to be nominated by the faculty and the Board, provided, however, that both may be filled by any of his lineal descendants, who may be in attendance upon the college at any time. The present scholastic year has been one of great harmony and has been marked by very satisfactory work. There has been no case of gross disorder or of dismissal. The attendance, while the smallest for a number of years, being 116, consisted of a superior class of students.

"Thanking you for your hearty cooperation during my term of office and recording my deep gratitude to our Heavenly Father for his blessing upon our united labors, it now becomes my duty to tender my resignation as President of Central College as the new work to which I am called by the church will demand my undivided energies."

During these years of administration the President was deeply concerned about the character of the student body and the religious life of the students. In his report to the Board on June 21, 1880, he refers to certain matters of discipline and says: "We are as unwilling that any of the students go out deficient in moral character as in scholarship." Again in 1881 he refers to the life on the campus: "The religious tone of the college is very marked and exercises a happy effect on the whole body of students. A large number were converted during the first term, and a daily prayer meeting for a half hour before chapel services in the morning has been maintained throughout the scholastic year."

In 1883 he mentions the fact that some students are being sent to the college because of the reputation for discipline and in the hope of reform. The policy of the administration is clearly stated: "When it appears to us that such students are honestly trying to do better we bear with them, but if they promise to prove an injury to others we promptly dismiss them if a proper occasion arises."

The President was always in control of the situation and he knew how to be firm in all matters of discipline. What influence were these duties as president of a college having on the man? He did not keep a daily record of his life in those years but his diary does reveal his inner growth and development.

January 5, 1880—Heard Moody and Sankey several times. The character of Moody impresses me well. Sankey has become somewhat self-conscious and is shorn of spiritual power.

May 17, 1880—My 34th birthday! My life of 33 years the same as that of my Master. Would that it possessed more of its breadth, as well as its length! . . . Returned from Cincinnati. While in attendance there on the Ecumenical Council preparatory to the great Ecumenical Methodist Conference in August, 1881, in City Road Chapel, London, I had an encouraging insight into the growing spirit of fraternity. . . . I venture the opinion that 1900 will see but one Episcopal Methodism in the country, with 3 or 4 General Conference Jurisdictions.

June 12, 1880—Today at 5 P.M. we laid away in the tomb the body of my dear brother Fremont. A year and a half my senior we have been inseparable during much of our lives. A noble, brilliant man with the brightest prospects before him as a naval officer or a businessman his earthly prospects were thwarted by pulmonary disease and observing a prescription for it until a habit of strong drink was formed. He died in peace, humbly penitent and trusting in Christ. It was my sacred privilege to be much with him the last week of his life and to close his eyes in death. May God graciously overrule his death for good!

June 25, 1880—Sought in my baccalaureate address to endorse the idea of the scholar, the priest and the soldier being the great factors of human history and those who most influenced their fellow-men represented in one the intellect, the sensibilities and the will all in harmony, or the scholarly, priestly and soldierly elements of character.

December 25, 1880—My heart was much touched this morning by a note or inscription in my little son's Bible, a present from his grandfather, who prayed that he may, if God so calls, become an earnest and able preacher of the Gospel. Have I allowed the first prayer for this end to ascend from other lips? Would I keep back from Thee, O my Savior, my only son? No! I give my own life and that of each of my family to Christ. Let my motto henceforth be that on the banner of an English regiment "Anywhere."

January 1, 1881—My great desire is to possess more personal holiness. I cannot influence men aright without greater conformity to the divine character. I am humiliated that I am not a better man, a riper Christian.

March 14, 1881—An anniversary day! Twenty-two years ago began my Christian life so that already two thirds of my life has been given to Christ as an avowed disciple. . . . Thank God that I have learned the great lesson of life, to commit my ways unto the Lord.

May 8, 1881—Returned this morning from Nashville. The outlook for missions was never more encouraging. We venture to appropriate $180,000. The Vanderbilt well equipped in buildings but lacks unity of design and the utmost harmony among its faculty. The Theological Department is its weakness because unwisely managed. Raw students required to attend lectures on Systematic Theology before the proper basis is laid. Our Episcopacy sadly needs strengthening. Wilson, Haygood, Granbery, and Parker the names most favorably mentioned. Brother Lambuth in Nashville and in miserable health—a noble brother who craves a grave in China.

June 1, 1881—During the past week I have reluctantly concluded not to go to the Ecumenical Conference in London, September 7th, on account of being absent at our college opening September 8th.

56

June 13, 1881—Returned today from a pleasant trip to Kansas City where I dedicated Lydia Avenue Church.

October 6, 1881—Much kindly talk of my future. Even asked if I would be willing to give up Central College for the Episcopacy. From the best light I now have I record my conviction that I can be more useful to the church for some years to come in my present position. . . . Am satisfied that my present position is a more congenial one and that the other would need to be undertaken in a spirit of self-sacrifice.

January 29, 1882—Without seeking anything at the hands of the church my mind is much exercised as the time for the General Conference approaches. . . . If Central College is to be my field for life I believe that I could be eminently useful here and have my children about me for years as they are being educated. If on the other hand I am called to the office and work of a bishop I may serve both the church and the college, but must scatter my energies and be much separated from my family. . . . I await the developments of God's providence and seek to do my duty faithfully here.

April 30, 1882—I leave tonight for Nashville, the seat of the General Conference. The election of bishops the all-absorbing topic. While my name is mentioned in the papers and in private correspondence I do not take it as any indication of election or even of a large vote as the number of names mentioned is large. But if I thought any improper motive influenced my going I would not dare attend the Conference.

May 28, 1882—Returned on yesterday from a month's absence at General Conference. Four choice men elected bishops and a fifth one, the greatest of them all, chosen but declined, shaming the truth in the saying, "No man is fit for any position until he is too large for it." Haygood's election a triumph but his declination a grander triumph. . . . Many kind expressions from the delegates about four years hence, all of which I appreciate without I trust over-appreciating the proposed possible honor. Haygood's preaching, addresses and private talks revealed a measure of self-conquest and devotion to Christ that drew me yet nearer to him. His declination not a surprise but in full keeping with my sense of the fitness of things and calculated to do great good to the Methodist World. Shall "Volo Episcopare" be the Methodist motto and "Nolo Episcopare" that of the Protestant Episcopal clergy with whom a declination is healthily common? We are in danger of giving undue prominence to one office.

January 29, 1882—"The Son of Man came not to be ministered unto but to minister." O that I may become a son of man, a servant of humanity, by precept and example helping men to live holier and more useful lives.

August 30, 1883—A busy day at Nashville with the Central Centenary Committee.

December 6, 1883—Our special services closed last night leaving me much worn but happy in a Savior's love and in His blessing upon the community. Many clear conversions and many awakenings! God's love a gracious theme in the pulpit.

January 20, 1884—Our Centenary Year has dawned at length. Ushered in with prayer all over the Connection and by special sermons on the doctrines and uses of early Methodism. . . . If it be a year of great spiritual power much will be gained every way.

March 16, 1884—I am too busy working for Christ and find too much of joy in that service to think of the rewards of Heaven. The Lord keep me faithful.

April 13, 1884—Attended the Church Extension Board at Louisville and helped to inaugurate the Centenary Church Extension Loan Fund . . . also the Board of Missions and the Centenary Mass Meetings at Nashville.

December 26, 1884—Home most sweet after some seventeen days absence in Washington and at the Great Centennial Conference in Baltimore.

March 14, 1885—Twenty-six years ago today I found peace in believing and was received on probation into the church. It was fully three years afterwards before I was received into full membership, owing to the disturbing influences of the war and the change of ministers. . . . From early childhood I desired a regularity in all my church life as well as moral conduct, trying to avoid any excess that would be unbecoming in one called to the holy ministry which call in my case I felt in my 15th year. . . . Now for twenty years I have tried to preach Jesus and His resurrection. This has been and still is the joy of my life. I have never refused an opportunity to preach unless physically unable or when I deemed that some one else could more profitably do so at the time.

May 17, 1885—I am thirty-eight years old today! . . . Before rising I thought of my life by decades. In the first my childhood when my character was forming under wise parental control. In the second my conversion, call to preach, and education, graduating at 20, the youngest in my class. In the third my professional studies, marriage, ministry in three important charges, tour of the world, and birth of two older children. In the fourth another pastorate, college presidency, much preaching and joy in Centenary celebration, and birth of two younger children. God will fill the blank as he has completed the decades.

May 31, 1885—Declined semi-official invitation to become Dean of Theological Faculty, with promise of Chancellorship at Vanderbilt, assured that my consent alone was needful to my election. Prefer Missouri on account of climate and my work now in hand.

November 11, 1885—Approached by Senator Proctor on the presidency of the State University at the request of the Board. Not inclined to do anything that will unfavorably affect the prosperity of Central.

April 14, 1886—Finished today payments on my Centenary offering of $5,000, as follows: Education $3,250, Church Extension $1,000, Foreign Missions $750. May I never give occasion to have it said of me, "He died possessed of too much money for a preacher."

May 30, 1886—Returned home on the 28th inst. from the General Conference in Richmond, Virginia, where on the 18th inst. I was elected one of the Bishops of the Methodist Episcopal Church, South. . . . The belief that it was the will of God led me to accept despite my more congenial work at Central College. I feel now that I belong to the Church as never before. May I never dishonor the high office to which I have been called, and which such holy men have filled before me. Our future home (if such it can be called on account of my future absences) will probably be in Kansas City.

No one familiar with the history of Central College can deny that President Hendrix saved the institution at a critical time and made it. Not only did he interest men of wealth like Mr. Barnes in St. Louis, and Mr. Hoagland in St. Joseph, but from many small contributors he secured funds for building an endowment which established the College. Even more significant than his strengthening of the College's financial position was his insistence on sound learning. More privileged than other young men of his day in his educational opportunities as a student he brought to Central College a zeal for sound learning and culture. He never ceased to grow in his own mental life and he was ever an evangelist for enlarging conceptions of truth. In an article he once wrote is a revelation of the passion which characterized his educational leadership: "Truth is alike the food and life of the intellect, and unless the intellect be fed it famishes. To bear witness to the truth brought the Son of God into the world, and his last command to his trained apostles was to go teach all nations. 'If the truth shall make you free ye shall be free indeed.' Error enslaves the intellect. Christianity alone makes thinkers. Satan rules men, as he first effected an entrance into the human soul, through the appetites and passions, or through the imagination and taste. The preacher who dares to compete with Satan on his own ground and with his own weapons cannot but fail. Sensationalism is something in which the devil is an adept. Christ declined Satan's pulpit even when it was the pinnacle of the temple. He who made the human mind knew that there was but one key to unlock it, and that was—Truth. 'Ye shall know the Truth and the Truth shall make you free.' His apostles must be disciples before they can become teachers. . . . What commercial integrity is to the merchant and what judicial integrity is to the judge, that and more should intellectual integrity be to the preacher. What intellectual honesty should forbid his preaching, if he does not believe it, the same integrity should forbid his preaching that or any other than what he is 'persuaded can be concluded and proved from the scriptures.' . . . This does not mean that more light is not to break from the Scriptures for us. Never was the sacred word more illuminated than now. It becomes every few years a new book to the studious and growing preacher. . . . What the wise preacher needs is to know just what higher criticism means. It is 'the criticism which is not purely linguistic or philological, but also takes into account the discoveries of history and archaeology, the teachings of comparative religion and the consideration of the ordinary laws of evidence, of documentary transmission, of psychology, and of human literature.' As Dr. Fairbairn puts it: 'The higher criticism is but a name for scientific scholarship scientifically used. If the Scriptures are fit subjects for scholarship, then the more scientific the scholarship the greater its use in the field of Scripture.' . . . We hold ourselves free to accept what is proved, for all truth is consistent with itself."

Any visitor at the home of the preacher, college president, or bishop soon found the conversation turning to books, and to the end of his days Eugene R. Hendrix was a teacher of truth. What he taught he learned in intensive study and he impressed all who heard him as a thinker. As he presided over an Annual Conference his preachers were often just his boys at Central College. Not only to that college but to the whole church he gave such an impetus for education and learning as few leaders of the church have been able to give. Never was an influence more needed than that of the man who transformed a school at Fayette into a college and sent men out into the world to demonstrate the power of thinking.

CHAPTER V

The Traveler

AS DR. Henry Van Dyke was returning to the shores of America after a tour of Europe he sang:

> Oh! it's great to see the Old World, to travel up and down
> Among its famous palaces and places of renown,
> To see its ancient monuments, its castles and its kings,
> But soon or late you have enough of antiquated things.
> So its home again and home again, America for me,
> My heart is turning home again and there I long to be.

Every man who loves his own country finds an echo of that song in his heart but there is a contribution to life which travel alone can make. Travel, as well as knowledge, maketh a full man. Scenes of physical beauty, unusual customs and widely different views, flowerings of genius in architecture and painting have a thrilling and a cultural influence, and one trip to Europe may be as valuable as a year in college. The convenience, ease and expense of travel make it possible today for thousands of Americans to know and see the old world. But in 1876 he was a courageous man who determined on a trip around the world. At the close of his pastorate in St. Joseph, Missouri, Eugene R. Hendrix left with Bishop Enoch M. Marvin to visit the mission fields of the Far East and to see the world of older civilizations. It was on the night of October 18, 1876, that the two travelers left Kansas City. It was in the day when the Pullman car was provided with a parlor organ and the passengers gathered around the organ in the evening to sing familiar songs.

It was on the morning of November 1 that the City of Alaska sailed on her voyage from San Francisco across the Pacific Ocean. The size of the boat greatly impressed her passengers, but it was small in comparison with a giant ocean liner today. She carried 750 persons, including passengers and crew, twelve beeves, fresh fruits and vegetables, and in her cargo 400 tons of flour and quanti-

Bishop and Mrs. Eugene Russell Hendrix. Pictures taken about the time of their marriage.

THE TRAVELER

ties of ginseng and quicksilver. It cost the ship $60,000 to make the trip from San Francisco to Hong Kong and back; there were 27 cabin passengers and 571 Chinese steerage passengers. It was the morning of November 30th, four weeks after sailing, that the shores of Japan were sighted. In his letter to America about his Japanese experiences Dr. Hendrix writes: "We were glad to obtain the following reliable statistics of missionary work in Japan up to October, 1876: Foreign missionaries, including 46 clerical, eight medical, and twenty-five educational, number 79; native missionaries, thirty-three; stations, forty; average weekly attendance, four thousand; baptized converts, one thousand; schools, nineteen; scholars, five hundred and fifty-seven; students for the ministry, forty; Sabbath Schools, ten; scholars, six hundred; a religious paper has one thousand one hundred copies in circulation." Ten days were spent in Japan and they were crowded with visits to native marts, and gardens and shrines; with investigations of missionary enterprises and preaching in churches and chapels; with conferences of missionaries and native Christians.

The approach to China is thus described: "Early on the morning of December 14 we were moving across the mouth of the Yangtse, her waters for all the world like those of the Missouri, and coloring the sea for miles around with sediment of mud brought down from the valley through which the river cuts her way. . . . We shortly turned up the mouth of the Woosung River, and crossing the bar, were only twelve miles from Shanghai. The Chinese village of Woosung, best known as the terminus of the only railway in the empire—a little line of twelve miles—lay off to our right. All about us were Chinese men-of-war, junks and other boats, nearly all of which had large eyes painted on their prows to enable them to see."

A Christmas Conference was held by Bishop Marvin at Shanghai, preceded by a conference of the laborers of that city at Brother Lambuth's house. The question discussed was the encouragements and discouragements of missionary work. Some of the encouragements mentioned were: When some of those present came to China thirty years before there was a single convert and now there are twelve thousand; only one or two cities could then hear the

63

gospel and now it is preached in a hundred walled cities, and five hundred villages; the schools have done well. The discouragements were: The slowness of the Chinese in understanding the drift of preaching, the harm done by foreigners from Christian nations who were not Christians, and the impatience of the church at home for large and speedy results.

There was a trip to Soochow and Hangchow, there were days in Hong Kong and Canton, and on January 18 the Bishop and his traveling companion left Hong Kong for Ceylon. Eleven days were spent in Ceylon and then the journey led to India. At Calcutta, Benares, Lucknow, Cawnpore, Delhi, Agra, Allahabad, and Bombay stops were made. The results of missionary work in India were given as follows: "Up to 1875 there had been raised up 311 ordained native preachers and 68,689 communicants of Christian Churches."

On March 12 boat was taken for Suez. As the English steamer made its way thought was given to the British control in the East. "What a vast empire England has acquired in the East! . . . English customs are beginning to prevail in the Orient. . . . The English language promises to be the spoken language of the world. . . . Those little crowded islands on the coast of continental Europe have found a grand outlet in this distant part of the world, and now rule ten times more people than their own population. What the English do, for the most part, they do well. Perhaps to no other nation in the world could the Almighty have committed so important a trust with as little danger of abuse, or as little liability to widespread corruption."

Cairo proved as fascinating as it always proves to visitors, and the same feeling of awe came to the Methodist preachers which every Christian experiences as he approaches Palestine. "Early on the morning of April 1st, Easter Sunday, we were in sight of the Promised Land. The mountains of Judea greeted my eyes as before sunrise I came upon the poop to get a first view of that land consecrated by the footprints and labors of our Lord. Here the incarnate God had lived, and taught and died. . . . Even the sepulchre hewn in these solid rocks was not able to hold his lifeless form when the hour had come for him to loose the bonds of death and come forth in divine triumph and glory." On approaching Jerusalem by road from Joppa came further reflections: "Bishop Marvin and I preferred to walk, for we had just passed the traditional Emmaus, where Jesus, on the day of his resurrection, had walked with two of his disciples. We also felt his presence, and our hearts burned within us as we talked by the way."

A week was spent in and about Jerusalem. There was the usual disappointment in the Christian life of the city. "The past week has been celebrated by the Greek Church here as Easter week, and many pilgrims from a distance have been present to witness the services. In the square in front of the Church of the Sepulchre was celebrated, on Thursday morning, the foot-washing. Olivet was represented by an olive-tree fastened to the wall some fifteen feet from the ground. The Greek patriarch, in his satin gown, ornamented with rich gold brocade, and wearing a jeweled miter, personated Christ; while twelve bishops, hardly less elegantly dressed, played the part of the apostles. . . . There appeared to be an entire absence of solemnity during these ceremonies. . . . On the following night the crucifixion took place, and at midnight on Saturday the resurrection, neither of which I cared to witness—a wax figure representing the body of the Lord. I did see, however, what was only less revolting, the kindling of the holy fire in the tomb of Christ."

After a visit to the Dead Sea and the River Jordan the pilgrims went north to Nazareth, and on to the Sea of Galilee. "Climbing the hills, we linger for another look at the historic lake which appears before us in all its dimensions. This, of all the localities in Palestine, Olivet alone excepted, is the most sacred to the Christians. How sacred these very names! But our hearts need not the tree-crowned mountain and the silent sea to help us to commune with Christ. An angel's voice calls from each, 'He is not here, He is risen,' while the believer replies:

"But warm, sweet, tender, even yet
A present help is He;

While faith has still its Olivet,
And love its Galilee."

With stops at Damascus and Baalbec the journey continued to
Beirut and then on to Europe by boat. Constantinople seemed to
have the finest site of any city in the world; Athens stirred mind
and soul with memories of Greek philosophers and Paul's sermon
on Mars Hill; the bay of Naples impressed with its beauty; Pompeii
brought amazement; in Rome was a cross-section of the centuries;
Florence was the embodiment of culture and the center of art;
Venice was picturesque; and the Alps inspiring. Such were the reactions of the travelers on their way to Switzerland and Germany.
One after another of the beautiful places of Switzerland was seen;
then the great cities of Germany, then the small countries of Holland and Belgium; then Paris and London; then Scotland and Ireland. In London the preachers of the day were heard and there are
these interesting comments: "One of the best sermons I heard in
London was by Canon Farrar, in Westminster Abbey—logical,
brave manly utterance. . . . I heard Mr. Spurgeon in his great Tabernacle before six thousand souls. The sermon was fresh, vigorous,
faithful. . . . Dr. Joseph Parker has large congregations; he is vigorous in the pulpit but his mannerisms offend; his delivery is unhap-
pily artificial and savors of the stage. . . . Dr. John Cumming, who
once had the ear of all London, and addressed thousands in Exeter
Hall, now preaches to a very small congregation in his enlarged
church near Drury Lane."

On reaching City Road Chapel it was found that Dr. Punshon was
preaching the annual sermon before the Lord Mayor and the high
Sheriffs. "The sermon was good, but gold lace and other insignia
of office seemed to divide the eyes if not the minds of the people,"
is the comment. The Wesleyan Conference was meeting at Bristol,
and Bishop Marvin and Mr. Hendrix received a letter in London
from the College of Bishops with the commission authorizing them
to go as fraternal delegates. They were impressed by the character of
British Methodism, and regarded these things as worthy of remembrance:

(1) The appointments were worked out by the Stationing Committee in advance of the Conference Session and could be studied with a view of adjustment during the Conference.

(2) The ministers were men of ability and sound scholarship, and the services of worship were dignified, the order of Service of the Church of England often being used.

After visits to Scotland and Ireland the travelers embarked at Cork on the Britannic and reached New York Harbor on the night of August 17, taking seven days, ten hours and fifty-three minutes for the ocean crossing. The tour of the world had been made in ten months and three days and the story of the journey ends with these words: "After a survey of the whole field the conviction strengthens—the world, vast as it is, is not too large a conquest to be made in the name of Christ." The volume descriptive of this journey had not yet come from the press when Bishop Enoch M. Marvin died; in an "In Memoriam" chapter Dr. Hendrix writes: "It was the prospect of his genial company that led me to take this tour around the globe when I did. . . . His sudden death throws back upon our delightful tour its only shadow. . . . How sacred will always be every league of the journey when I remember that the companion with whom I measured it has passed to his reward."

The journey of Bishop Marvin and Mr. Hendrix made a great impression on the church. The purpose of the journey was a study of the advance of Christ's Kingdom, and it was the first time ministers of the Methodist Episcopal Church, South, ever went around the world on such a mission. It was not the last but only the longest journey of Eugene Russell Hendrix. To Mexico he went as the Bishop in charge of the work of the Methodist Episcopal Church, South, in 1893, 1912 and 1913. He was in Europe in 1900, and again in 1914. In 1895 he visited the Orient to study situations and the work of Methodist missionaries with a view to the opening of new stations. In 1899 he went to Brazil as Bishop in charge of the work. Each of these journeys was memorable in his life and in the history of his church.

In 1893 he called on President Diaz in Mexico City. There is this record of the visit: "His strong and wise government is doing much for Mexico and I expressed to him my high appreciation of it. He was exceedingly cordial while quite willing that the interview should be of service to the Republic by producing a kindly feeling toward Mexico."

He went to the Orient in 1894 with a special letter from President Grover Cleveland. This put every United States consulate and ministry at his command, and he had remarkable contacts with the leaders of the Orient. There were audiences with Li Hsi, King of Korea, and Li Hung Chang, the foremost Asiatic of his day, and there were visits to many sections of Japan, Korea and China. There is a detailed account in a diary of the trip to Brazil in 1899. Sailing first to England he was present at a Fourth of July Dinner in London at which Ambassador Choate, Cardinal Vaughan, Lord Dartmouth and Mark Twain were the speakers; he was the guest of Canon Holland at Canterbury; and he was entertained by those great leaders of Wesleyan Methodism, D. J. Waller and Hugh Price Hughes. He sailed for Brazil from Southampton via Lisbon. Through the United States legation and the missionaries he met many of the leaders of Brazil and rendered great service to the churches and church schools of that Republic. In 1900 he went to England as fraternal messenger to the British Wesleyan Conference, preaching in many Wesleyan churches, and strengthening the ties of friendship with the leaders of British Methodism. The visit to Mexico in 1912 brought about an adjustment of territory between the Methodist Episcopal Church and the Methodist Episcopal Church, South, and marked the beginning of a friendship with President Madero. On the trip to Mexico in 1913 the train on which the Bishop was riding was attacked by bandits and lives were saved by the courage and composure of the railway engineer. Perhaps no travel experience was so thrilling as the journey to the Peace Conference at Constance in 1914. Representatives of the churches of Protestant lands were meeting in the German city at the outbreak of the World War. There were thrilling experiences in Holland in the efforts to get home, perils from icebergs in the North Atlantic, and danger from German cruisers necessitating sailing without lights. Few conferences in the history of the church have been more idelistic than the Peace Conference at Constance with all Europe mobilizing for war, and among the great leaders of that conference was Eugene R. Hendrix.

A service of thirty-six years in the episcopacy took Bishop Hendrix to every section of his own country. He kept a careful record of the sermons preached and the texts used, and in almost every one of those years he was preaching in the East and the West, the North and the South. It is true that no Bishop of the Methodist Episcopal Church, South, ever traveled farther, and few Methodist preachers have journeyed as many miles in the service of the church. In a typical year we find him preaching in Arkansas, Louisiana, Missouri, Kansas, Tennessee, Virginia, Maryland, North Carolina, Montana, Washington, Oregon, California, Arizona and Kentucky as he administers his work!

What does travel do for a man? It educates him. It gives him a knowledge of geography and history. There are those who insist that the geographical configuration of a country determines its history. There are undoubtedly other factors that enter into the development of a nation's life, but its shape and its mountains and its water-ways and its neighbors have much to do in the determination of its history. The conflict of Norway's mountains with the North Atlantic's stormy waves has produced a race that is not only sturdy in physique but strong in character. Palestine's location has made it a bridge across which the armies and caravans of Egypt, Babylonia and Assyria have moved; each of these civilizations has had its influence on Palestinian life and religion. Not only is the traveler educated in geography but in history as well. He can read histories of England for years, but historical figures come to life as he travels across the channel with William the Conqueror, lingers for a day at Canterbury and stops for a week in London. I heard a man say that he learned more of English history in a day at the Tower of London than in his course in college. One knows from his reading that Florence is a city of culture, but he sees in a few days there enough to explain the love for that city in the heart of every student of art. Why has Florence been such a center of culture? The traveler learns that a conference was held in that city between a Pope of

Rome and a Roman Emperor from Constantinople under the patronage of a Medici prince. The Pope was anxious to extend the influence of the Church of Rome, and the Emperor from Constantinople wanted assistance against the threatening Turks. In the train of the Eastern Emperor were clerks and attendants who were scholars versed in the classical lore of Greece and Rome. When the conference was over many of these scholars stayed in Florence to teach the classics to Florentine youth, and there came to Florence and to Europe the Renaissance. For the traveler the past is peopled with real persons, and history is more than a series of dates.

And travel multiplies friendships. A man is often made by the people he meets. Each year a group of American clergymen goes to Europe under a leadership that brings contacts with European leaders. The work of any such leader is better understood when he himself discusses his objectives, and anyone who has met him in person is enlarged and changed. Even the casual traveler understands any land he visits if he is fortunate enough to find a friend in that land who will talk.

Furthermore, travel destroys prejudices. The most prejudiced person in the world is one who is born and dies in the same region, with no opportunity to get far away from home. The citizen of a foreign land is not like the caricature of him which is often drawn. The policy of another nation is often very different from the representation of it. The disrespectful names given to foreign citizens cannot be used when the civilization and culture of their native lands are known.

Finally travel makes a man a citizen of a larger world. Paul of Tarsus was a citizen of no mean city, and he is proud of the city of his birth; but Paul was not a real citizen of the Roman Empire until in his journeys he went far beyond the limits of Tarsus. Goethe used to long for that culture and that knowledge which would make him at home in any land, and the horizon enlarges for that man who finds it possible to get away from home. He who travels becomes a citizen of the world.

Travel exerted all these influences on the life of Eugene R. Hendrix. He had the best university and seminary training of any Methodist preacher in the south, but his travel added to the knowledge which he acquired in college. In almost every sermon or address he turned for an illustration to some land beyond the sea. His acquaintance and friendship with the great leaders of other countries enabled him to speak with authority as he quoted them. His success in securing interviews with those who shaped policies in Mexico, and Brazil and the Orient helped his church and its missionaries. But it did more than that! It made his church known in other lands as it had not been known.

Most of the bishops of the Methodist Episcopal Church, South, have been leaders only in their own denomination and their own section. Few of them have been known in the North or East, but Eugene R. Hendrix was as heartily welcomed and almost as well known in New York, Chicago or Syracuse as in Birmingham or Dallas. A bishop can go to a mission field and come home without any discovery of his presence on the part of the country's leaders. It was not so when Bishop Hendrix went! The leadership of any land he visited knew that a bishop of the Methodist Episcopal Church, South, had been in that land. It was all because he knew his way around and was at home in the lands he knew by travel.

Many great men have small traits, but travel destroys narrowness and prejudice. Dr. James W. Lee used to tell a story about a Georgia Methodist preacher who was quite conceited about his election as secretary of a District Conference. When his attitude became unbearable Dr. Lee took him for a walk one night and engaged him in conversation. One after another came these questions: "Have you ever been in Atlanta? Have you been out of Georgia? Have you ever looked at a map to see how small a part of the world the United States is? Do you know that the star we see is so far away that it takes two thousand years for its light to reach the earth? I wanted you to mediate a little on the size of the universe." Eugene R. Hendrix never made a fight for a petty cause. There were times when some of his listeners were irritated by his reference to his travels or his acquaintance with world leaders, but such listeners were usually those whose outlook was limited and whose background was provincial. Small men found it difficult to get close to him, particularly

71

if they sought his support for some small cause, and so he was not popular with such groups. But a study of his leadership in the church will reveal his alignment with the constructive forces and his support of the large causes in the church controversies of his day.

He lived in a large world. He could see city and state and nation and world in proper perspective. He was loyal to his church and no leader ever supported the denominational program and interests more faithfully. But he never lost sight of the fact that the Christian Church is larger and of more value to the world than any unit of it. Above all, his loyalty of loyalties was a devotion to his Lord. His Lord must increase even if in that increase the church should decrease. He lived in God's world, and the world for him must be the world as God made it. Frederick F. Shannon has a lovely interpretation of truth when he says that in the Galilee of Jesus a bird was more than a bird, a flower was more than a flower, and rain was more than rain. A bird could not fall to the ground without the Father's notice, and flowers revealed the beauty and goodness of God, and rain fell on the just and the unjust. So the world was God's world, and the church Christ's church for Eugene R. Hendrix. The exaltation of Christ was a favorite theme and the incarnation a continuous subject of study; so the church must be thought of as Christ's body, a spiritual agency for a spiritual ministry! He said once: "Methodism is the least part of the great religious movement of the 18th century under the Wesleys." We live in a world of neighbor states, and every individual must be a world citizen. It was not so before the World Wars, and the man who came to such citizenship made a place for himself by pushing back the horizons. When the horizon is pushed back for every one no one is recognized as a conspicuous leader who is not a citizen of the world, and one wonders how the world could have seemed so large and lands beyond the seas so far away.

There was a time when distances were great and frontiers could not be passed, but Southern Methodism furnished in Eugene R. Hendrix one who pushed the sky back on either side. Of such service as his was the poet thinking when she wrote:

72

THE TRAVELER

"The world stands out on either side
No wider than the heart is wide;
Above the world is stretched the sky—
No higher than the soul is high.
The heart can push the sea and land
Farther away on either hand;
The soul can split the sky in two,
And let the face of God shine through.
But East and West will pinch the heart
That cannot keep them pushed apart;
And he whose soul is flat—the sky
Will cave in on him by and by."

CHAPTER VI

The Bishop

AT THE General Conference of the Methodist Episcopal Church, South, at Atlanta in 1918, Dr. E. W. Alderson, of Texas, was discussing the weaknesses and failures of the episcopacy in the Methodist Church. He was saying that the Bishop of the Southern Methodist Church had more authority than any ecclesiastical official in the world except the prelate of the Roman Catholic Church; that he frequently abused the trust reposed in him by using his office to appoint to influential churches political friends and supporters; that the office is so much larger than the man who is usually elected to it. At the beginning of his address the speaker said to the presiding officer: "I am sorry, Sir, that I must make these remarks with you in the chair. If all our bishops had been as worthy of the office as you, and if they were all as capable of filling it, we would never have had in the church the criticism of the episcopacy we hear on every hand." The chairman of that morning's session was Bishop Eugene R. Hendrix, who was concluding thirty-two years of service in the episcopacy. Was the speaker right?

There were times in his episcopal career when there was much criticism of the Bishop. There was a time when he was involved in a controversy over the control of Central College in Missouri. Many Missourians thought he was wrong in his effort to control that institution, and spoke of his autocratic use of power. But he lived to serve the conferences in Missouri as presiding bishop from 1914 to 1918 and when he finished his quadrennium he was respected, honored and loved from one end of the state to the other.

He was widely criticized for his gesture of friendship at the General Conference of the Methodist Episcopal Church in Saratoga Springs when he and Bishop Cranston clasped hands as symbolic of Methodist unification. Years have passed since then, and unification has come at last. And when it came the Hendrix who was criticized was hailed as a prophet.

He was criticized also when as Chairman of the Board of Trust of Vanderbilt University he refused to join his colleagues in the episcopacy in a lawsuit to test the ownership and control of the University. The present has all but vindicated the wisdom of his position, because it is doubtful whether any other General Conference since would have done what the Conference in Oklahoma City did in 1914. If the present has not vindicated him, the future will.

Categorical statements are not sufficient and we must go into the record of his administration and examine his own reactions, as well as those of others, to his duties as a bishop of the Church.

He ordained to the ministry of the church more than 1,600 candidates and dedicated 287 churches. Through the years of his episcopacy he kept a record of the places at which he preached and the texts used. There is a record of 2,696 sermons, or about 75 each year of the thirty-six years of his episcopacy. This means that his average was more than a sermon a week. During the last four years he preached only 104 times, or an average of a sermon every two weeks. For the first thirty-two years of his episcopacy the average number of sermons a year is thus found to be 81.

Far more remarkable in this record is the number of special sermons at colleges or conventions.

June 6, 1886, Central College
June 26, 1887, Wesleyan University
October 19, 1887, Vanderbilt University
July 7th & 10th, 1888, Northfield Assembly in Massachusetts
July 14, 1889, Monteagle Assembly in Tennessee
June 20, 1891, University of Virginia
June 12, 1892, Wofford College
August 14, 1892, Ocean Grove Camp Meeting
June 18, 1893, Vanderbilt University
June 17, 1894, Central College
June 1, 1895, Emory College
May 31, 1896, Cornell University
June 14, 1896, University of Alabama
February 14, 1897, University of Missouri
June 6, 1897, University of Mississippi
May 1, 1898, University of Virginia
June 5, 1898, Central College

75

June 11, 1899, Emory College
July 2, 1899, Westminster College in London
April 24, 1900, Carnegie Hall in New York
June and July, 1900, Belfast and Dublin in Ireland
  Oxford and London in England
July 15, 1900, City Road Chapel in London
October 21, 1900, Vanderbilt University
June 1, 1901, Southwestern University
June 15, 1902, Cornell College in Iowa
April 20-24, 1903, Quillian Lectures at Emory College
April 26-May 3, 1903, Cole Lectures at Vanderbilt
June 14, 1903, Hendrix College
June 14, 1904, Southwestern University
October 16, 1904, World's Fair at St. Louis
February 5, 1905, Princeton University
February 6, 1905, Union Theological Seminary
February 7, 1905, Drew Theological Seminary
November 12, 1905, University of Missouri
June 2, 1907, University of North Carolina
May 23, 1909, Tuskegee Institute
January 1, 1910, Student Volunteer Convention in Rochester
February 12, 1911, University of Kansas
September 28, 1911, Garrett Biblical Institute
June 6, 1912, Baker University
June 9, 1912, University of Arkansas
June 16, 1912, Wesleyan University
October 11, 1912, Dedication of Barnes Hospital in St. Louis
December 4, 1912, Fullerton Hall in Chicago
August 2, 1914, Peace Address in Constance, Germany
October 29, 1915, Southern Methodist University
June 15, 1916, Albion College
October 8, 1916, Vanderbilt University
June 17, 1917, Wesleyan University
November 14, 1920, United States Naval Academy

Not only was he in demand as a preacher at colleges and universities but he was invited by the leading churches of his denomination for sermons at regular and special services. At St. John's Church in St. Louis he preached seventeen times and in his home church, Melrose of Kansas City, one hundred and five times.

It is equally interesting to read the list of the churches of his own and other denominations in which he preached. A part of that list is noted:

May 23, 1886, First Presbyterian Church in Richmond
March 13, 1887, Presbyterian Church in Fulton, Missouri
November 23, 1890, St. Paul's Methodist Church in New York
November 30, 1890, Hyde Park Methodist Church in Chicago
November 13, 1902, Sixth Avenue Methodist Church, Brooklyn
July 9, 1905, Central Presbyterian Church, Denver
November 19, 1905, Central Congregational Church, Brooklyn
August 30, 1908, Linwood Boulevard Christian Church, Kansas City
December 6, 1908, Arch Street Methodist Church, Philadelphia
February 14, 1909, Second Presbyterian Church, Chicago
March 26, 1909, First Methodist Church, Omaha
December 30, 1909, Asbury Methodist Church, Rochester
January 2, 1910, Central Presbyterian Church, Rochester
February 4, 1910, Third Baptist Church, St. Louis
May 8, 1910, First Presbyterian Church, Asheville
July 16, 1911, First Congregational Church, Kansas City
December 6, 1911, Metropolitan Methodist Church, Toronto
December 12, 1911, First Presbyterian Church, Pittsburgh
April 5, 1912, Linwood Boulevard Presbyterian Church, Kansas City
May 10, 1914, First Presbyterian Church, Oklahoma City
June 25, 1916, First Methodist Church, Rochester
November 5, 1916, Old John Street Methodist Church, New York
February 4, 1917, First Methodist Church, Evanston
November 2, 1919, First Presbyterian Church, Shreveport

In a study of the texts used in the sermons preached at Melrose Church in Kansas City it is remarkable to see how few times a text is used a second time. There are twelve texts used a second time in the period of thirty-six years; this leaves ninety-three texts used by the Bishop at Melrose Church, and his preaching there is a cross section of his preaching ministry. Sixteen of these texts are from the Old Testament, and there are seventy-seven from the New Testament. The texts are chosen from these books:

The Gospel of John	18	The Epistle to the Hebrews	9
The Gospel of Matthew	14	The Epistle to the Romans	4
The Gospel of Luke	8	First Corinthians	3
The Gospel of Mark	4	Book of Acts	3
First Epistle of John	3		

There are two texts from Colossians, two from 1st Timothy, 2 from 2nd Timothy, Revelation, and one from 1st Peter, one from James, and one from Galatians. Of the Old Testament texts the selection is from these books:

Psalms	5	Nehemiah	1
Isaiah	4	Proverbs	1
Joshua	1	Genesis	1
Ecclesiastes	1	Samuel	1
	Joel	1	

It is astonishing to a preacher of today that a student of the Bible should miss the riches of the Old Testament in his search for texts. Bishop Hendrix was a New Testament preacher, and even there he was most interested in the mystical and theological. He turned also to those passages which discuss the mystery of the incarnation and the function of the Christ in man's redemption. The gospel stories of Mark and Luke which tell the life history of Jesus and which emphasize a ministry of human helpfulness are not sought as Matthew, which seeks to prove that Jesus is the Messiah, and John, which seeks to interpret Jesus as the Word and the Son of God.

At Melrose Church the Bishop sometimes preached a sermon he had used a few days before at an Annual Conference; sometimes he preached there a sermon he intended to preach at an Annual Conference. He preached to the church what he preached at Melrose, and the denomination came to regard him as a New Testament preacher, with an inclination to the philosophical and theological. He was not always understood, but from one end of the church to the other he was regarded as a great preacher. In the years of his episcopal service a bishop's chief qualification was his ability to preach. A little earlier, perhaps, it was almost the sole qualification for the episcopacy. In later years administrative ability has been considered a prime requisite, and the bishops who are approved by their conferences and their denomination are those who can direct other men and get results in increased gifts and membership. Bishop Hendrix served for so many years that his episcopacy touches both the era of episcopal preaching and episcopal administration. He was not lacking in administrative ability. His experience at Central College, and his association with men of affairs prepared him for an effective ministry as an executive officer of his church. He presided over every conference in the connection and his business judgment was often needed. To evaluate his episcopacy it is well to know not only what he thought of the function of a bishop, but how he reacted to his responsibilities as he went about his work. It is better still to know what the church, its ministers and its members, thought of the Bishop. We will attempt now to follow paths which will lead us to a knowledge of what the Bishop thought of his work, and what others thought of the Bishop.

There are these records in the diary which reveal the Bishop's attitude toward his work.

July 29, 1886—On July 1st met the Bishops at the Sea Shore Camp Ground near Biloxi, Mississippi. Learned to love and confide in my colleagues whom I find delightful friends and wise counsellors. . . . A delightful religious atmosphere and I enjoy hearing and preaching the word. May God help me to magnify my enlarged opportunity of usefulness!

October 2, 1886—Enjoyed my new duties while presiding over the Kentucky and Louisville Conferences on account of the gracious presence of the Master. His grace sufficient amid many perplexities and grave responsibilities. The sessions were religious and harmonious. The appointments received much attention and were generally satisfactory, only five out of 250 expressing any desire for a possible improvement.

October 17, 1886—Had a delightful time at the Tennessee Conference. Enjoyed much of the Divine Presence and everything seemed to move smoothly. Stationed about 160 preachers and did not hear a single word of complaint.

February 8, 1887—Returned on the 1st instant from a ten weeks' trip to Alabama, Georgia, and Florida. . . . This completes my round of conferences during which I have ordained 59 deacons and 26 elders and received 56 preachers into full connection and stationed over 800 preachers or more than 1/5 of the whole traveling connection with complaints from less than 1%. Enjoyed the work of the conference sessions which were seasons of spiritual profit.

June 12, 1887—Two months and a half of ceaseless travel and labor. . . . but this is the chief sacrifice I can make for the Master together with the giving of my income over and above a moderate living "unto Him."

December 31, 1887—I have seen enough of my new duties during the year and half of my labors as a bishop in the church to know somewhat of both the trials and joys of the office. A consciousness of integrity indispensable to peace of mind amid such grave responsibilities. What I do will depend largely upon what I am. I feel concern for both my intellectual and spiritual habits. I must be more a student of the word and live a more consecrated life properly to preach or impress and influence men. . . . And now, O my Prophet, Priest and King, I humbly accept Thy teachings, implore Thy intercession and consecrate myself anew to Thy service.

May 17, 1888—My colleagues warn me that I am attempting too much and I suspect that they are right. Declining chautauqua and college engagements to give the more time to church work.

September 16, 1888—Have held three of my six conferences and find that my work the second year satisfies me much better than the first as I know both the men and the charges better. Have greatly strengthened the Denver Conference, consolidated the Western Conference and revitalized the Missouri Conference by healthy pruning and changing leaders. . . . A wise movement inaugurated among the laity to increase their own efficiency.

March 14, 1889—The death of Bishop McTyeire has filled my heart with great sadness and a sense of increased responsibility. Added duties fall to his colleagues at a time when great wisdom is needed in administering the affairs of the church. Have been carefully reviewing church history during the past two months, thereby broadening my sympathies and strengthening my faith.

October 20, 1889—Have enjoyed my trip to the Indian Mission Conference where I ordained five Choctaws and Creeks, and twelve Americans. The civilized tribes as curious about each other and the wild tribes as we are. Started some of the charges on a self-supporting basis.

March 14, 1890—The thirtieth anniversary of my conversion finds me assisting in a protracted meeting at Melrose where all my family are members of the church. Some religious interest in our different churches here this winter without many conversions. The tide of worldliness is stayed but that is not enough, the church must do more for the conversion of sinners.

July 13, 1891—The cornerstone of the Training School laid July 3 with addresses by Dr. Lambuth, C. F. Reed and Dr. W. H. Potter. . . . The Board of Managers held an important meeting and unanimously elected Miss Laura Haygood as Principal.

October 25, 1891—Returned on the 22nd instant from the Second Ecumenical Conference in Washington, a grand and inspiring occasion.

January 1, 1892—I enter upon the new year with the desire and purpose to grow in grace and in the knowledge of our Lord Jesus Christ. To this end I shall be a more diligent student of the word in the original and strive by meditation and prayer to know more of the mind of Christ. I dread arrested development as damaging to intellectual and spiritual life. . . . I enjoy my work despite the care of all the churches.

February 28, 1892—I had a delightful religious talk with Mr. R. A. Barnes (in St. Louis) who has been so liberal a friend of the College (Central) for the past twelve years.

September 14, 1892—The Scarritt Bible and Training School was formally dedicated today in the presence of a large congregation.

February 5, 1893—My exegetical studies this winter are in John's Gospel having been in Romans last winter. The three mid-winter months my longest period of uninterrupted study always looked forward to with great pleasure.

December 30, 1893—Bless God for his grace during the peculiar trials of the last half of the year. Have been better able to sympathize with businessmen in their perplexities and losses from own first serious experience. The financial stringency still widespread.

April 24, 1894—Am just leaving for Louisville and Memphis at which latter place I report to the General Conference after my eight years in the episcopacy following my eight years as college president which followed my eight years as pastor. How each experience has prepared for the one that followed. I sought to be pastor even when a teacher and I am now both as never before. . . . I have believed that the theologian is more than the preacher and the scholar more than the writer and have sought to increase my resources while I have been in labors abundant.

October 9, 1894—At home again after my six conferences. Made many changes, especially in Missouri where I gave much attention to the manning of the leading stations and the retiring of less competent men from places of responsibility. . . . A delightful meeting with the Trustees of the Barnes Hospital at the Planters House, and the discussion of location and policy had.

March 1, 1895—Busy in my winter's work of exegetical study and in historical theology, especially the history of doctrine in the Greek Church and what Methodism owes to the belief in the Divine immanence. Am grateful for a God not apart from the Universe, but who is immanent.

December 27, 1896—Returned on the 22nd instant from my fall conferences in Texas, Mississippi and Louisiana where I greatly enjoyed friendship with my brethren, seeking to save them from overprofession and arrested development. I have felt called to preach Christ Jesus as Lord in all the fulness of his power to give abundant life to the whole man and not simply to stir his emotional nature.

December 12, 1897—At home after holding the three conferences in Arkansas. . . . Many changes rendered necessary by brethren having too little resources for the pastorate. Advised the disuse of canned goods and the killing of a beef. A type of religious fanaticism in the White River Conference needed to be checked by the presentation of the whole gospel.

March 26, 1899—Returned on 20th from a memorable visit to St. Louis where on the 18th I gave an address on Methodist Catholicity before the St. Louis Conference of the Methodist Episcopal Church in Union Church. . . . On Sunday night Mr. Samuel Cupples gave me $26,000 for Central College.

May 21, 1899—Twentieth Century Movement growing in favor as seen by mass meetings in Nashville and Birmingham addressed by my beloved Galloway and myself. . . . Enjoy preaching at these gatherings which are so full of hope to the church.

October 20, 1901—A good time in St. Louis at cornerstone laying of the new St. John's Church and at meeting of Curators of Central College to put College on better financial basis. Cupples and Scruggs gave $25,000 each, Carleton $7,500, Governor Stevens $1,000 and others enough to reach the aggregate sum of $70,000.

May 30, 1902—Returned two days ago from our fourteenth General Conference held in Dallas. Despite the great interest preceding the session the general policy outlined by the episcopal address was wisely pursued. The inevitable "War Claim" disposed of. . . . Bishop Galloway and I cemented our Damon and Pythias friendship.

October 5, 1902—Returned on the 15th instant from the dedication of the Travis Park Church in San Antonio, Texas, having raised $12,400 on September 30th.

December 30, 1907—Seven busy weeks during which I held five conferences, giving fifteen addresses, dedicated eight churches, five of them in two and a half days.

May 18, 1911—The 25th anniversary of my election as bishop celebrated by a notable reception and the presentation of a loving cup by the Missouri Methodists.

October 11, 1912—Today I laid the cornerstone of Barnes Hospital, St. Louis, for which my old friend Robert A. Barnes left $900,-000, now grown to $2,000,000.

July 4, 1913—Returned from Waynesville Assembly where I raised $151,200 for missions.

These comments on his episcopal service reveal Eugene R. Hendrix as an indefatigable worker. He gave himself to his tasks and was away from his home most of the time. He held his conferences, frequently attended district conferences, and responded to calls for dedications and the laying of cornerstones. Through most of his episcopal career he held from five to eight conferences a year, and met all of the extra engagements that came to him. He was firm in his presidency of a conference, and he did not hesitate to make changes in appointments if they seemed necessary for the good of the church. Never was there a selfish motive in any of his appointments; he seems never to have had in mind the building up of any sentiment for himself, and no man's appointment depended on his standing by the administration. He was in demand as a leader of financial campaigns, and his ability as a businessman was of great service to his church. In the later years of his episcopal administration he had an open cabinet, and insisted that preachers be given the opportunity to discuss with their presiding elders changes in their appointments. There may have been more dissatisfaction with his appointments than the Bishop learned, as he refers to less than one per cent of dissatisfied preachers; but those who knew his episcopal administration will agree that his judgment and his sense of justice did bring about harmonious adjustments in appointments. There were dissatisfactions but it is remarkable that there were so few complaints against his administration in the Committee on Episcopacy at the General Conference which reviewed his official conduct.

When he was elected bishop congratulations came to him from friends around the world, but he kept only a few messages. One of those preserved is from Dr. Nathan Scarritt: "I know of no office in church or state in which there is greater need of Divine guidance than that of a Methodist Bishop. It is a great work—a very great work. It is a work in which is involved the eternal destiny of many immortal souls whom you must meet at the judgment bar." In the spirit of that message he served his church. Miss Belle Bennett wrote him at the time of his election as President of the Federal Council of the Churches of Christ in America, "I have learned to prize your Christian judgment, wise counsel and ever enlarging vision of the world's need and how to meet it." Dr. James Atkins, afterwards a Bishop, expressed his appreciation of the Bishop's work at the Holston Conference: "The abundance and high quality of the work which you did there through the week was enough to break one down temporarily, but I was much about the city where I could witness the influence of that work, and I doubt whether you ever touched a city in which the high quality and abundance of your work were ever more appreciated or had a more enduring effect on the preachers and the people."

When the Bishop retired a daily newspaper of Kansas City carried an editorial with the title, "Full of years and service." These sentences come from that editorial: "He was an ecclesiastical statesman. . . . The career of Bishop Hendrix has been marked by unusual accomplishment. . . . He served with vision and rare effectiveness a wide church constituency."

One of the most impressive hours in the history of the General Conferences of Southern Methodism was that in which Secretary A. F. Watkins read at Hot Springs in 1922 a message from Bishop Hendrix. That message is a classic and deserves a place in the church's archives. It breathes the spirit of the Bishop and his episcopal administration.

My Beloved Brethren, Greetings:

While absent in body I crave to be with and among you in the fellowship of the Spirit, by whose leadings and guidance you have met and will resolve and act together. Only the constraining authority of a trusted doctor and those of my own household restrain me from attempting the journey I must needs make to meet and fellowship with you. Some of you know the fervency of my hope to have done so. Again, Greetings: And this for the last time! For I have heard the command, "Unarm, the long day's work is done, and we must sleep." God speaks in no uncertain voice. But I rejoice that his work does not quit nor slack. And while my heartbeats weaken, I know there are younger and stronger men and women all alive under the inspiration of God's spirit, to love, companion and pasture his flocks.

To my companions of the Episcopacy: May our Heavenly Father endow you daily with holiness and wisdom and mercy and strength.

And to the faithful pastors: May they come also to the rejoicing bringing their sheaves with them.

And to the men, women and children with whom we labor and whom we love, of every race, clime and condition, our brethren for whom the riches of the infinite lovingkindness of our Heavenly

Father have been abundantly poured out: To them what may I say?

Bid these, my brethren, that they love one another, and share together the joys of the life that now is and of that which is to come, in a wholesome security of a living faith that they are God's children and the subjects of His constant love and care. They shall not want, for He is the Almighty One who holds the infinities in His hand.

Kindly relieve me, my brethren, as my God has done already, of the further labors of my Episcopal office. With joy have I lived and with joy have I died, and I lay myself down with a will. I have your several faces and characters in affectionate and joyous remembrance. All good words and works be yours! Let me in my daily prayers remember you and each one of you in the face of our Heavenly Father. Take from my outstretched hands and a full heart my faithful benedictions.

May God's richest blessing be and abide with each and every one of you now and evermore! Amen! Fraternally and affectionately, your retiring bishop,

EUGENE R. HENDRIX.

And thus did the most honored and most influential bishop in the history of the Methodist Episcopal Church, South, come to the end of his episcopal labors.

CHAPTER VII

The Missionary Leader

A MEMBER of the class of '67 at Wesleyan University wrote the newly elected Bishop Hendrix: "How much I would like to get near enough to you to let my heart throb against yours. You were even in the old college days just such an earnest, truthful soul, loyal with uncompromising fidelity to every noble conviction, transparently clear and clean. . . . The Bishop was in you. . . . Don't you recall some of the old Band Meetings now? Don't you remember how we used to wait on the Lord and how that though we were scarcely more than boys nevertheless 'the blessing' came upon us, and our hearts were thrilled, filled and surcharged with spiritual power?" The praying band at Wesleyan sought not only spiritual growth for its members, but it was eager to serve God by holding services in neighboring towns and in churches without ministers. Here was born that missionary zeal which was to characterize the ministry of Eugene R. Hendrix. The trip around the world with Bishop Marvin in 1876 brought an acquaintance with missionaries and the missionary enterprise, thus deepening the zeal.

Mrs. A. P. Parker, the wife of the great missionary to China, has told of that wintry night in Missouri when her husband and another young man by the name of Hendrix prayed far into the night for China and its people, the result of that prayer being Parker's decision to go to China. More than one minister of the church faced similar decisions in the presence of this missionary enthusiast. When Young J. Allen in China heard of his election as bishop he wrote him: "I am not so sure about the other new bishops, but I feel sure that you will, as in the past continue to feel and take ever a more active interest in our operations in the Far East."

In the year 1884 there was observed the centenary of Methodism as an organized movement in America. As the program for that year, emphasis was laid on spiritual growth and missionary expansion. President Hendrix of Central College was a member of the Central Centenary Committee. In the diary, under date of January 20, 1884, he writes: "Our Centenary Year has dawned at length, ushered in with prayer all over the connection and by special sermons on the doctrines and usages of early Methodism which have contributed under God to her spiritual power."

As indicating his further activity in the Centenary Movement are these entries:

April 13, 1884—Attended the Church Extension Board at Louisville and helped to inaugurate the Centenary Church Extension Loan Fund. Also the Board of Missions and the Centenary Mass Meetings in Nashville.

May 25, 1884—Centenary Day one of great joy and profit at Fayette in Centenary Chapel. Some eight thousand dollars given as Centenary thank offering. Our hearts overflowed in Love Feast. A remarkable day. Praise God! May the church be blessed as largely.

October 13, 1884—Have been very busy at the three conferences looking after College and Centenary interests. Missouri gives $200,-000 as a Centenary offering, an inspiration to the rest of the church.

December 26, 1884—Home most sweet after some seventeen days absence in Washington and at the great Centennial Conference in Baltimore. The Christmas Conference a great success. . . . The honor of presiding during one session I esteem for my children's sake and for the pleasant memories the fact recalls.

After his election Bishop Hendrix put forth every effort to carry the Christian message to the world. He was in charge, at different times, of the mission conferences in the Orient, in Mexico, and in Brazil. His supervision was more than a visit to the countries. His letters to missionaries on the field after his return home indicate how effectively he handled all the problems faced. When Dr. and Mrs. A. P. Parker were sent to the Anglo-Chinese College in Shanghai he wrote to Mrs. Parker, September 30, 1898: "Shanghai gathers strangers from Japan, Korea and all the twenty provinces of China. Why may we not reach many of these in an institution which has cost the church so much money? A practical educator could solve the problem provided he understood the genius of the Chinese people. Men who had been successful in America were beyond the language learning period and were apt to make serious blunders in seeking to conform everything to American models. . . . I ventured to cast myself on your high sense of devotion to God and His church, and ask you in the spirit of self-sacrifice to undertake this great work."

Bishop Hendrix was responsible for the creation of the Korean Mission and on May 14, 1897, he wrote to Dr. C. P. Reid: "It gives me pleasure to say that the Board of Missions separated the work in Korea from the China Mission Conference by creating the Korean Mission and you are hereby finally appointed Superintendent, the first session to be October 6th." He sought expansion of the work in China during the years of his administration, and one of the happy experiences of his missionary labors was the gift of $3,000 by Mr. Julian S. Carr, of Durham, North Carolina, to send Dr. and Mrs. J. B. Fearn to open a new station in Changchow. On July 29th, 1897, he wrote to them: "Dr. Fearn's letter of June 30th reached me this week, and I have just read Mrs. Fearn's letter of April 26th giving an account of your April trip to Changchow. Mr. J. S. Carr has been so impressed with the opening and opportunities of Changchow that he now offers to do even more than before, namely to meet Dr. Fearn's salary for three years at Changchow. With this wholly unsolicited offer on his part, inspired by the Holy Spirit and the Lord of the Harvest, we feel that the same Divine agency has given us two admirably equipped agents in the persons of Dr. and Mrs. Fearn. . . . No other mission in the Kiangnan Province is so fortunate in having as man and wife such suitable agents for opening this great and important city to the gospel. . . . It does seem that after fifty years we should do more than we have done in occupying the Kiangnan Province and now the way is open for us to enter this new field and center which brings us the coveted opportunity of enlargement which will quicken the whole church. So far from losing faith in the work in China we are entering another important center and proving the efficiency of medical work in thus opening the door for the gospel. . . . You go to your new field with our prayers and sympathies. . . . Your heroic spirit is firing the missionary zeal of the church at home." In commenting on the work of

Dr. and Mrs. Fearn he wrote to another missionary: "The occupancy of Changchow will do much toward impressing the church that we believe sufficiently in the evangelization of China to extend our work which has been too long congested in only two or three centers. 'Plan great things for God; expect great things from God' is as wise and worthy a motto as when uttered by Carey a century ago." He never had any illusions as to the difficulty of the missionary's task. To Dr. S. H. Wainwright, who has done such a remarkable work in Japan, he sent this letter, Dr. Wainwright having at the time a great educational opportunity and a heavy responsibility at the Kwansei Gakuin, Methodism's leading school in Japan: "I am always glad to hear from you and my sympathies go out to you in the midst of your responsible work. . . . In carefully watching and aiding Kwansei Gakuin I recognize that we are protecting and strengthening our entire work. I am anxious for the influence of the institution to be widely felt and am glad to learn that you have projected something like University Extension work under its auspices. I rejoice that you are getting the ear of the people where you have gone, especially the teachers of Japan. It is by showing the supremacy of Christian philosophy we may hope to attract their attention to Christianity itself. Thinkers can be reached only by thought. Commonplaces do not seem to have any place in missionary work. It is not until the truth takes a deep hold on the religious teacher who sees in it something more than a mere statement that it can impress others whether in Christian or heathen lands. The bane of our pulpits is the barrenness of thought. . . . The secret of our Lord's ministry was its freshness. It was not so much anything new that he taught as the force of his teachings because of the hold of truth on Himself."

He was deeply conscious of the difficulties the missionaries faced through the failure of American residents abroad to live Christian lives. He used his influence to have the United States name devoutly Christian men to diplomatic posts in the Orient. Since he had organized the Korean Mission he could write to Dr. C. F. Reid, the Superintendent, this happy letter: "While in Washington in September on some other business with the President I expressed to him my great joy that he had expressed his purpose to send only Christian men to represent our nation in the capitals of heathen countries as our diplomatic representatives. He replied, 'I think I have made an excellent appointment to Korea.' I said, 'Mr. President, you could not have done better. I know the great esteem in which Dr. Allen is held both by foreigners and the Koreans as a Christian gentleman.' "

He watched carefully the developments in the Far East and was aware of their influence on the missionary enterprise. He writes to one missionary: "The changes occurring in Asia I am watching with deep interest but with faith in the God of Nations. Revolutions? Yes! But God has ever sown the seed of His Kingdom in the furrows of revolutions. Change of dynasties? Why not, when all are to bow before the King of Kings. It is not for us to concern ourselves unduly about the political aspects of Eastern Asia but to give them the gospel of light and love."

There were two problems in administration which the Bishop constantly faced. One was the problem of relating the work of the General Board of Missions to that of the Woman's Board of Missions; friction would sometimes develop between the representatives of these two boards. The other problem was the jealousy in one field of another field; a missionary to China opposed the opening of a mission in Korea, and a missionary to Japan was keenly disappointed that a large collection at a missionary conference should go to a Chinese college rather than a Japanese school. Such jealousy is easily understood; each missionary, consecrating his life to his field, would look on his work as the most important in all the world.

In meeting the situations arising in such friction and controversy the Bishop used tact. His personal relations with men on the field were very close. Sometimes he found it necessary to be very firm, and to administer a rebuke. Sometimes he showed a tenderness that surpasses that of a woman. He wrote to the missionaries; some of these letters are intimately personal, and carried no suggestion or consideration of work. Among the messages which indicate the yearning of his heart over those who have gone afar to serve their Lord are these two, the one written to a missionary whose child had died and the other written to the father of a young man just ready to leave for China. To Rev. W. O. Davis in Japan he wrote on learning of his child's illness: "A great compensation in such a time is the knowledge of having tender and devoted friends. Happy are we that such friends stand ready in our hours of helplessness to do everything for us and in our very consciousness they are our eyes and hands and feet." When word came that the child had died he wrote again to Brother Davis: "Your wife and yourself have the sacred honor of being parents to one who is forever with the Lord. . . . Your family circle is forming rapidly in the skies where both of your parents have preceded you."

To Rev. J. M. Cline, of Benton, Arkansas, whose son was leaving for China, he wrote this fine letter: "I have been much touched in reading your letter of the 15th inst. I too have an only son and can well understand a father's devotion, especially when the son's success at home has been so encouraging. I remember meeting both you and your noble son when I last held the Little Rock Conference and being most favorably impressed. I am sure that your father's heart was made glad when you knew that God had called your only son to the ministry. Now his Lord calls him to a post of great honor and responsibility in helping to win China to Christ. He will find difficulty in acquiring the language if he delays his going even for a few years. His heart is in the work, he offered his services to the Board and has been accepted. He is greatly needed, and while your heart is sad at the thought of parting I am sure it responds to the heart of God who so loved the world that He gave His only begotten Son that whosoever believeth on Him may not perish but have everlasting life. How much your son can do to add to your own many years of rejoicing!

"He will be distant from you only a month, and even a few days less, as I frequently get letters from China that have been less than a month on the way. Send him out with his father's blessing and prayers that he may labor in hope and joy for his Lord."

No finer letter was ever written in such a time, and in my judgment, Bishop Hendrix never wrote a better letter, with the possible exception of the perfect letter he wrote to Rev. W. W. McMurry in his last illness and the farewell message to the General Conference at Hot Springs in 1922. When the Bishop undertook the supervision of mission work in Brazil in 1899 he had to meet the opposition of the Roman Catholic Church. The missionary task there was very different from that in the Far East. To Rev. E. A. Tilley, our missionary in Brazil, he stated his justification of missionary work in Brazil: "As regards the question which so much perplexes you I do not see that we can reorganize the church of Rome in Brazil as a church of Christ and remain in Brazil. Our very mission there is to give Christianity to a people who would otherwise be without it. Whatever the church of Rome may be in America we know that in Brazil it is Christianity without Christ. . . . The synagogue which universally prepared the way for Paul and other missionaries was a teacher of the law which was the schoolmaster to bring men to Christ. Rome has had true believers in spite of her priests rather than as the result of their teachings, especially in Brazil. . . . I wish an annual visit were possible so as to keep the church at home in more immediate touch with the church in Brazil until the time comes when you can stand alone, a true church of Christ in Brazil, if not the Brazilian Church."

The Bishop was as zealous in securing recruits for the service in Brazil as he had been while in Asia. In company with the missionaries he visited the different sections of Brazil and on his episcopal visit in 1899 he traveled 20,000 miles. He sailed to England, and from there to Brazil. Even if the Atlantic crossing is included in the 20,000 miles there was a journey which took him 2,000 miles by land and water in Brazil. He gave to the church at home his ideas about the mission fields and his thinking was most influential in shaping the thinking of the church. Since the days of his missionary journeys the church has been rethinking missions. It might not indorse his indictment of the church of Rome in Brazil and it might not approve his conclusions as to the politics and policies of China and Japan. But there were some emphases in message and administration which mark Eugene R. Hendrix as one of the missionary statesmen of the church of Christ. He sought to supplant sentimentality and fanatical enthusiasm as missionary motives;

93

when he went to China and Japan, and when he went to Brazil missionaries were thought of as journeying to other worlds, and the slogan of many a missionary campaign was "We must save them; they are dropping into hell, millions every year, and thousands every hour." There were missionary enthusiasts who expected the conversion of the world to Christ within a few years. The Bishop never lost his enthusiasm for evangelism and he felt it was a great mistake to establish schools or churches whose missionary leaders would settle down for life; a missionary would lose his religion in the Far East if he did not seek the conversion of sinners, and every mission station must keep its passion for expansion and growth. Yet it is characteristic of his leadership to urge out-thinking the native religions; Christianity does not deserve to survive in a non-Christian land if it cannot outlive and out-think other religions. He recognized the great truth each of the religions had brought to the world, and in many of his utterances he anticipated the liberal reactions of students of comparative religion; in his spirit he approached very closely to the Stanley Jones of today.

Furthermore he was concerned lest the missionary enterprise should be a process of Americanization. He anticipated the native churches, and was very anxious to develop in each land a Christian movement which would create its own traditions and even its own creeds. He stands in the succession of missionary leaders whose work has been creative and constructive. His work in the church at home was as truly kingdom-building as the opening of Korea or South Brazil.

In the fall of 1889 he spent much time in the Indian Territory, now the state of Oklahoma. He ordained "five Choctaws, one Creek, and twelve Americans" to the ministry and his tireless efforts laid the foundation of a self-supporting church. During the year 1890 he assisted Miss Belle Bennett and Mrs. M. D. Wightman in arousing enthusiasm for a missionary training school. The General Conference of 1890, meeting at St. Louis, gave its endorsement to the Training School plan. The Rev. Nathan Scarritt was a member of that General Conference and he was greatly interested in the Training School; he died just after returning from the Conference but his family determined to carry out his wishes, and gave liberally for the establishment of the school in Kansas City. The cornerstone of the new building was laid July 2nd, 1891, and the new building was dedicated September 14, 1892.

At the time there was celebrated the twenty-fifth anniversary of Bishop Hendrix's election as bishop the faculty of the Scarritt Bible and Training School presented an address with these sentences: "We wish to express to Bishop Hendrix our appreciation of his service not only as a Bishop but as President of the Board of Managers of this institution, which, under his wise guidance is fulfilling its great mission of usefulness. He was an inspiration in the pioneer days; he has been our friend and adviser throughout nineteen eventful years."

To him, more than to anyone else, must go the credit for creating the office of deaconess. One of the interesting documents in the history of that movement is a letter to Miss Belle Bennett under date of August 16, 1902:

"After having Miss Gibson and Mrs. Hargrove over last evening and devoting several hours to the careful consideration of the deaconess question they agreed with me that the best thing to do to get the work before the whole church in a dignified and correct way would be to limit the recognition and consecration of all deaconesses to the Annual Meeting of the Women's Home Mission Society where you can annually have the services of one of the bishops or other connectional officers. This will secure you against the violation of any of the proprieties or the confounding of the consecration with an ordination. The certificates given should be signed by one of the bishops just as is done now with missionaries going to the foreign field.

"Inasmuch as the General Conference did not authorize a regular order of service for the consecration of deaconesses I question whether we had better anticipate such action by publishing one. I have examined the one used in the Methodist Episcopal Church. That form or a similar one can be used during the three occasions between now and the next General Conference at your annual meetings when deaconesses are consecrated. . . . Before the time

95

comes for the first setting apart I may be able to suggest some improvement on the Methodist Episcopal Service.

"Your by-law to correct the weak place in the action of the General Conferences is worthy of Talleyrand. It so completely neutralizes the action of the General Conference that you are liable to indictment for infanticide! Now following on the heels of that to publish a form of consecration service which the General Conference never ordered might lead to a life sentence anyhow. Therefore, I think a tentative service such as I propose will meet the needs admirably and save you from any more protests on the floor and in the press."

This is the letter which is more responsible than any other document for the deaconess consecration. It is delightful to find a leader who finds a way to circumvent a bit of foolish conservatism in a General Conference, and a Bishop who has humor enough and enough of loyalty to a progressive cause to smile about the method. In the same letter the Bishop advises Miss Mabel Howell to attend the University of Chicago before taking up her duties at Scarritt Training School—and that was in 1902 when it took courage to mention the University of Chicago!

Perhaps the most valuable service Bishop Hendrix rendered to the cause of missions was his support of and leadership in every forward movement in the home church. Looking back on his visit as Bishop to the Orient he recorded in his diary, August 5, 1896, this reflection: "One year ago I sailed on the Empress of India for Japan, China and Korea. Today I begin to see some of the definite results of my mission, especially with reference to a new mission field. . . . The Virginia and Missouri Leaguers have each promised $1,500 for Korea. . . . My soul rejoices at the blessing of God upon my voyage to Asia and the efforts to enlist the church in America in behalf of the new field." The Bishop's missionary task was twofold; he must inspire the missionaries and advance the lines on the missionary field, but he must also inspire the church at home and hold its interest in missions.

As he was returning in 1899 from his service in Brazil he was not only happy over the work done there, but he was rejoicing in the plans for the Twentieth Century Fund Campaign in the home church. He came home with more than $10,000 subscribed in Brazil for the Twentieth Century Thank Offering, and in his home church he took the field for that movement, raising one thousand dollars.

From Kansas City he started on a journey which took him all over the church, in behalf of missions and the forward movement. The climax of that effort was the great Missionary Conference in New Orleans, where, after a memorable address by Bishop Charles E. Galloway, there was a subscription of $54,000 for Soochow University. That collection overshadowed all else at the Conference, but Bishop Hendrix made a great address and he was partly responsible for the creation of sentiment and atmosphere. During the years of his episcopacy Bishop Hendrix was invited to address the great conventions of the Student Volunteer Movement. Perhaps the most influential of all these conventions was the one at Rochester at the holiday season of 1909-10. There were 722 institutions represented; there were present 329 professors and teachers, 2,678 students and 165 missionaries. Notable addresses were given by James Bryce, Robert E. Speer, John R. Mott and Eugene Hendrix. In inviting Bishop Hendrix to speak Dr. Mott characterized him as one of the great missionary leaders of the generation. When the convention was over Dr. Mott wrote: "On behalf of our Committee I write to thank you most sincerely and heartily for the invaluable help which you rendered at the Rochester Convention. Your message was exactly what was wanted. Evidence has come to my attention from many sources showing that your words came with mighty power to the Convention."

Under date of July 4, 1913, is this entry in the diary: "Returned from Waynesville Assembly where I raised $151,200 for missions, besides interesting many volunteers for mission work and the laymen's movement came into its own. New Orleans in 1901 recalled and surpassed." This was probably the climax of the Bishop's service to the cause of missions in the home church, but there was a consecrated effort in Missouri during the 1914-1918 which deserves to rank with it. Within that quadrennium fell the year 1916, the hundredth anniversary of the founding of Methodism in Missouri. To celebrate and commemorate that founding the Bishop launched a "Go Forward" Movement in Missouri. The entire program of the church was urged on all the congregations, and in connection with the movement there were two remarkable happenings. Neither was a part of the movement and yet both belong to the endeavors of Bishop Hendrix. On October 14th, 1914, Benefactors' day was celebrated at Central College in Fayette, Missouri. Under the courageous leadership of President Paul H. Linn, ably supported by Bishop Hendrix, there was raised an endowment fund of $300,000 for Central College, increasing the endowment of that institution to $500,000.

On November 5, 1914, Bishop Hendrix dedicated Barnes Hospital in St. Louis. There was a crowd that overflowed the spacious lobby of the new building, erected twenty-two years after the bequest of Mr. Robert A. Barnes. The trustees had wisely held the amount originally given until it had increased to a sum which would provide a building and an endowment. The address of Bishop Hendrix at the dedication has these paragraphs: "For over twenty years the administration of nearly a million dollars (now become over $2,150,000) has been the honor and joy of leading citizens, like Richard M. Scruggs, Samuel Cupples, Smith P. Galt, Samuel Kennard, Murray Carleton and Lon V. Stephens. Half the number have already ended their high stewardship and the other half, with S. M. Kennard as the only survivor of the original trustees, live to see the happy consummation of their great plans, and to see the inauguration of the Robert A. Barnes Hospital . . . a hospital for sick and injured persons, without distinction of creed, under the auspices of the Methodist Episcopal Church, South. After years of thought the trustees have wisely enlarged the work of Barnes Hospital by making it a teaching hospital, where disease will be studied in the most scientific manner, alike in its origin and treatment. By a wise affiliation for a term of years with the Washington University Medical College, men of the highest order of ability will devote their entire time to the service of the patients, whether in the wards or the private rooms, but not to the exclusion of the private physician or surgeon whom the patient may desire to have called in consultation. For sufficient reason the trustees can veto the services of any member of the medical staff of the hospital. They, too, employ all nurses or discontinue them, as may be deemed wise. Every interest of the hospital will be under the vigilant care of the Trustees."

The Protestant Church can never maintain a hospital without large endowment and that the Trustees of Barnes Hospital knew. As this hospital ministers to sick and injured persons the statement is sometimes made, "Barnes Hospital is getting away from the church." What could the Methodist Church do with it that it does not do when the church administers it for sick and injured persons? Bishop Hendrix had sense as well as sentiment when he approved the agreement under which Barnes Hospital operates. His friendship with Mr. Barnes was largely responsible for this gift to the Methodist Church.

CHAPTER VIII

The Vanderbilt Controversy

IN THE long history of the Methodist Episcopal Church, South, no controversy has aroused such bitterness as the Vanderbilt controversy. In one form or another, it came before the General Conferences of 1898, 1906, 1910, and 1914. From 1905 to 1914 it was the major issue before the church, and we may be still too close to it to see in proper perspective the men and the measures involved, to evaluate properly its influence on the church, the university, and the cause of education. Among those engaged in that controversy none was more conspicuous, and none played a more difficult role than Bishop Eugene R. Hendrix. Never was he criticized more severely and never was he praised more highly. It is not necessary to discuss here all the issues nor to trace in sequence all incidents of the controversy, but the story must be complete enough to show the relationship of Bishop Hendrix to its various phases.

In the fall of 1871 eight or nine of the Annual Conferences of the Methodist Episcopal Church, South, appointed committees to confer with each other "in reference to the establishment and endowment of a Methodist University of high grade and large endowment." In January, 1872, the committees met in Memphis, and, after a discussion of three days, adopted resolutions prepared by Bishop H. N. McTyeire. These resolutions proposed the establishment of an institution of learning of the highest order; the naming of the institution the Central University of the Methodist Episcopal Church, South; the raising of one million dollars, the securing of half of that amount being a condition of opening any department; the leaving of the location to the College of Bishops; the creating of a Board of Trust of twenty-four members, seven constituting a quorum; making the Bishops a Board of Supervision.

The Bishops agreed to locate the institution when five hundred thousand dollars should be secured, but decided that they could "take no official relation to the Central University that will dis-

E. R. Hendrix at his home, 3242 Norledge Place, Kansas City, Mo.
With him are two of his grandchildren.

criminate between it and every other institution of the church."
On June 29, 1872, the individuals named on the Board of Trust
filed their petition for incorporation in the Chancery Court at
Nashville. On August 6, 1872, decree was entered on the petition
constituting the charter. On August 22, 1872, the Board of Trust
met at Iuka, Mississippi, accepted the charter, and adopted by-laws.
One by-law reads: "Since the charter leaves the property of the
Board in its own power, we request the several Annual Conferences,
cooperating, to nominate at least four representatives from each.
So soon as this shall be done, the present Board will reorganize in
such manner as to secure the elections of trustees so nominated,
and that hereafter, when vacancies occur, they shall be filled by
nominations by the several Annual Conferences and confirmed by
the Board."

On March 26, 1873, at a meeting of the Board of Trust in Nashville, Bishop McTyeire submitted a letter from Cornelius Vanderbilt, dated March 17, 1873. In this letter Mr. Vanderbilt agreed to
give at least five hundred thousand dollars for the establishment
of a university, on certain conditions. These conditions were that
Bishop McTyeire was to serve for life as President of the Board at
a salary of $3,000; that at the Bishop's death the Board should elect
a President; that the President should have the right of veto of any
action of the Board, and that any act thus vetoed must be carried
by a three-fourths vote to be valid; that the amount set apart as an
endowment be forever inviolable and safely invested; and that the
institution should be located in or near Nashville.

On April 23, 1873, a petition to amend the charter was filed
in the Chancery Court at Nashville. The principal amendments
sought were a change of name from Central College to Vanderbilt
University, and a striking out of the words "or the resolutions of
the convention at Memphis set out herein, which resolutions are
hereby adopted as a part of this charter."

On January 14, 1874, the Board of Trust accepted the amended
charter, and after an address by Bishop McTyeire, passed the Garland
resolution: "Forasmuch as the charter of Vanderbilt University
confers upon its Board of Trust the exclusive right and power to

fill vacancies that may occur in its own body, and as this power cannot be delegated to any other body of persons whatsoever; therefore, be it resolved, That this Board will now proceed to fill the vacancies which have been created by the death of the late Dr. Green, and by the transfer of the Reverend W. C. Hearn to the Denver Conference. But in order to maintain the closest connection with the patronizing Conferences, the Board submits these and every other election to fill a vacancy in its own body to the confirmation of the Annual Conference from which it is made." In 1895 certain changes in the method of electing trustees and in the constitution of the Board were made, so as to relate the University more closely to the whole church; each of the patronizing conferences was allowed one trustee, and the eight vacancies thus created were to be filled by the selection of representative men, without regard to geographical limitation. In 1897 it was proposed that all members of the Board of Trust be selected from the church at large, to be confirmed by the General Conference. A committee of three Bishops presented a memorial on this subject to the General Conference of 1898, and the General Conference passed this resolution: "The General Conference of the Methodist Episcopal Church, South, hereby accepts the proposed relation and control of the Vanderbilt University and commits to the General Board of Education the confirmation of all trustees selected by the Board of Trust of Vanderbilt University."

In 1905 the Board repealed the by-law making the Chancellor and Bishops ex officiis members, and passed another by-law making the Chancellor and five Bishops, according to seniority, members of the Board. After the action of the Board of Trustees in 1905 there was created in the church an uneasiness as to the control of the University. Consequently, the General Conference of the Methodist Episcopal Church, South, meeting in Birmingham, Alabama, in May, 1906, passed resolutions with these paragraphs:

"There can be no question as to the ownership of the University by the Methodist Episcopal Church, South, or as to the charter rights of all the Bishops; but in view of certain questions which must be authoritatively decided, we recommend the appointment by this

General Conference of a Commission of five laymen of the Methodist Episcopal Church, South, as follows:

(1) To inquire into and determine the present relation of the Vanderbilt University to the Methodist Episcopal Church, South.

(2) To take legal steps, if necessary, to perfect the transfer of the University from the patronizing Conferences to the General Conference of the Methodist Episcopal Church, South.

(3) To define the charter rights of the Bishops of the Methodist Episcopal Church, South; and, when so defined, the Bishops are hereby instructed to enter on the same."

When the resolutions were adopted the Commission was composed of Judge Edmond Orear, of Kentucky, Judge John A. Rich, of Missouri, Judge E. D. Newman, of Virginia, Judge Joseph A. McCulloch, of South Carolina, and Honorable Creed F. Bates, of Tennessee. The new Commission reached these conclusions, after investigation and study:

(1) That the petitioners who applied for and obtained the charter of the University, and who were thereby declared to be the "body politic and corporate" were not the members of the corporation, but that the Memphis, the Tennessee, the White River, the North Carolina, the Alabama, the Mississippi, the Louisiana and the Little Rock Conferences of the church were the real members of the corporation of the Central University of the Methodist Episcopal Church, South; and

(2) That the University was not founded by Mr. Vanderbilt at the Memphis Convention, and

(3) That since 1898 the General Conference, as assignee of these Annual Conferences, had been the member and the sole member, of the corporation . . . and

(4) That the trustees of the University . . . are and were agents, at the first of the Annual Conferences . . . and that these Conferences had and have full power, authority and control over the Board of Trust, their committee or agents; and

(5) That, while the Bishops had no authority in law or power under the charter as members, either of the Corporation or of the Board of Trust . . . nevertheless by virtue of the ninth of the

Memphis resolutions, made part of the charter, the Bishops were visitors of the University, with common law visitorial powers (so long as the Board of Trust did not violate the law of the state, or the charter, or the purposes of "the settlers of the trust" the Bishops could not interfere with the internal management of the University under their visitorial powers). The Conferences of the Church accepted these conclusions. The Board of Trust of Vanderbilt University passed these resolutions:

WHEREAS the Commission has concluded its labors, and reported the result of its deliberations to the Board of Trust of Vanderbilt University:

Resolved, 1. That we cordially receive the same, and direct that it be filed with the records of the Board. 2. That we hereby express our appreciation of the ability and fidelity with which the members of the Commission have discharged their important duties. 3. That, recognizing and rejoicing in the ownership of the church in the University, and all the responsibilities arising therefrom, we welcome any supervision by the College of Bishops that may aid us in executing the great trust committed to our hands so as to insure the observance of the charter, the conditions of specific gifts, and the statutes of the state.

From these resolutions it is apparent that the Board of Trust did not accept fully the conclusions of the Commission. When the General Conference of the church met in Asheville, North Carolina, in May, 1910, Judge E. C. Orear was elected Chairman of the Committee on Education. He insisted, as Chairman of the Education Commission, that Bishop Hendrix call a meeting of the Vanderbilt Board of Trust in Asheville, or in Nashville if the law required a meeting in Tennessee, to accept fully the conclusions of the Commission as settling the Vanderbilt issue.

Bishop Hendrix, as Chairman of the Board of Trust of Vanderbilt University, could not agree to such a committal. Then the General Conference, under the leadership of Judge Orear, passed resolutions accepting the findings of the Commission, and nominating three men as Trustees of the University. The Board of Education of the church was instructed to take any steps necessary to sustain the findings of the Commission in the courts, and Judge Orear, as Chairman of the Committee on Education, led the General Conference in a decision to add $25,000 to the annual assessment for education to be used by the Board of Education at its discretion. In discussing this proposed action Judge Orear stated that the money would probably be needed for litigation. At Asheville, it was perfectly apparent that everything possible was done to embarrass Bishop Hendrix, and that Judge Orear and his supporters were determined to enforce their views as to the ownership and control of Vanderbilt.

On June 11, 1910, at a meeting of the Board of Trust, two of the three men, elected by the Asheville General Conference as Trustees, appeared on their own behalf and on behalf of the third man elected, and demanded that they be seated. The Board asked the Chair to appoint a committee of seven to determine the right of these men to membership on the Board and to recommend procedure. In the report of the committee is this language: "We are of the opinion that the General Conference acted without lawful authority when it undertook to elect members to fill vacancies on the Board of Trust. We are further of the opinion that it is the duty of the present members of this Board by election to fill all vacancies thereon which may now exist." The Board adopted the resolutions offered and elected three men to membership. The issue was joined. Who were to be the Trustees of the University, the three men elected by the General Conference at Asheville, or the three elected by the Board of Trust?

At the October term of the Chancery Court of Davidson County, Tennessee, in 1910, action was brought by the College of Bishops (except Bishop E. R. Hendrix) and by the three men elected by the General Conference at Asheville against the Board of Trust of Vanderbilt University. A decree was sought recognizing the right of the General Conference at Asheville to elect Trustees and enjoining the three elected by the Board of Trust from serving as Trustees, and granting any other such further general relief as the facts of the case may demand. The trial of the case, and the arguments of council took more than one month. In deciding the case, Chancellor John Allison gave as his opinion:

1. That the Methodist Episcopal Church, South, acting through its several Annual Conferences, was the founder of the University.

2. That the Memphis resolutions are a part of the Charter.

3. That the General Conference acted within its legal rights in electing Trustees.

4. That the Bishops have visitorial powers, and can annul actions of the Board of Trust.

5. That no man can be a Trustee unless elected as the General Conference determines.

This decision upheld the views of the Bishops of the Church, and the Board of Trust appealed the case to the Supreme Court of Tennessee. In the opinion rendered by that court on March 21, 1914, it is held that two questions are involved—whether the General Conference has the right to name members of the Board of Trust of Vanderbilt University, and whether the College of Bishops has visitorial powers and the right to veto the actions of the Board. The Court decided:

1. That Commodore Vanderbilt was the founder of the University.

2. That the Bishops have no visitorial powers and no right of veto.

3. That the Board of Trust is a self-perpetuating body and can elect to fill its own vacancies.

The opinion of the Supreme Court was a complete reversal of the opinion of Chancellor Allison, and put an end to the legal controversy. The Supreme Court had held that the General Conference, or its General Board of Education, had the right to confirm the Trustees elected by the Board or to refuse confirmation. When the General Conference met in Oklahoma City in May, 1914, there were different opinions as to what should be done. There were some who felt that the General Board of Education should refuse confirmation until Trustees of their liking were elected; there were those who thought the General Conference should return to the original patronizing Conferences all rights received from them in the resolution of the General Conference of 1898; there were others who believed the Conference should pass a resolution of refusal to co-operate further in the control of Vanderbilt University. The third group won, and all church cooperation with Vanderbilt University was ended by the action of the General Conference. Thus was concluded a controversy which created almost as much interest as the celebrated Dartmouth College case. As indicative of the strong convictions held by both sides are the two court decisions. One court holds for the Bishops on every controverted point, and the higher court holds for the Board of Trustees on every issue. In all probability there was never a case in the South with such an array of distinguished counsel, and never were issues the cause of more bitter debates. Outside of the courtroom, on conference floors and in church papers controversialists voiced their opinions, and the church was in a ferment for years. The able editor of the Nashville *Advocate* during the heat of the controversy was Dr. George B. Winton, a member of the Board of Trustees of Vanderbilt and sympathetic with the position of the Trustees. Bishop E. R. Hendrix, as Chairman of the Board of Trust of Vanderbilt, did not join the other Bishops of the Church in the suit. So Bishop Hendrix and Dr. Winton were regarded as the leaders of the Minority in the church, who felt that the Bishops were wrong in their attitude and that the church had all the authority and ownership it needed to exercise. We are interested in the part Bishop Hendrix played in the controversy, and in the opinions he held.

The outstanding figures in the controversy were Chancellor J. H. Kirkland and Bishop E. E. Hoss, representing the different views of church control. Those who agreed with Bishop Hoss claimed that Chancellor Kirkland was opposed to church control and that he sought to alienate the University from the church. By those who agreed with Chancellor Kirkland it was asserted that Bishop Hoss was actuated by personal pique, and that he made a church issue of the university control because of his personal dislikes. The part played by Bishop Hendrix was not so conspicuous but it was very dramatic. He was Chairman of the Board of Trust and agreed with the position it took. He was a Bishop of the Church and did not agree with his colleagues in the suit that was brought;

but when the suit was brought by the College of Bishops he could not be put in the position of Hendrix the Bishop bringing suit against Hendrix the Trustee. So he resigned as a Trustee of the University and refused as a Bishop to have anything to do with the suit. No other course could have been followed by a man of keen discrimination and a man with loyalty to his convictions. He was often in a position of difficulty, and he was many times accused of contradictions in his opinions and in his testimony. The principal criticisms of him have been:

(1) He accused Bishop Hoss of personal animus, and of prejudiced action in the Vanderbilt controversy, and it is contended that his attitude was unbrotherly and unworthy of a Bishop.

(2) He is criticized as vacillating and inconsistent when he refused to call a meeting of the Vanderbilt Board of Trust at Asheville in 1910, to consider the report of the Commission.

(3) He has been attacked for refusing to join the other Bishops in the suit against the Board of Trust, and has been represented as disloyal and almost a traitor.

In the light of letters and documents in the files of Bishop Hendrix I want to examine each of these criticisms. These letters, many of them, have not been made public before, and some of them I would not care to publish since they are very confidential. Was Bishop Hendrix justified in feeling that Bishop Hoss was motivated by personal prejudice? On January 18, 1905, Bishop Hoss wrote a letter from Dallas, Texas, to Bishop Galloway as the latter was taking up his responsibilities in Nashville. In that letter are these sentences: "Before you go, I hope you will fully acquaint yourself with local conditions. It is a great opportunity, but it means a fight from the word go. Between you and me, Vanderbilt is almost lost to Methodism. Bishop Hargrove's administration has been impotent in recent years. . . . You will not see everything at first glance. The surface indications are misleading. But the whole inner drift and spirit of the University has been away from Methodism, and nothing short of a revolution can restore the original and true status. . . . Pardon me for saying these things. You have not asked any counsel from me about the situation, and it is a little presumptuous in me to offer suggestions without being solicited to do so. . . . I have engagements covering the whole time up to May 1st. Some day I long for a little of freedom and cessation from toil. That will come long after I am in the Kingdom. I am almost tempted, however, to ask you to nominate me for the Brazil Mission this year, so that I may get the benefit of a sea voyage."

In a letter from Bishop W. W. Duncan, written from Spartanburg, South Carolina, and dated October 7, 1905, Chancellor Kirkland is informed: "I received this morning a letter from Bishop Hoss, written evidently under considerable excitement. He wants me to inform you, even by wire, that I withdraw my signature from the new charter of the University. He is most emphatically opposed to it and will fight it even to the Supreme Court of the United States. I expect to meet him at the Holston Conference and I will then find out what he means, for I really do not understand." On October 11, 1905, Bishop Galloway wrote Bishop Hendrix: "I take the liberty of enclosing to you the letters received from Bishop Hoss. So far as I know, no objection was expressed by any other former member of the Board. . . . Bishop Hoss has appealed to Dr. Ward and perhaps others to withdraw from the petition (for a new charter). I cannot express my amazement and grief at this whole matter." On the same day Bishop Galloway wrote to Bishop Hoss, "My suggestion is that you prepare a statement to be laid before the Executive Committee setting forth your views of the whole case. . . . Of course you know it will have the fullest and most careful consideration. Indeed I earnestly solicit your judgment in the case." In this letter Bishop Galloway crossed out one sentence, which, he thought, apparently, might hurt or antagonize Bishop Hoss. Yet the sentence can be plainly read under the cross. "Personally I should deplore newspaper discussion, or legal proceedings, or General Conference debate in such an issue."

To Bishop Galloway's letter Bishop Hoss made a lengthy reply. Among other things he protested against the action of the Board of Trust, and in determining that the Chancellor and the five Bishops in the order of seniority should be members of the Board. Among other things he said: "The Chancellor is a learned man, but he is not a Chief Justice, and his opinion, ad rem, in the absence of a judicial deliverance, is not worth the white paper it is written on. . . . A careful examination of the whole matter forces the conclusion that the prime motive was to get rid of the Bishops. For myself, whatever others may do, I wish to say that I insist on remaining in the association with gentlemen who have sought to thrust me out of their company, my answer is that I am not there by their grace, not to please them, but to discharge an obligation put upon me without any volition of my own by the providence of God. . . . If a fight must come on, that is one which is raised by the Board itself, why, I will fight in the newspapers, in the conferences, and in the courts."

On October 26, 1905, Bishop A. W. Wilson wrote to Chancellor Kirkland: "It is said that my name is in the list of signers of the petition for a change in the charter of Vanderbilt University. I do not recollect that I signed though it is quite possible that I did. . . . One aspect of the case I overlooked at the time. I am put in the attitude of praying that the majority of my colleagues may be removed from the Board while, under the provisions of the new Charter, as proposed, I am retained. . . . I now ask that my name be withdrawn from the petition." On November 16, 1905, Bishop J. S. Key wrote Chancellor Kirkland that he had received additional information about the proposed charter and wished to withdraw his name as a signer of the petition. Bishop Hendrix believed that letters from Bishop Hoss to Bishops Wilson and Key, similar to the one received by Bishop Duncan, were responsible for their change of mind. How could he draw any other conclusion?

After the session of the Tennessee Conference in the fall of 1905 Bishop Galloway wrote Bishop Hendrix, "We had the Vanderbilt University matter before the Conference in the form of a memorial prepared by Dr. H. M. Hamil. The course of Dr. Hamil, I must say, commands my indignation. . . . He has helped to circulate, if not foment, criticism in the University as to its orthodoxy. Any man who, in this day, teaches the old theory of verbal inspiration, and almost the inviolability of the Authorized Version is an intellectual anachronism. The action of the Conference was evidently a distinct blow to him." Senator W. R. Webb wrote to Bishop Hendrix a long letter about the history of Vanderbilt, in the course of which he said: "I have felt that Bishop Hoss acted unwisely in his course. As Dr. Hoss he was fighting the institution. I recall that when the citizens of Nashville presented the statue of Vanderbilt . . . Dr. Hoss had scarcely a notice in the *Advocate* and the daily papers were full of the great event. I recall another Vanderbilt occasion when Dr. Hoss was severely criticized by the orator of the Alumni Association. He sat near me. . . . At the close of the speech he showed great excitement and said in a loud voice, 'If Vanderbilt wants a fight they can get it, but they ought not to shoot off firecrackers at me; let them send out a big gun.'"

Several letters are in the files of Bishop Hendrix, written by ministers and laymen in Nashville, saying that there was a bureau in Nashville carrying on propaganda through the conferences, with the approval, if not with the leadership of Bishop Hoss.

On September 11, 1907, Bishop Hoss wrote to Bishop Galloway, and to Bishop Hendrix short letters of protest against the election of new Trustees by the Board of Trust because they were not Methodists. On October 12, 1907, Bishop Hoss wrote Bishop Hendrix a longer letter of protest because the Board of Trust did not, as fully as he thought it should, accept the decision of the Educational Commission. He closed the letter with this paragraph: "All the issues are bound to be settled quietly, and the sooner the better. If they can be settled quietly among ourselves I shall be most happy. But if not, they must go to a tribunal that has the power to enforce decrees. . ."

With the death of Bishop Galloway in 1909 Bishop Hendrix became the Chairman of the Board of Trust of Vanderbilt University. Chancellor Kirkland wrote him on November 2, 1909, in the heat of the controversy: "You are at liberty to say that I repudiate definitely and emphatically the attempt of Bishop Hoss to set forth my views or he misrepresents them. . . . Bishop Hoss makes the positive statement that our first movement in the matter of amending the charter was with the intention of 'eliminating every semblance of the church's authority over the University.' There is only one thing to say about a statement of this kind and that is that it is absolutely false."

On June 28, 1910, Bishop Hoss wrote a letter to Mr. Samuel Cupples, and it was sent on to Bishop Hendrix. It closes with this paragraph, "In bringing suit we shall need to examine the records of the Board of Trust. Of course we can get an order of Court giving us access to them, but we hope it will not be necessary for us to take that step." Many other letters came to Bishop Hendrix telling him of the attitude and activity of Bishop Hoss. I have no desire to recall a controversy that is ended, and I know Bishop Hoss was earnest and sincere. No one can read the records of the controversy, however, without sensing the personal animus in it and without concluding that Bishop Hendrix had reason to believe what he said in his testimony about the attitude of Bishop Hoss. In the closing weeks of 1911 Bishop Warren A. Candler, in a very brotherly way, sought to mediate between Bishops Hendrix and Hoss, and the correspondence does credit to the character of each of these leaders. Bishop Hoss suggested that the settlement of their difficulties and differences be left to three of their colleagues. On December 20, 1911, Bishop Hendrix wrote to Bishop Candler from Nashville: "I cannot tell you how much I appreciate your visit here today as peacemaker. . . . I cheerfully withdraw any language of mine that implies that Bishop Hoss was actuated by personal motives only in his part in the Vanderbilt controversy."

In dealing with the criticism of Bishop Hendrix for refusing to call a meeting of the Board of Trust of Vanderbilt at Asheville, the seat of the General Conference of 1910, I present two telegrams. One is from one of the ablest lawyers who ever served on the Board, W. T. Sanders, of Athens, Alabama: "If the Vanderbilt Board of Trust is called to meet in Asheville in response to the suggestion of the Conference, I shall not be able to attend. . . . If my attitude as a trustee shall be embarrassing in the settlement of the questions at issue, you are at liberty to tender my resignation to the Board." The other telegram is from W. R. Cole, at Nashville: "Stokes (attorney) advises in his opinion meeting of trustees cannot be legally held outside of Tennessee." Bishop Hendrix was acting on what he considered competent legal advice in his refusal to call a meeting.

The criticism of disloyalty to the church is met by the many commendations of Bishop Hendrix for his courageous stand. His files are full of letters like this one from Miss Belle Bennett: "I want to write and assure you of my appreciation of your position and my confidence in your leadership. You may have to suffer, and for a time be misunderstood, but it will only be for a time."

It was the hope of Bishop Hendrix, until the suit was filed, that he could bring about a solution of the problems. Anxious for the church to keep Vanderbilt, and anxious for Vanderbilt to sustain that relationship to the church which it had long enjoyed, it was his conviction that controversy had blinded judgment. But the years of 1909 and 1910 were not a period for judicial weighing of opinions. In a letter to Bishop Hendrix Chancellor Kirkland had written in 1906: "The relation of the University to the church grows out of the whole history of the movement that brought the University into being. The relation of Vanderbilt to the General Conference is one that was established by general agreement in 1898. . . . The relation of the University to the Church is a much wider question than the relation of the University to the Conference. . . . The Board of Trustees has been the interpreter of this relationship and has endeavored to make the University serve the interests of the church in the best possible way." Such was the view of Bishop Hendrix. Had the Vanderbilt controversy come in 1930 instead of 1905-1914 it would have had a different issue. There are those who hope the Methodist Church, can yet rectify the mistake it made in 1910 and 1914. Whether, even for the sake of history and attitude, we can ever recall what was done, time will continue to lift Eugene Hendrix into a more and more exalted position of leadership. Forgetting the personal bitterness, and refraining from criticisms of those who fought and opposed him, it is surely a fact that Bishop Hendrix seems to those who look back twenty-five years a wiser leader than he seemed to some of his contemporaries. Would that the Church had followed Galloway and Hendrix in those distressing days!

After his return from the General Conference at Oklahoma City in 1914 Bishop Hendrix made this entry in his diary under the date of May 25, 1914: "Somewhat stormy session over the Vanderbilt case, but hope for quiet and harmony. . . . Several of my colleagues now share my views after four years of loneliness, while scores of delegates believe my position from the beginning to have been the only correct one. Have tried the work of a peacemaker, and hope to know its beatitudes."

Chapter IX

The Unification of American Methodism

THIS chapter is being written in Molde, Norway, during a session of the Norwegian Methodist Conference. The nestor of the Conference said to me, "I was a delegate to the General Conference of the Methodist Episcopal Church at Saratoga Springs in 1916 and the scene I will never forget was the clasping of hands by Bishop Earl Cranston and Bishop Eugene Hendrix as they pledged themselves to work for a united Methodist Church in America." Every living delegate to that General Conference cherishes the same memory. Each of those bishops was nearing the end of his service but both were looking forward.

Some years later Bishop Cranston said to a Joint Hymnal Commission, representing three Methodisms, "I am glad we are to continue to have one hymnal. I wish we could have one church. I remember how Dr. Lewis of the Methodist Protestant Church has stirred us all by his eloquent pleas. In my heart has always been a deep love for the Southern Church, and I explain it in this way. In the months before I was born my parents lived in Louisiana. My father was a government engineer and he was assigned to work on the Red River. The people of Louisiana were very kind to my mother during her residence there, and while she came back to her old home in Ohio before I was born, she often said that the kind people of Louisiana made her months of pregnancy so much easier. I suppose she transmitted to me before I was born that love of the Southland that was hers. It is a part of my very nature, and I wish I could live to see a union of our churches in the north and the south."

The father of Bishop Eugene Hendrix was born in Pennsylvania and his mother in Maryland. When he went away to college it was a New England Methodist University he attended. In vacation time he often visited his grandfather's homestead in Pennsylvania. Union Theological Seminary in New York City was the place of his training for the ministry. His first pastorate was in Leavenworth, Kansas, when the feeling between the North and the South had run very high. The southern church was not as strong as the northern, and the young pastor of the southern church knew what it was to suffer; but there were friendships from the first week in Leavenworth that made up for all the heartaches, and the experiences in Leavenworth did not hamper the enthusiasm for more fraternal relations between the great divisions of Methodism. The two men who clasped hands at Saratoga Springs were a man from the South, whose education was in northern schools, and a man from the North who had inherited a devotion to the South. In themselves these two men embodied the aspirations and hopes, as they understood the barriers and difficulties in the way of union, of the two great sections of Methodism in the North and the South. Twenty-three years must pass before the dreams of that historic moment were to become reality in the Uniting Conference of 1939. But those two men at Saratoga Springs were more than prophets of a union; they were leaders in the effort to make it reality.

In the years that were to follow John C. Broomfield and James H. Straughan were to assume leadership in the Methodist Protestant Church, and to become earnest seekers of a united church. In the Methodist Episcopal Church William F. McDowell and Edwin Holt Hughes were to assume the same kind of leadership while the leaders in the Methodist Episcopal Church, South, were to be Edwin D. Mouzon and John Monroe Moore. Much as United Methodism owes to these six men they themselves would be the first to acknowledge their indebtedness to T. H. Lewis, Earl Cranston, and Eugene Hendrix. To understand the work of this trio one has to remember something of the history of unification efforts.

The separation of the Methodist Episcopal Church and the Methodist Protestant Church took place in 1828, but this separation was overshadowed by a still more bitter controversy that led to the separation of the Methodist Episcopal Church and the Methodist Episcopal Church, South, in 1844. When the War Between the States was over there was an exchange of fraternal messengers between the North and the South; perhaps the most significant addresses of the first twenty-five years after the war were those of Dr. Lovick Pierce before the General Conference of the Methodist Episcopal Church, and of a layman, General Clinton B. Fisk, before the General Conference of the Methodist Episcopal Church, South. Each voiced hopes of reunion in the seventies, shortly after the war.

The most dramatic incidents in the working out of plans for Methodist union belong to the years between 1914 and 1939. It was at a General Conference of the Methodist Episcopal Church, South, at Oklahoma City in 1914 that resolutions were passed proposing unification by reorganization. Between that date and the meeting of the General Conference of the Methodist Episcopal Church in Des Moines in 1920 the first Unification Commission to work out a plan prepared a scheme for reorganization. After much discussion this plan was unacceptable to the Des Moines General Conference. While it was discarded a proposal was made there for a convention in which the churches would have larger representation than could be possible in a commission. I do not believe the members of that General Conference really favored a convention; it was only a proposal that seemed to save face after a plan for union by reorganization was discarded.

When the next General Conference of the Methodist Episcopal Church, South, was held at Hot Springs, in 1922, the negotiations for unification were at a critical stage. Those who were opposed to union were saying, "The Methodist Episcopal Church has turned down a plan for union. Let us now drop all negotiations." I was not only a member of the Committee on Church Relations in that General Conference, but I was named as Chairman of a small Committee of Nine to propose to the larger committee the action the General Conference should take. On that Committee of Nine were five who favored unification and four who opposed it. The leader in that group of opponents was Judge John S. Candler of Atlanta. I know intimately this chapter which was a strategic time in southern discussion of unification, but it has never been told before. The unification majority on the small committee decided to support the proposal for a convention that came from the North until such time as our four opponents would consent

117

to a compromise. Night after night we held to our contention for the convention until finally Judge Candler said, "If you will drop the idea of that convention we will consent to any reasonable proposal." Then I asked, "Will you agree to the naming of a new Commission on Unification, which is not to be hampered by any Oklahoma City resolutions, but which will be free to negotiate?" When he and his three associates agreed we wrote our report and presented it to the larger committee. The anti-unificationists were astonished but we got the report adopted for recommendation. When it was on the calendar for action by the General Conference I went to the Chairman of the Committee on Church Relations, Dr. Paul H. Linn of Missouri, and suggested to him that we ask Judge John S. Candler to represent the Committee on the floor of the General Conference. Again anti-unificationists were so astonished that one whom they had counted as their leader should advocate a Commission to negotiate for union that they were easily defeated. One of their speakers had expressed surprise at Judge Candler's change in attitude, and he did it in such a way that the Judge was moved in a second speech to a strong advocacy of unification. So far as the South is concerned that second speech of Judge John S. Candler at the Hot Springs General Conference was the turning point in unification discussions. There was constituted the second Commission on Unification by the action of that General Conference and action of the General Conference of the other church. The plan produced by that Commission came before the General Conference of the Methodist Episcopal Church in Springfield in 1924 and was overwhelmingly endorsed. Then a special General Conference of the Methodist Episcopal Church, South, was called to meet in Chattanooga in the early days of July, 1924. It was a dramatic session but it gave the constitutional majority to the approval of the plan by the Southern Church. While a majority of the bishops of that church favored the plan the minority was in charge of the larger conferences in the Deep South. In some of them a sufficiently large number of negative votes was recorded to defeat the plan. The discussions were very bitter and the controversy was an important factor in the selection of delegates

118

to the General Conference in Memphis in 1926. While the unificationists were in a majority there was a very large minority and the
feeling was so bitter that it was decided unwise to name a new
Commission on Unification. It was not until 1934 that the Third
Commission to produce a plan was named. It was my privilege to
present the proposal for such a Commission then as I had presented
the proposal for the former Commission at Hot Springs in 1922.
There was little opposition since the bitter controversy of earlier
years had died down, and we had new members in the Episcopal
College. This Commission was composed of men named by this
General Conference at Jackson in 1934 and by men named by the
General Conferences of the other churches. The able leadership
given by Bishop Edwin Holt Hughes, Dr. James H. Straughn,
and Bishop John M. Moore, together with the willingness of the
representatives of all three churches to adjust and compromise,
produced a plan which won the approval of the General Conferences
and the Annual Conferences of the three churches. The Uniting
Conference was held in Kansas City in 1939; and there was formed
one Methodist Church where for many years there had been three.
I was a member of that Commission and I can recall how Bishop
John M. Moore would always come to the meetings with his proposals carefully written out. The language of the present plan of
union is very largely the language of John M. Moore. The leadership of Bishop Hughes and Dr. Straughn was responsible for many
of the adjustments in attitudes that were necessary to secure
approval.

I have sketched the dramatic events in the Methodist Episcopal
Church, South, in the period of 1914 to 1939 and I remember so
vividly the heated arguments and the breaking of friendships over
the issue of unification. For many years there had been the exchange
of fraternal messengers; apparently the three churches were on the
friendliest of terms; there had been created a new hymnal of the
churches in the early part of the twentieth century. There seemed to
be no reason why the churches should not soon unite after the publication of the new Joint Hymnal. But there were undercurrents of
feeling. Some Methodist Protestants felt that they were repudiating

their history by coming into a church with an episcopal form of government, and many of their members were suspicious of the liberal theology in the Methodist Episcopal Church. Between the North and the South there was some overlapping of territory. The Southern Church had gone into Illinois and the Pacific Northwest following its members. The Methodist Episcopal Church had likewise followed its members into many southern states having episcopal areas centering in Atlanta and Chattanooga. Long years before a Commission had adjusted boundary and property disputes between the two sections, but there was an undercurrent of feeling that each church had violated the spirit of agreements; certainly there was a very strong feeling against the Methodist Episcopal Church in many sections of the South. Then the Methodist Episcopal Church had three hundred thousand negro members, many of them in the South, and had elected a negro bishop in 1920. Of course, there was practically segregation in that church because the negro churches were in separate conferences and the negro bishop was to preside over negro conferences. Nevertheless, there was a fear in the Deep South that the color line might be broken, and negro bishops come to preside over white conferences. This assertion was made again and again to influence people of the South against unification.

In any plan for church union the obstacles are frequently psychological and sociological; they are not in the field of polity or theology. Methodist Protestants had come to a sense of freedom in their local congregations and had grown used to the authority of congregational meetings. The laymen had a very influential role in church affairs. In that church there was a real fear of authoritorian influence of bishops and district superintendents. In sections of the North there was a theoretical attitude toward race relations which was impatient of what was considered a reactionary attitude in the South, whereas in the South there was a fear that those in the North might act as they were saying Christians should act in dealing with race problems. Then there had been an identification of the church's cause with the nation's cause in the War Between the States and in the post-war struggles. The American flag was waved too often in church services to suit southern sentiment, and there was a feeling that the church in the North was too politically minded. A noted northern divine had been quoted in the South as saying that John Brown deserved a place in Christian tradition with the Apostle Paul. On the other hand there were many in the north who felt that the southern influence would retard the liberal movement in theology as it might very well hinder the preaching of the social gospel and render of little effect the great pronouncements of the Social Creed of the Churches, the creation of leaders in the Methodist Episcopal Church. It was this undercurrent of feeling that for so long kept the Churches apart, as such undercurrent does in any discussion of church union. The hurdles which appear are not the real hurdles.

As one takes into consideration the strong manifestations of emotion in the period between 1914 and 1939 he can understand the resentment against Bishop Hendrix in the South when in 1916 at Saratoga Springs he took the hand of Bishop Cranston and indicated that the Southern Church was ready for union. On every hand in the South questions were raised. What right had Bishop Hendrix to speak for the whole Southern Church? Did he not know that many people in the South were opposed to union? Was he not aware of the fact that the last preceding session of his General Conference had said that union was possible only on certain lines? Was not Bishop Hendrix always inclined to take too much for granted, and was he not dramatizing too realistically his own liberal attitude? As these questions were raised Bishop Hendrix was more severely criticized than for anything he ever did save when he took a position against his colleagues in the episcopacy in the Vanderbilt issue. As we look back on this historic moment at Saratoga Springs we may revaluate in the South our judgment on the action of Bishop Hendrix. He was ahead of his church, and he was giving prophetic leadership. We think of the picture of Bishop Hughes and Dr. Straughn and Bishop Moore at Kansas City in 1939 and for many of us that picture symbolizes union. But another picture belongs with it and that is the picture of Bishop Cranston and Bishop Hendrix clasping hands at Saratoga Springs. We must go back a bit beyond 1916, as we have been thinking about the years since, before we can fully grasp its significance. The separation of the northern and southern sections of Methodism in 1844 brought heartaches to many, but, with the coming of the War Between the States, the separation seems providential. The Southern Church was able to serve in the South as a national church could not have served. The Methodist Episcopal Church had a similar mission in the North. However, it is undoubtedly true that each of these churches identified itself so fully with the political and social ideals of its section that the separation was an ever-widening gulf between the Methodism of the North and the Methodism of the South. In the days of reconstruction there were some northern commanders in occupied territory and some northern ministers who used high-handed methods in taking over churches and property of the Southern Church. There are several incidents of this kind in a border state like Missouri and as Eugene Hendrix returned from the seminary in New York to take his first pastorate in Leavenworth, Kansas, he must have heard many stories about what had happened to southern churches in St. Louis and other sections of the state. One of the churches of the Methodist Episcopal Church in this state continues to carry the name Union Methodist Church. On the other hand there were attitudes of bitterness on the part of southerners toward Methodists from the North who might be residents of the community.

The Methodist Protestant Church knew no separation in those tragic days and was able to function as a national church. For this reason that church could appeal to both the northern and southern branches of the Church. This is a very important fact as one studies the role of the Methodist Protestant Church under the providence of God in the promotion of Methodist union.

Not only did the war leave bitterness in hearts in both the North and South, but there were serious disputes about property ownership along the border. Though an effort was made after the separation of 1844 to divide the property fairly and honestly, there were still some instances of disputed ownership when war came. The war created other problems, brought about largely by seizure of certain properties. As fraternal messengers were bringing messages of brotherliness to successive General Conferences, beginning immediately after the war, commissions were set up to adjust property claims, and in the Congress of the United States Methodists from the North often aided Methodists from the South in pressing their claims for damages and destruction during the war. One of the most celebrated claims was that of the Publishing House of the M. E. Church, South, against the Federal Government. The bill to pay this damage claim was finally passed at the turn of the century and it brought on one of the most serious controversies in the Southern Church during the years of Bishop Hendrix's episcopacy. The lobbyist had been paid a considerable per cent, and there were accusations of dishonest representation brought against at least one of the Publishing Agents. That whole controversy brought to the Southern Church again many of the debates over some of the issues of the war.

The tragic era of reconstruction days left memories in some sections of the South which lingered for many years. In the special session of the General Conference of the M. E. Church, South, at Chattanooga in 1924, all the clerical and lay delegates from South Carolina were voting against proposals to endorse the plan for unification, with the exception of one lay delegate, President Henry N. Snyder, of Wofford College. As the unificationists accused the South Carolinians of narrowness and prejudice Dr. Snyder arose to their defense in one of the great utterances in the history of Southern General Conferences, beginning with the sentence, "I do not agree with my brethren from South Caorlina but I do understand them." Again and again in the discussions of unification was Bishop Hendrix reminded of the grievances of some southern communities. It was the most natural thing in the world for Methodists in the North to sense an obligation to the negroes in the South who had been emancipated. Money was raised and missionary teachers were dispatched to the South to work among the negroes. To raise more money and send more teachers in this worthy enterprise it was necessary to picture conditions in the South in such a way that reports of what was said reached those who resented very much the critical attitude. Whether or not the term was used in a wise way southern people did not like to hear it said that missionaries were being sent from the North into southern territory. Soon after the war the negro Methodists of the South were organized into the Colored Methodist Church. That church was aided from the beginning by the Methodist Episcopal Church, South, and there were special schools and social service institutions established by the Southern Church to aid negroes. While there was full appreciation by some of the fine service rendered the institutions established by money from the North there was a widespread feeling in great sections of the Southern Church in the early years of this century that many Methodists in the North assumed that nothing had been done and nothing would be done by Methodists for the southern negro unless they of the North did it. Some of his episcopal colleagues who did not share the views of Bishop Hendrix about unification never lost an opportunity to remind him that in their judgment he was forgetting too many things when he talked so much about more brotherly relations with northern Methodists. In attempting to recover the atmosphere in which the bishop from Missouri was called on to defend his views on unification I do not forget the very harsh things that were said by at least three of the southern bishops during the early discussions of the first Commission on Unification. They were very critical of both attitudes and conduct in the northern section of the church. While they were all strong men, with strong convictions, and spoke from their own particular points of view there is no doubt about the fact that they spoke for a much larger section of the church at that time than could Bishop Hendrix. He rarely engaged in any controversy with his colleagues over this issue, but he went on saying the things that were in his mind and on his heart about the need to unite the Methodist Churches of the United States. In his native Missouri, one of the border states, he encouraged a plan for comity agreements between the two Methodisms to avoid building altar against altar. Presiding as bishop over the first session of the Missouri Conference after union I reaped the harvest of that policy. In many communities only one Methodism served and in most of those where both Methodisms had been serving it was not difficult to work out mergers. Bishop Hendrix was not presiding over the

Missouri Conferences when many of the comity agreements were made, but he did reside in Kansas City from the date of his election in 1886, and his influence was always felt in the state.

Many of us in the South were deeply disappointed when the vote in the Annual Conferences defeated the plan for union approved by the special session of the General Conference in 1924, but it was providential. A substantial section of the Southern Church would not have gone into the United Church at that time. After fifteen years of waiting, with opportunities for discussion and with a chance for many of the opposition to change views, it was possible to bring practically the entire southern group into the United Church. Some of us had feared even then that we might lose as many as fifty thousand members, but we were mistaken. The loss has been only a small per cent of that. However, there was opposition in 1916 and Bishop Hendrix was made to feel the weight of that opposition when he came back home after the dramatic clasping of hands with Bishop Earl Cranston, and the symbolizing of the desire for union. His church was far from the position it was ready to take in 1938 and twenty-two years of argument and debate must pass before the delegates of the General Conference at Birmingham in 1938 were willing to commit the church to the program which Bishop Hendrix thought in 1916, and for years before, his church should take. He died before the consummation of union but there seems to be a peculiar fitness in the fact that the Uniting Conference met in Kansas City, the home city of the Bishop.

One can understand the enthusiasm of the Bishop on that day in Saratoga Springs. His own family belonged to both the North and the South, and he knew the Methodisms of both sections. His college education was at a northern institution of learning and likewise his seminary education. Among both teachers and students he had intimate friends whom he loved and whose Methodist convictions were as deep as his. To some of them he felt so close that they were really in the same church.

Then his pastorates were in the border states of Kansas and Missouri, and he lived in Kansas City for many years. He had seen the folly of building altar against altar, and more than once he had said, "What a Methodism we could have in Kansas City and Missouri if we had been united years ago." His last period of episcopal service in Missouri was in the quadrennium of 1914 to 1918, and the Conferences of 1916 commemorated the hundredth anniversary of the coming of Methodism to Missouri. In each of the three churches entertaining the Annual Conferences he had a bronze tablet put on the wall calling attention to the establishment of Methodism. Those churches were, of course, southern churches; they and the Annual Conferences were reminded of the fact that the two Methodisms in Missouri had a common origin. Then his experience in the Federal Council had raised a question: "If all the large communions in the United States can join together in the creation of the Federal Council has not the time come for the Methodisms in America to forget their differences?" He knew well the negotiations and plans of the years since the war for the deepening of understandings and the elimination of differences. In the thirty years of his episcopacy, between 1886 and 1918, things had happened which seemed to Bishop Hendrix to justify the stand he took at Saratoga Springs. He was not giving expression simply to a personal conviction.

It was as far back as 1874 when the fraternal messengers of the Methodist Episcopal Church brought to a General Conference of the Methodist Episcopal Church, South, assurances of brotherly interest, but in those years immediately after the war the Southern Church was made to feel that it had withdrawn from the Methodist Church and formed a new organization. In the Southern Church was the conviction that in the separation of 1844 both churches carried the main tradition, and one was as much the original church as the other. That issue had to be settled before there could be any hope of reunion. In 1876 the Southern Church sent its fraternal messengers to the General Conference of the Methodist Episcopal Church. In 1891 at Cape May in New Jersey a Joint Commission of the two churches declared: "Each of said churches is a legitimate branch of Episcopal Methodism in the United States having a common origin in the Methodist Episcopal Church organized in 1784." That was an authoritative statement of the historic situation, and after that statement discussion of uniting the churches became continually more earnest. In 1894 a Commission on Federation was proposed by the General Conference of the Methodist Episcopal Church, South, and after approval by the General Conference of the Methodist Episcopal Church in 1896 such a Commission was set up. It settled some disputed matters and considered some property claims but its most important work was a plan for a common catechism, a common order of worship and a Joint Hymnal. The publication of the Joint Hymnal and a common order of worship brought congregations all over the nation into a closer fellowship. As congregations in the North read the names of the southern representatives on the Hymnal Commission, and congregations in the South read the names of the northern representatives on the Commission people everywhere sensed the fact that they belonged to the same church. There is no surer way of bringing people together than uniting them in worship, and in all ecumenical gatherings the worship service is the medium for a real experience of unity. So it was in the Methodist Churches, North and South; one cannot overemphasize the publication of the Joint Hymnal as a step in the unification of the churches.

In 1910 the Commission on Federation appointed representatives to explore the possibility of union, and there was more serious consideration of the possibility. The differences still seemed great, but it was a General Conference of the Methodist Episcopal Church, South, which declared "union is feasible and desirable" on a plan of reorganization. Stress is laid on the fact that a Southern General Conference meeting at Oklahoma City in 1914 passed such a resolution, not because there is a desire to show the Southern Church as officially taking the lead in the matter of unification, but as proof that Bishop E. R. Hendrix was justified in extending a right hand of fellowship to Bishop E. R. Cranston, at the Saratoga Springs General Conference of 1916, as an assurance of southern readiness for union. The last preceding General Conference of his own church had declared union both possible and desirable. Those in the South who criticized him as misrepresenting the southern attitude and giving unjustified assurances need to read their own church's history and especially the wording of the Oklahoma City resolutions.

They indicated a union through reorganization, but they also stated the desire of the Southern Church for union. Under the inspiration of the dramatic meeting of the two bishops the General Conference of 1916 agreed to the naming of a Joint Commission on Unification. The real work on a plan began soon after that.

Those of us who have lived through the days of the Uniting Conference of 1939 are so impressed by its drama and significance as to forget history. We may go back beyond the days when Edwin D. Mouzon gave leadership to the same cause. But we either do not know or we have forgotten the service of Eugene R. Hendrix, and years before him of Lovick R. Pierce. It is amazing that Bishop Hendrix had leadership in so many fields. A pioneer in church educational efforts he served at Central College and on the Board of Trust of Vanderbilt University; making a trip around the world with Bishop Marvin he acquired that knowledge of missions which made him a missionary statesman in his administration of Methodist Missions in the Orient and South America; in the field of church cooperation he was a leader and he was the inevitable choice as the first President of the Federal Council; in the uniting of the Methodist Churches he was a prophetic leader when the triumvirate was T. H. Lewis, Earl Cranston and Eugene Hendrix. It is surely true that in the long history of Southern Methodism no man gave evidences of more conspicuous ability and wiser leadership in so many fields of endeavor. When the full story of the unification of American Methodism is written the name of Eugene Russell Hendrix will appear again and again. For fifty years he was at the heart of the movement, sometimes seeking cooperation as a pastor in a local community with bitter antagonisms, and sometimes as the advocate of union before large audiences in every part of the country, and sometimes as a witness to the necessity of a deeper fellowship among the churches in the building of a stronger nation. Always and at all times he refused to be a sectarian or a sectionalist. While loving both the South and the Southern Church he was ever at home in the larger church. While he was surrounded all through his ministry by many who were Methodists of the North and Methodists of the South he was always at heart an American Methodist.

Bishop Hendrix in later life.

Chapter X

The Federal Council

AFTER the meeting in Philadelphia where the Federal Council of the Churches of Christ in America was organized a popular American magazine carried an article which opened with this paragraph: "November, 1908, was a notable month. On its third day the American people elected a president. It is not generally known, however, that during the following month occurred an event of even more importance to the American people. This was the assembling in Philadelphia of four hundred earnest men, representing more millions of constituents than the combined population of Spain, Portugal, Greece, Denmark, Switzerland, Scotland, Sweden, Norway and Canada—forty millions in all, or nearly three times the number of voters registered at the presidential polls. The delegates formed the Federal Council of the Churches of Christ in this country, acting for over one half of the population—one person in every two among the men, women and children in the United States being a church member or a church contributor." While the magazine writer may have exaggerated a bit in his figures the significant thing is that he writes of this church gathering with such enthusiasm and considers it more important than the election of a president. The United Brethren in Christ at their General Conference the following May referred to the organization of the Federal Council as "the most Christian measure ever taken in America."

The subsequent history of the organization has more than justified these words of approval and expectancy, but we are concerned here with the early years of the Federal Council because Eugene Russell Hendrix was its first President. In the histories prepared for the Federal Council by Dr. E. B. Sanford and Dr. Charles S. Macfarland, as well as in an address of mine on the thirtieth anniversary delivered in Buffalo in 1938 are to be found most of the facts relating to those early years. There were cooperative efforts among the churches and certain organizations which prepared the way for the Federal Council. Perhaps we may speak of the Evangelical Alliance as the real precursor. There was a world Evangelical Alliance before there was a branch of it established in the United States, though much of the leadership in the world movement came from America. As early as 1838 a Lutheran leader, Samuel Schmucker, appealed to Protestant bodies to form an alliance and the great scholar of the Reformed Church in the United States, Philip Schaff, is quoted by Dr. Macfarland as saying: "Federal or confederate union is a voluntary association of different churches in their official capacity, each retaining its freedom and independence in the management of its affairs, but all recognizing one another as sisters with equal rights and cooperating in general enterprises, such as the spread of the gospel at home and abroad, the defense of the faith against infidelity, the elevation of the poor and neglected classes of society, works of philanthropy and charity and moral reform." In view of the conservative attitude of the Lutherans one hundred years later in the formation of the World Council of Churches it is significant that one of their number took such interest in forming the World Alliance. The first session of this World Alliance was held in London in 1846, and previous to the organization of a branch of the movement in the United States international conferences were held in London in 1851, Berlin in 1857, and Geneva in 1861. Shortly before the fifth international conference held in Amsterdam the branch in the United States was organized January 31, 1867. The first president was the great layman, William E. Dodge, who served until 1883. He was later succeeded by his son, who served until 1903. The international meeting of the World Alliance was held first in this country in October, 1873, and it brought together the most distinguished religious leaders of that day—ministers, university presidents and prominent laymen of the business world. Subsequent meetings were at the Centennial Exposition in Philadelphia in 1876, at Basle in 1879, at Boston in 1889, at Florence in 1891. By the turn of the century it was felt that the cooperative movement should be reorganized in America and in New York in 1900 was held a meeting looking toward such reorganization. At the meeting of the National Federation in 1902 it was recommended that a Committee be appointed to secure the naming of delegates from the denominational bodies to meet in 1905. Up to this the meetings and organizations brought together interested individuals. It must be remembered that cooperation among Mission Boards of American denominations had begun and that such organizations as the Y. M. C. A. and the International Sunday School Movement were promoting interdenominational cooperation. The two men who were most active in the promotion of the meeting in Carnegie Hall were William Henry Roberts and E. B. Sanford, but in any list of founders must be included Eugene Russell Hendrix, who served as Chairman of the Business Committee at that important conference which assembled November 15, 1905. There were 436 delegates appointed by 29 Evangelical denominations. The laymen who were present were men of great distinction and included President Woodrow Wilson of Princeton, Judge Henry Wade Rogers of Yale, Dr. Robert E. Speer, Dr. John R. Mott, Mr. Charles Evans Hughes, Judge Peter S. Grosscup, Governor James A. Beaver of Pennsylvania and Governor M. Sim Bruce of New York; perhaps it was the most distinguished group of laymen ever brought together in a religious conference in the United States.

As Chairman of the important Business Committee which organized and directed this Conference served Eugene Russell Hendrix, a bishop of the Methodist Episcopal Church, South, and one of its delegates. The Conference took steps in the formation of the Federal Council, and approved this resolution: "It shall be the duty of each delegation to this Conference to present this Plan of Federation to its national body, and ask its consideration and proper action. In case this Plan of Federation is approved by two-thirds of the proposed constituent bodies the Executive Committee of the National Federation of Churches and Christian Workers, which has called this Conference, is requested to call the Federal Council to meet at a fitting place in December, 1908." The basis for membership was stated as the desire to manifest "the essential oneness of the Christian Churches of America in Jesus Christ as their Divine Lord and Savior" and to "promote the spirit of fellow-ship, service and cooperation."

When the organizing meeting was held in Philadelphia there were among the delegates some differences of opinion as to the basis of federation. What should be the relation of the national organization and the state federations? Should the evangelical basis for membership he established? These were the two most debated issues. As Chairman of the Business Committee Bishop Eugene R. Hendrix closed the debate on the issue of the evangelical basis for membership with these words: "The question has been raised: Is this Plan on a Trinitarian basis? On behalf of the forty men representing every Church in this Great Federation of Christians, and after prayer and much careful consideration, I most emphatical-ly in their name say 'Yes.' It was called on that basis. Its whole proceedings have been conducted on that basis, and on that basis the Committee voted this morning, with only one dissenting vote, to adopt the words, 'Our Divine Lord and Savior.'"

The vote was taken and the only negative vote was that of Prof. J. Q. Dealey, the distinguished Professor of Sociology at Brown University. Professor Dealey had offered this amendment: "Nothing in the phraseology contained in this plan of union shall be construed to imply any doctrinal basis whatever, save that implied by the broadest Christian unity."

The growing interest in international cooperation created by a conference that had met from time to time at Lake Mohonk and the emphasis on the social gospel in the writings and work of Josiah Strong and his associates created in large measure the intel-lectual and moral atmosphere of the first session of the Federal Council. The scene on the platform was impressive with a choir of 500 so arranged as to form a cross in the center. In the Assembly were 352 delegates and alternates representing 33 separate denomi-nations. Bishop E. R. Hendrix was at once unanimously elected the first President of the Federal Council. That honor was merited not only because of the position he held in the ranks of Protestant Churchmen in his day but because of the able leadership he had given at the Carnegie Hall Conference in 1905 and at this first meeting of the Federal Council.

The Committee on Organization and Development proposed some plans which were too ambitious for the early stage in organization. The nation was to be divided into four districts each with office and staff, and a central office was to be established in New York. Perhaps the most significant action taken was the adoption of a "Social Creed" which had been approved for churches of that denomination a few months before by the General Conference of the Methodist Church, and this carried with it the creation of a Commission on the Church and Social Service. That Commission was in after years bitterly attacked at times in church assemblies and by individual churchmen, but in 1908 its creation was approved without a dissenting vote. That is as much a matter of interest as the activity of the Lutherans in the early days of the World Alliance of Evangelical Churches.

The objects of the Federal Council were stated in these simple words:

I. To express the fellowship and catholic unity of the Christian Church.
II. To bring the Christian bodies of America into united service for Christ and the world.
III. To encourage devotional fellowship and mutual counsel concerning the spiritual life and religious activities of the churches.
IV. To secure a larger combined influence for the churches of Christ in all matters affecting the moral and social condition of the people, so as to promote the application of the law of Christ in every relation of human life.
V. To assist in the organization of local branches of the Federal Council to promote its aims in their communities.

Seldom has a great movement been launched with more enthusiasm, but the working out of the plans is in contrast with the dreams of the years from 1905 to 1908. Dr. E. B. Sanford acted as Corresponding Secretary and the search for a permanent Secretary began. When the first meeting of the Executive Committee was held in Louisville in 1909 only 27 members were present and only $9,000 of the $30,000 budget had been secured. Bishop Hendrix took the chair at that meeting and had to make use of his administrative ability as well as his tact to prevent an attitude of frustration. His address at that time, with his vigorous leadership the following year, turned the tide of frustration, and the meeting of the Executive Committee in Washington in 1910 showed the enthusiasm of earlier years. The third meeting of the Executive Committee at Pittsburgh in 1911 selected Charles S. Macfarland as Secretary of the Commission on Social Service and he soon became Acting Executive Secretary. Substantial progress was recorded in the promotion of city and state Federations of Churches. The second session of the Federal Council was held in Chicago in 1912. The four years had revealed the fact that many can dream dreams but only a few can face the hard and difficult task of making dreams realities. President George W. Richards, a member of the Council from the beginning, once characterized another period of church history as "the days of small things and big men." One of the big men in the first quadrennium of Federal Council history was Eugene Russell Hendrix and there were times when his interest and zeal alone kept the new organization alive. The meeting of the Executive Committee in Pittsburgh closed with a service at the First Presbyterian Church which was announced as a "great mass meeting." There were only fifty people present and even the pastor of the church failed to appear. It seems impossible that the enthusiasms of the 1905 Conference at Carnegie Hall, and the Assembly in Philadelphia in 1908 could so far decline.

At the meeting of the Executive Committee in Louisville in 1909, a year after his election as President, Bishop Hendrix delivered an address which takes rank among the historic addresses in Federal Council history. The courage and vision of this man had so much to do with saving the Council and preserving it for its future mission that I want to quote at length from his message: "A generation ago the eloquent Pere Hyacinthe said: 'In the sixteenth century the Church saved Christianity by separation. In the twentieth century Christianity will save the churches by bringing them together.' What seemed far distant in Europe then seemed equally far distant in America. What seems far distant in Europe now, seems an already accomplished fact in America. The seer could not see how or how far this closer relation was to be brought about. But what has been so wonderfully accomplished in the United States may have a gracious influence in bringing about closer relations among the great Protestant Churches of Europe. The great divisional names of the Churches in America were imported as our ancestors brought them with them to America. What have been added since are subdivisions for the most part of a comparatively small number of great divisions which were in existence in Europe before our ancestors left. We are resolved to find a basis of agreement among them, and have already found it.

"Federation in America is federation at the top, federation of Churches rather than individuals. . . . This is doubtless possible in a large measure because there have never been any religious waves in America. The Churches themselves have often been rivals and their competition not infrequently in the past has been marked by earnest debates on differences in polity and in doctrine; but there has never been any blood-shed. But in Europe more Christian blood has been shed by Christians than by all the non-Christians and Mohammedans combined. In fact, most of the wars in Europe have been religious wars with rival candidates of different religious beliefs. 'Holy Wars' they called them, not only when Protestant and Papal armies and navies were called out, but even when Protestant Scotland and England differed and when Covenanter and Churchman were as fierce as Huguenot and Papist, and sought to decide their differences in battle. . . . The close relationship of Church and State in all Europe made the church a party to, and often the cause of civil and foreign wars. It has taken many a Triple Alliance, and more than one session of the Hague Tribunal to keep the peace of Europe."

Within a few years after the delivery of that address the First World War began and there has been little peace in Europe for a generation. Neither World War was a religious war, but the organization of the World Council of Churches in Amsterdam brought to the surface differences among churches in Europe which can be traced, many of them, to the bitter conflicts and religious wars of earlier days. The churches in America can thank God that they have no religious wars in their history, though they have as part of their heritage the religious struggles in Europe.

Bishop Hendrix went on to say in Louisville in 1909:

"Happily for America we have never known a religious war, and the churches have never been tempted to seek the control of government. Their mission is not to be established by the state, but to seek to establish the state. With a growing passion to obey their Lord's teachings, whether in the Sermon on the Mount, or in his parables of the kingdom, or in his last great commission, they have been working together at home and abroad until they have heard each others' voices in the harvest field or on the watch towers in distant lands, and until they have learned to esteem each other highly in love for their work's sake. Federal Councils, although under another name, began to be held in China and Japan and Central Asia before America became ripe for hers. It thus came to pass almost without observation that the kingdom came among us in New York and Philadelphia, because the churches were ready. Perhaps it was God's method of saving the churches themselves by federating them for their sublime and world-wide mission, and so fulfilling the words of the eloquent Pere Hyacinthe. Who knows but that we have come into the kingdom for such a time as this to be the leaders of the Lord's hosts? . . . The churches which seek to save their lives by separation are in greater danger of losing them, just as the corps which refuse to be mobilized with the main army are in most danger of being cut off by the foe."

In discussing the attitude of the Federal Council toward the union of churches Bishop Hendrix said in that same address: "Organic union of the churches is not the province of the Federal Council, although organic union will follow between some of the same name or polity. Nor on the other hand is it the province of the Council to disintegrate any body of believers, large or small. All these matters are left to the several churches. Our gospel is not like that of John the Baptist, the gospel of the axe, but like that of our Lord, the gospel of the leaven. It makes much of the 'time-spirit.' It is the gospel of love and of spiritual fellowship, not of outward forms of worship or of ecclesiastical machinery. There is no attempt to define the church any more than to appraise any church save on the basis of its works. The mark of a true church is that it makes saints and vinebranches. As a wise and devout leader in the Protestant Episcopal Church said: 'It is not what we think of other churches whose zeal and good works far outrun our own that is of moment, but what do those churches think of us who pretend so much and who produce so little.' The value of a church is best measured by estimating what we would do without it. . . . A church may be spared as no longer needed that makes loud claims but lacks Christ's spirit, that clamors for more territory but neglects what it already has, that embarrasses its fellow-workers by over-lapping and so creating waste and confusion in any community. It may even die 'by request' and unwept. The ability to live together in the same community is a good test of civilized men and also of the Churches of Christ, and is one of the best fruits of our holy religion. Neighborliness is a good thing in men and in churches."

It is doubtful whether the historic attitude of the Federal Council toward the promotion of church union has ever been better stated. At the close of my term of office as President of the Federal Council I made a plea for the Council to take a greater interest in the uniting of the churches, and insisted that a step should be taken beyond federation. After much discussion the Biennial Meeting of 1936 approved the creation of a "Commission For the Study of Christian Unity." I became the Chairman of that Commission, the only one the Federal Council has ever had in all the years of its history. While the Commission succeeded in doing some very fine things and set the stage for a unification effort among several communions it was never able to influence the thinking of the Federal Council about its own obligation in the field of promoting union. In the Council are some members who want to see a larger Protestant Union; there are several influential churches whose attitude was stated a generation ago by Bishop Hendrix.

In speaking of unity in diversity and diversity in unity Bishop Hendrix used these words: "It was the Allied Armies that won the battle of Blenheim and the battle of Waterloo, which did so much to make Great Britain and to make Britain great. Trafalgar was fought for Europe, not for England only. It is the Allied Armies of our Lord that are to win the world-conquest. Called to do what seems impossible of accomplishment we grow great in attempting the impossible task side by side with our fellow soldiers of every regimental color but fighting under one banner of the cross. We learn from each other how to be valiant soldiers of the cross as we are inspired by the same bulletins of hard-won victory. We are beginning to learn how much we have in common in the great hymns of Christendom as well as in the great prayers which have lifted the saints of all ages nearer to God. Thus it was Calvin's liturgy that enriched the English Prayer Book with its exhortations and confessions and even its absolution. The Lutheran Ritual gave part of the beautiful marriage service. The Puritan, Edward Reynolds, a Westminster Assembly divine, gave the noble Thanksgiving, while the Morning Prayer is not complete without the prayer of St. Chrysostom. It is the allied forces of our Lord of Hosts who enrich all saints with the fruits of their faith. No wonder Paul prayed for the Ephesians that they might comprehend with all saints, for unless we comprehend with all saints we do not comprehend at all. We need that catholicity of spirit and of experience and of view that enables us to see truth from the stand-point of our fellow believers of whatever name. It is usually given to each church to see strongly some phase of truth but only those who comprehend with all saints can see the whole truth. . . . We doubtless can better wield the Sword of the Spirit which is the word of God by reason of the help that has come in understanding it from the best and most spiritual men of all the churches. . . . Robert L. Stevenson used to tell many of the short-comings of one he called 'my little brother'—short-comings due to inexperience and often to prejudice. He would join in the laugh raised at his 'little brother's' expense, and would then explain that his 'little brother' was himself before he had seen more of the world and was better prepared to make proper allowances for his fellow-man. . . . If some of our brethren of other churches are still a little 'belated' in their spirit of fraternity let us remember that our 'little brother' was once the same way. So too, were John when he wanted to call down fire from heaven on those who did not think as he did, and Peter also, who was very careful about what he ate and with whom he ate, until after a memorable noon-day nap on a house-top in Joppa, with the Mediterranean in the back-ground, he had quite a change of heart. 'The sea grows always greater' says Tintoretto. It helps us the better to think the thoughts of God. It becomes a bond and not a barrier as we remember that God made of one blood all nations of men to dwell on all the face of the earth. It helps us to renew our interest in the human race when we hear the voice from over the sea speak of 'the other sheep which I have but which are not of this fold.' But there shall be one flock and one Shepherd."

That address voices the faith of the first President of the Federal Council, and it is doubtful whether any President since his day has ever echoed more sympathetically the opinions of those with whom he was associated.

In the membership of the churches were many who were not conscious of the great movement, and even among the church leaders were many who were indifferent. There was a small group of men who saw far beyond their time and were in the truest sense prophets of a new day in Christian fellowship. The last service of Bishop Hendrix to the Federal Council was at a meeting of the Executive Committee in Columbus, Ohio, December, 1915. The First World War had begun. The President of the United States, Woodrow Wilson, met with the Executive Committee as he had been interested in the Federal Council from its beginning. The Executive Committee placed on record this resolution, "As these sessions draw to a close we place on record our appreciation, first of all, of the presence with the Executive Committee of Woodrow Wilson, the President of the United States. We tender to him hearty thanks that amid the multitudinous cares of the State he has taken opportunity thus to express his deep interest in the welfare of the Christian Churches of our country." As was most appropriate the message was handed to the President by Bishop E. R. Hendrix. When the fortieth anniversary of the Federal Council was observed at a memorable Biennial Meeting at Cincinnati in December, 1948, the gavel for the Presiding Officer was the one used by Bishop Hendrix at the first session in 1908 and was presented to President Charles P. Taft by Bishop Arthur J. Moore of the Methodist Church.

In its forty years of history the Federal Council has given prophetic leadership again and again. It is difficult to imagine how the churches could have ministered to the country or the world without it during the two periods of world war. Through its Commission on Chaplains it served the nation's armed forces as well as the Protestant Churches. It gave valiant support to the League of Nations after the First World War and sought to guide the thinking of the United States and the world through its Commission on a Just and Durable Peace when the Second World War was devastating great areas of the world. It was evident through all the trying years of war that God's Spirit had led the creators of the Federal Council.

In the midst of the depression when preachers and people alike were losing heart about the church the Federal Council launched in the fall of 1936 the National Preaching Mission. It was the greatest crusade of evangelism the United States ever knew. As the missioners went from city to city they were humbled by the crowds which attended the services. They were amazed at the response of the non-church community and the amount of space which metropolitan newspapers gave to the Mission in every city visited. They saw a new radiance in the faces of discouraged preachers, twenty-five thousand of whom attended the services. There was a new earnestness in the hearts of Protestant Church members, two million of whom came to the meetings. The response was beyond any anticipation or dream. In an editorial which appeared in a daily paper of a city visited were these sentences: "Crowds have attended the services of the National Preaching Mission. Why? Life is desperate these days for many people. The preaching of this Mission is desperately earnest. No missioner seems to be concerned about his reputation or about his prestige or about what men think of the sermon he preaches. When we think of fifteen men coming to our city for the announced purpose of changing currents of life we are inclined to say that it is silly and foolhardy. On second reflection we are bound to say that it is breath-taking in its magnificence. There are questions which must be answered. Even a hard-boiled newspaperman, through whose fingers flows the news of the world, must wonder in these days if religion has the answer. Perhaps it has. This we know, that the questions must be answered if the world is to go on."

It is a little difficult to select a third achievement of the Federal Council which deserves to rank with the war and post-war service, and with the National Preaching Mission of 1936. Perhaps one would name the contribution to the ecumenical movement. Through the early years of the Federal Council the Commission on Social Service was the most significant development in church cooperation, its position of influence being taken later by that on International Justice and Goodwill. The Commissions on Worship, on Race Relations, on Marriage and the Home, on Religion and Health, on Field Work and Organization, on Radio, on Research and Education have made great contributions in the Christianizing of unchristian areas of American life. But the Department on Relations with Churches Abroad gave every support to the great world conferences of Protestantism for years before the organization of the World Council of Churches at Amsterdam in 1948. The Commission For the Study of Christian Unity brought together the secretaries of all the cooperative agencies in American Protestantism and is largely responsible for the movement to merge all these agencies into a new structural unity to be known as the National Council of Churches. Working for the elimination of duplication and for the increase of efficiency in the service of the churches in America, while at the same time it was seeking to deepen fellowship and create a kind of spiritual Una Sancta throughout the world, the Federal Council has made the largest contribution of any agency in the world to the development of the ecumenical movement. Without the Federal Council there could not have been the great chapter in church history of the last forty years. Those who established the Federal Council in 1908 builded more wisely than they knew. The first President, Eugene R. Hendrix, and the first Secretary, E. B. Sanford had been students together in Wesleyan University at Middletown, Connecticut, and they had been close friends since college days. That friendship had brought great dreams and served as a strengthening influence in the lives of both men when the initial enthusiasms for the Federal Council cooled. Sanford gave an endless amount of time to personal contacts and numerous letters. Hendrix gave his administrative ability and his wide experience in the work of the church. The two of them together, with the zealous support of men like William H. Roberts, George W. Richards, Frank Mason North, and Charles L. Thompson, guided the Council through the days when it was learning to walk. Such were the "founding fathers."

William Adams Brown once wrote: "It is difficult to exaggerate the importance of the contribution to Christian unity which was made by the formation and development of the Federal Council. By its adoption of the federal principle a precedent was set which was destined to be followed years later in the creation of the World Council." Frank Mason North, on the eve of his election as President of the Federal Council, said: "To those who in the period from 1894 to 1908 looked and worked toward such an organization as the Federal Council that notable Assembly in Philadelphia seemed a consummation. The ascent, however, to that summit brought them and the churches they represented not to a mountain peak but to a plateau. What to aspiration had seemed a height of vision, to achievement became the broad plain of opportunity. Through the intervening years, as atmosphere has cleared and action has developed energy, the horizons have lifted and the unbroken light has revealed at once the forces and the tasks of the Churches of Christ." Continuity through the years has been given to the work of the Federal Council by the two men who have served as Executive Secretaries, Charles S. Macfarland and Samuel M. Cavert, each serving the Council for approximately twenty years. Both are men of genius whose great abilities have made possible the work of this great agency of the churches of America. The Presidents have been Eugene R. Hendrix, Shailer Matthews, Robert

E. Speer, Frank Mason North, S. Parkes Cadman, Francis J. Mc-
Connell, Albert W. Bevan, Ivan Lee Holt, Edgar DeWitt Jones,
George A. Buttrick, Henry St. George Tucker, Luther E. Weigle,
G. Bromley Oxnam, Charles P. Taft, John S. Stamm. But Secretaries and Presidents alike would pay tribute to those men who
had the vision to create such an agency, and the courage to see it
through its opening years. In the front rank of these men stands
Eugene Russell Hendrix. In the churches of America are some
who have not yet seen the vision that was his forty years ago. The
tragedies of recent decades have brought others to convictions
about church cooperation which were his because of his concept of
the church and its mission in the world.

In the midst of his term as President of the Federal Council Bishop
Hendrix gave the Episcopal Address to the General Conference
of the M. E. Church, South, in 1910. In referring to the Council he
said: "Our own church, true to her catholicity and religious spirit,
has had no small part in this great Federation of Churches, our
General Conference being the first of all the chief judicatories to
endorse it. . . . The once lonely watchmen are now seeing eye to
eye and together are they lifting up the voice to sing."

CHAPTER XI

The Preacher and Lecturer

WITH the completion of his round of Annual Conferences in the fall Bishop Hendrix would return to his home in Kansas City for the holiday season. Then during the remainder of the winter he spent days and weeks in his study and among the books of his large library. There were two or three months of almost uninterrupted reading and study and he was as methodical in his study as he was active in his work. There were prepared his addresses and sermons. When he spoke his voice was clear and his enunciation distinct. He was not as eloquent as Bishop Galloway but his thoughtful utterances held the attention of the congregation. Both his experience and his travel gave him a wealth of illustrations and his wide reading is revealed in apt quotations.

His sermons were always logical and very carefully outlined, while the development of his thought was the expression of a trained intellect. The listener might not experience many emotional reactions, but he would likely remember the sermon and its outline for a long, long time. Yet there were passages of sublime pathos when audiences were moved to tears, and also paragraphs of real eloquence which would provoke listeners to high resolves and enthusiastic purposes. He never resorted to shallow sentimentalism, but he could reach into the depths of the human soul, far beneath the disturbances and tumults which other preachers might create who were incapable of such deep thinking. The emotions he stirred were not of the surface.

His books were volumes of lectures he gave at colleges and universities—Christ's Table Talk, Skilled Labor for the Master, and The Holy Spirit. It is not easy to select one of his lectures or sermons from the number of able ones, but I have chosen from among them the one reproduced here. It is an address on "Arnold of Rugby."

"The mightiest forces which the world has ever known have not been material and physical, but intellectual and moral. Matter yields to spirit. Thought gives shape to granite and steel, makes channels for rivers, outlets for seas, courses for storms; makes the stars disclose their secrets, harnesses the lightning, rules the whole material world. The study of these material forces, fascinating as it is, is far less interesting than the study of the spiritual forces which control them. Man, who is God's vice-gerent on the earth, is peculiarly an embodiment of these ruling spiritual forces. As a mere physical being he by no means has dominion in the earth.

The fly with its eye of two thousand facets excels him in accuracy and the eagle in strength of vision. The spider surpasses him in the delicacy of touch, and the bloodhound or bee in keenness of scent. The mole is far more acute of hearing, while a hundred animals excel him in strength. As a mere physical being he is at the mercy alike of beast and insect and he would be helpless before the fury of brute or storm. And yet he rules the world. The whole face of the earth has been changed by human skill. Forests have given place to cities and prairies to forests and wild beasts have disappeared at the approach of man. Our own land bears testimony with the world at large to that power in man which has enabled him to subdue the earth and to exercise dominion over it. The secret of that supremacy is man's spiritual, or his intellectual or moral nature.

Mere Intellect

Of these spiritual forces which thus rule the world mere intellect is not, as is generally regarded, the chief. Intellect by means of mechanical inventions comes in contact with dead, inert matter and shapes it at will. But mind is most powerful not in ruling matter, but in ruling mind. Thought, while never powerless, may be weak for lack of moral support. A man may be majestic because he thinks, but his may be a sceptre before which few shall bow. His character may weaken the force of his influence and he learn with Satan that "to be weak is miserable."

In these days of civil service reform adulations of official honesty would have but little force if spoken by a venal politician and the praises of compassion, if uttered by a Robespierre, would awaken but slight response.

The mightiest of spiritual forces, and hence the most potent thing in the universe, is character. It is not what a man is reputed to be, or professes to be, but what he is. It is the embodiment of what he thinks, of what he feels and of what he wills. Intellect, sensibility and will all combined find their truest expression in the man's character.

Character organizes and disorganizes society. Character reforms and corrupts, destroys and resurrects. It gives tone and vigor to thought and action. It inaugurates enterprises or thwarts them. It is constantly communicated to and colors every human thought and deed. From its throne of power it rules through the intellect and will even master mechanical forces. A man's house or invention is frequently a true expression of what he is just as the material universe with its evidences of adaptation and design for the happiness of those creatures which obey its laws and the punishment of the disobedient shows forth the unmistakable attributes of the Deity.

Mental and Spiritual Forces

Many of the principles regulating physical forces hold in the realm of these spiritual forces embodied in character. Whether or not the relation existing between the physical and mental forces may be strictly defined as a correlation, yet there is something like a correlation and conservation of these mental and spiritual forces themselves.

We may not be able to learn from some delicately-constructed apparatus that not the smallest amount of spiritual force can be created or destroyed, and that every force disappears only to be found without increase or diminution in some other form. There are no crucibles or balances for testing and weighing influence and thought. But though we may not be able to trace them with such accuracy as in the case of material forces, yet we believe that not a thought or impulse or influence which enters into or is the product of a great character is lost.

There were radiated from John Newton's character influences

that are felt in Cowper's poetry, in Buchanan's logic, in Judson's glowing zeal, in Scott's reverent exposition of the Scriptures. Richard Baxter's thoughts wrought through Doddridge to Wilberforce, to Edmund Burke, to Leigh Richmond. Augustine has been reproduced in Calvin and Edwards and Hodge.

As in the material world heat, light, electricity and magnetism are modes of motion which are capable of mutual conversion, heat being transformed into electricity or electricity into heat; so in the higher realms thought kindles desire, desire arouses zeal and zeal is transformed into action. Character is imperishable. Elijah's mantle falls on Elisha; Stephen lives over again in Paul, and Paul's life is reproduced in Timothy.

Is Melanchthon dead? Is Knox dead? Is Wycliffe dead? Is any man that was ever fit to live dead? Physical science assures us that not a particle of matter which composed their bodies is destroyed, but lives in some new form and to serve some useful purpose; and much more certain are we that those spiritual forces constantly radiated by their characters are imperishable. And while mere physical force can only reproduce itself these higher forces seem capable of giving birth to yet sublimer thought and mightier influences. A great character imparts without losing, may seem to grow stronger by the very power which is given out. In the spiritual realm there is that which scattereth abroad and yet increaseth.

Arnold of Rugby

It is to a character thus embodying the greatest forces known to the world—clear thought, intense feeling and determined will, all in harmony with each other and with God, a character grand in itself and reproducing itself in hundreds of others, losing nothing while so generously giving, and fathering power with each succeeding decade, that I would call your attention. His name is one of the most cherished of modern times—Arnold of Rugby.

It matters but little when or where such a man was born. He belongs to all time and to every place. The star which a half century ago, by its clear, pure light fixed the gaze of the Christian world, was only sublimated into ethereal and eternal beauty when men whispered, with choking utterance, Arnold is dead. The light and beauty of that character have not left the world, though the manly form is no longer visible among men.

A true man, such as he, belongs to no century, no country, no profession, no sect.

It is not, then, as the "prince of schoolmasters" that we consider him at this time; nor as the fearless and eloquent preacher; nor as the reverent and profound theologian; nor as the able historian of Rome, leading Macaulay and Grote to follow his graphic method of contrasting ancient events with modern, giving freshness to the former and intenser significance to the latter; nor as the professor of modern history in Oxford University, awakening an enthusiasm unparalleled in England; but as Thomas Arnold, the man, a brother to every other man of whatever calling and the benefactor of all who study his noble, manly character.

Manhood needs no professor's gown, nor clerical robes, nor rank, nor title to dignify it. It is that which dignifies every calling and ennobles every place. The flashing jewels of a coronet cannot supply it and the coarse garment of a peasant cannot hide or degrade it. It matters but little just where in the firmament or in what constellation, if any, a star is placed, so that its light shines upon every part of the revolving earth.

His Manly Character

It was not Arnold's scholarship alone, accurate and painstaking as it was, nor his position as headmaster of Rugby school, nor his reputation as a historian, nor his eloquence as a preacher, but his manly character that gave him so powerful an influence over the hundreds of those most intimately associated with him and over a wide circle who never saw him.

He stood forth in all the symmetrical proportions of a noble manhood, nothing little or narrow, as in Bacon's case, to make him the "greatest, wisest, meanest of mankind," but with a heart full of warm impulses, as his lips were of brave sentiments, he left his impress forever upon all who came in contact with him. Dr. Arnold's example would arise in the minds of his pupils in whatever exigency, and what he would have done, or what would please him, determined their conduct as they cited the principles of right action which they had so often heard from his lips or seen as the rule of his life.

The devotion which Arnold inspired has not a parallel, unless it be in the case of Napoleon. But Arnold had not the pageantry of arms, the recollections of splendid victories, the attraction of a world-wide renown with which Napoleon inspired the ardent military French. His was simply the influence of a great character overcoming the antagonism too often existing between teacher and pupil, opposing cherished traditions and principles most welcome to depraved human nature and inspiring in the minds of thoughtless schoolboys a love of truth and a devotion to himself as the champion of right which made them almost worship him as hero while living, a devotion, which would have led them to suffer almost any personal violence for their assailed and persecuted leader; and dead has made sacred pilgrimages to Rugby and dropped hot tears and formed high resolves over his sepulchred remains.

The News of His Death

It was this which hushed the breath and started the tears of thousands as the fearful news of his death spread only too rapidly across the Empire. The hundreds of young men who had gone out from under his instruction to Oxford and Cambridge, and thence out into positions of influence in the world, when the sad tidings came wept over the death of one who had inspired in them the true idea of life, and had taught them by his example how to live.

If you would see his monument I would respond in the epitaph of another of England's honored sons, "Look around you." But his is not like Sir Christopher Wren's a monument of stately but perishable marble, the admiration of the world for its architectural beauty. Arnold's monument is found in the character of those Laleham and Rugby pupils who today, among England's noblemen and in her universities and pulpits, adorning bench and bar and legislative hall, show forth the manly, unselfish qualities of their honored teacher.

Great Britain owes Arnold a debt which was not paid in the

tribute to his memory erected by the gratitude and generosity of all classes of her citizens; not met in the esteem in which his services to the nation are still held. It is a debt which his native land alone cannot pay, but which the Christian world shares with the island which gave him birth. This debt rather increases with the years, and the influence of such a character is more powerful today, multiplied as it is in the characters of hundreds who have been inspired by the moral grandsur of a true, fearless, self-poised manhood, than it was in Arnold's lifetime, when the popular tide turned in his favor and multitudes gathered around him in Oxford to listen and revere.

The Homage of Minds

Such a character is the embodiment of forces more powerful than all the physical forces known to the world, for it alone secures the homage of mind which rules these physical forces. Shall such forces be less worthy of study and analysis than electricity or heat or magnetism? Nor must we be surprised if our analysis shall show the elements of such a character to be like the elementary material forces —very simple. It is their harmonious combination which gives them such power.

The first element in Arnold's character which we notice was his fidelity in his lot. It mattered not to what place he was called, whether humble or conspicuous, he was faithful in the discharge of his duty there. One is astonished at the obscurity from which he emerged to enter upon his great life work at Rugby.

A graduate of Oxford University, filled at the beginning of his career with a lofty ambition which contemplated as the great object of his life to become the prime minister of a kingdom, the governor of a nation or the writer of works which should live in every age and country, he did not waste his life by neglecting the possible in the vain endeavor to perform the impossible.

For thirteen years after his graduation, four of which he spent in his fellowship at Oxford and nine at Laleham, he was content to continue in the office of a private tutor fitting young men for the universities, but all the while engaged in those studies which made him the ripe scholar, the well-furnished and disciplined thinker. But thus early he had developed and was acting upon those principles which made his life so illustrious.

The Foundation of His Character

In the calm harbor he was building the staunch vessel which should weather some of the fiercest storms known to man. A distinguished scholar who saw how well Arnold was laying the foundations of his own manly character and how faithfully he was testing his principles of action, thus unobserved by the world, recommended him for the vacant headmastership of Rugby, with the expressed opinion that if he were elected he would change the face of education all through the public schools of England. Even when called to this important place many who recognized his great abilities would say: "What a pity that a man fit to be a statesman should be employed in teaching schoolboys!" But Arnold did not cry with Archimedes for some other place to stand upon that he might move the world, but he used his present position as his fulcrum and cast himself upon his present opportunity as his lever, and few statesmen have done more to move the world than he.

Rugby was a miniature world to him. Just as he reached the entire school of three hundred by his well-known.sixth form of thirty, so he endeavored to abate the evils which cursed the nation at large by checking the corresponding vices among schoolboys. Among them as among their sires were to be found want of reverence for law, selfishness and thoughtless waste, insolence and want of sympathy shown by the wealthier toward the poorer classes. He hoped to avoid and abate the evils of the church by developing true devotion and manly piety among his pupils. With Sir Launfal he found the Golden Grail at his own castle gate.

The man who is not faithful at his carpenter's bench would disgrace a nobleman's coronet. Elisha behind his twelve yoke of oxen is preparing for the prophet's place. David, like Moses, was all the better a "king in Jeshurun" for having been so faithful with the shepherd's staff. Cincinnatus was all the more efficient as Roman consul for having been so good a farmer. The plow handle fits the hand prepared for a sceptre. Place cannot make men. A king may be like a dot or a cipher rendered important only by his position. Pigmies perched on Alps are pigmies still. The block must be dressed in the quarry before it is fit to become the head of the corner. Leonidas was greater at the head of his three hundred Spartans than Xerxes with his unwieldy millions. Fidelity in little things insures success in great enterprises. Napoleon taught the world that great victories are well-planned campaigns carried out in all the minuteness of the studied details. His battles were all fought over in his mind before the first gun was fired.

"Weighing What He Might"

Thus it was with Arnold that while writing histories, editing classics, governing the whole school and taking the liveliest interest in the great social, religious and even political questions of the day, he had his eye upon every individual scholar, weighing what he might become as a factor in the future of Church or State, and endeavored personally or through others to shape wisely the character of each.

None were unimportant in his eye, for he knew not which would become the greatest power for evil or good. Unlike Samuel, he was as willing to pour the anointing oil of consecration to a royal mission upon the head of the untried lad as upon the more manly sons of promise. It was a memorable day in the history of the Rugby schoolboy when he realized for the first time that the doctor took an interest in him personally and that he was a member of a great institution.

Such a feeling is akin to that which comes upon a man when he discovers for the first time that there is not one too many in the world and he that one—with no work to do, no mission to perform. Up to that time the timid soul has been constantly apologizing to the world for his existence. The influence of the great has made him despair and the success of others has but filled him with despondency. It has been the rayless night of existence until this morning star of promise heralds the approaching day, when he, even he, may work. Henceforth, hopeless inactivity gives place to resolute action.

Every Atom to Its Place

God has not made one atom too many or too few. One more or one less would change the universe. Each has its place, and an important one. The annihilation of one, were it possible, would create a vacuum that would affect every other atom. One less or one more star in the firmament would alarm the world, as all other stars must find new orbits and adjust themselves to the change. Would God adjust every atom to its place and yet send a man into the world with no place to fill, no life work to do?

Would God make a star without a determined orbit and without definite and important relations to every other star, and yet place in the world a human soul, the mightiest of forces, with no orbit in which to move, and like some lost planet, jostling others in their courses and spreading destruction on every side? It was thus that Arnold saw for every pupil a life work as grand as the divine purpose could make it or as disastrous as such powers misused could effect.

In his eye no event in a human life is unimportant, no place that brings a man into influential relations to a single fellow-man is insignificant. If the stamp of a foot communicates an electrical influence which reaches the stars, if the voice of a child excites vibrations in the atmosphere which extend throughout the universe, no duty was too small for a man like Arnold to perform for in its performance the world was not just the same as if it had been left undone. He knew too much of values to esteem anything as altogether worthless. He thought with Wordsworth:

> "He who feels contempt
> For any living thing, hath faculties
> That he hath never used: and thought with him
> Is in its infancy."

Fidelity in His Lot

This element in Arnold's character, of fidelity in his lot, is an element of real greatness. No man is stronger than his greatest weakness at this point. In most enlightened countries of the present day there will probably henceforth appear few towering minds. The means of information are no longer monopolized by the scholar but are in the reach of the people. The masses are being elevated to so high a level that the mountain peaks will not long have the rays of sunlight ere they bathe all the plain below.

Eminent men, in the sense of former centuries, will rarely appear, where one man does the thinking for a nation or rules by his imperial will a people only too glad to serve. The path to greatness is fidelity in little things that develops a character which in a crisis is found to be a granite fortress, ribbed with steel, no part left unprotected because of its supposed lack of importance, but buttressed against any possible attack.

Gibraltar, under the careless Moors and Spaniards, was once and again taken by the enemy; but under the vigilant English, a three years' battle by land and sea told the world that it was impregnable.

Another element of Arnold's character was the constant presence of a controlling purpose. Life was to him no nameless reverie. He believed with Lord Bacon: "In this world God only and the angels may be spectators." Not only was his whole career an illustration of "unhasting, unresting diligence," as described by one of England's great authors after a visit in Rugby; it was more, it was a life of untiring industry, because it was labor performed for some useful end.

There is a kind of employment that is simply negative. Reading may be an excuse for not thinking. The thoughts which pass through one's mind from the open page may be streams which set no wheels in motion, but babble idly along their accustomed bed. Such minds utilize nothing because they have no object in view. If they write their thoughts may be beautiful but cold as "the fanned snow that's bolted by the northern blasts twice o'er."

They chill you with their faultlessness, though they be as "chaste as the icicle that's curded by the frost from purest snow, and hangs on Dian's temple."

A Warm Heart

But there was the pulse of Arnold's warm heart in everything that he wrote or said. Some patriots are nations individualized. National interests are felt to be personal interests. It was thus that Arnold became Rugby and Rugby was forgotten in Arnold. He was Rugby individualized so completely did he throw his great spirit into his life work. He rarely drew his bow at a venture. Because he felt so deeply he spoke and acted so positively. Because he pulled his bow-string with such might his arrows went so far and sank so deep.

If, as Buffon says, "the style is the man," no one can read Arnold's writings without seeing this controlling purpose. The directness and simplicity of his style best answered the end in view. It may be said of him as of Lyman Beecher, that like the Yankee schoolmaster, when he went to use the birch rod he stripped off all the leaves.

In times of great public interest Arnold was heard more than once to say, "I must write or die," and as we read the pamphlets which came from him at such times we can well believe it. Nor was Arnold simply content to pay the debt, which Lord Bacon says every man owes to his profession. Aside from his great work at Rugby, both by his principles and example changing, as was predicted of him, the whole system of public school education throughout England, his histories and sermons and pamphlets and editions of the classics were all prepared with a well-defined end.

A master purpose utilized all the results of his studies, and made him intensely practical. If he wrote histories it was to show the bearing of ancient events on the great social problems of his own day. If he preached it was to bring religion into common life and to apply the warning of prophets and apostles to the vices of his own time.

If he taught it was to give a Christian character to the education of the youth of England.

In short, this controlling purpose was present like a Napoleon to concentrate every force and faculty of his being and hurl them against whatever foe until he had won the field. Without such a master purpose the powers of the human mind are unorganized and incapable of achievement. They are dispersed like the French troops under Marshal Berthier in the campaign of 1809, awaiting the enemy to destroy them in detail, until the born commander appears with his fierce swift order for concentration and attack.

A Ruling Purpose

The man without a purpose never has the right-of-way. He steers for no port, and is the prey of whatever tempest. A ruling purpose knows how to hold the helm in the fiercest storm. For forty years it sustained Copernicus as he developed his theory of the planetary motions. Having supported Keplar all through those arduous labors of discovery, which gained for him the title of "legislator of the skies," it enabled him to say, as he completed his "Harmonies of the World," "The book is written to be read either now or by posterity, I care not which. I can afford to wait a century for a reader since God himself has waited six thousand years for an observer."

Such a purpose sustained Arnold in carrying out his principles of government amid almost universal opposition, and he sounded the keynote of his life in that memorable reply to the almost mutinying pupils of Rugby: "It is not necessary that this should be a school of three hundred, or of one hundred and fifty, or of fifty boys; but it is necessary that it should be a school of Christian gentlemen."

Arnold was not content with announcing great truths and unpopular, or even revolutionary, principles which he felt to be right, but he acted on them amid the hurling weapons of malignant foes. He well knew that such principles, combating popular prejudices, are

> "Hard to shape in act;
> For all the past of time reveals
> A bridal dawn of thunder peals
>   Wherever thought has wedded fact."

Decision of Character

To fidelity in his lot and to the constant presence of a controlling purpose Arnold joined decision of character. John Foster could not have found a man better combining all the constituents of this commanding quality—confidence of opinion, energy of feeling and the full agreement of all the powers of the mind.

Yet with all these elements Arnold was a man of the most refined sensibilities and of the kindest affections. He was one of those self-poised men who only wanted to know that he was in the proper orbit. A man who yearned for sympathy, he would not sacrifice the smallest principle of right to secure it. He would have preferred being a constellation rather than have all eyes fixed on him in his solitary place in the heavens.

With Milton his soul was like a star and dwelt apart, but its clear, steady light inspired wonder and reverence. Every individual soul was made to move in an orbit really its own. Every atom of matter stands apart from every other atom. They only seem to touch. Natural philosophers tell us that there is attraction up to a certain point and then repulsion.

The human soul may try to sink its individuality in the mass of humanity, but in vain. The consciousness of another separate existence attests its own. But men become identified with the multitude by common opinions and actions.

Men move in masses with one thought, no common man daring to think or act for himself. But the man of decided character by his own clear convictions becomes separated from the crowd. If he be right and immovable the star which has thus shot from the nebulous mass becomes in time the center of a system, as other stars hasten to revolve in its light.

Coleridge says that every great and original writer, in proportion as he is great and original himself, must himself create the taste by which he is relished: he must teach the art by which he is to be seen.

It was thus that Wordsworth stood alone for long desolate years, the butt of Byron's sarcasm and the jest of the critics, his unsold poems counted as a loss upon the booksellers' shelves until the educated taste of England at last placed the laureate's crown upon his silvered head.

To Stand Alone

Because Arnold dared think and act apart from the multitude, he, too, during a large part of his life, was compelled to stand alone. But there was grandeur in his solitude. "The elements so mixed in him that nature might stand up and say to all the world This is a Man."

His manly character in his loneliness stood grand and erect like Eddystone lighthouse, defying every storm and radiant with light in the midst of darkness and tempest.

Arnold only needed to know that he was right and that his feet were on the rock, and he could stand alone against the world. It was this desire to know his position thoroughly, for when he took it, it was for life, that made him so cautious in the adoption of his opinions.

Confidence of opinion with him came only after the most careful examination of every link in the chain of argument. His hesitancy in early life in placing himself upon some of the fundamental and usually accepted doctrines of our holy religion arose from just that decision of character which adopted no opinon except to proclaim and defend it. Those most intimate with him at this period of his life often said, "One had better have Arnold's doubts than most men's certainties."

When his doubts were finally resolved into certainties nothing could shake his well-grounded opinions. He might well have been the original whose portrait Tennyson paints:

> "One indeed I knew
> In many a subtle question versed.
> Who touched a jarring lyre at first,
> But ever strove to make it true:
> Perplext in faith, but not in deeds,
> At last he beat his music out.
> He fought his doubts and gathered strength,
> He would not make his judgment blind.
> He faced the spectres of his mind
> And laid them: thus he came at length
> To find a stronger faith his own."

Clear Convictions

It was Arnold's clear convictions which gave such intensity to his feelings, and a man who thought so clearly and felt so strongly only needed manly courage to make him stand firmly though he stand alone. This undaunted courage no one could deny to the moral hero of Rugby. There was a period of four long, desolate years when, because he dared be true to his convictions, he could hardly take up a newspaper but it contained some attack upon him.

His administration of Rugby school was assailed. He was charged with heresy. A man with the most ardent love of truth, he was accused of falsehood. Of purest life and irreproachable character, his enemies charged him with indifference to the moral law.

He felt that greatest of human sorrows, what it is to do well and suffer for it. He was looked upon with suspicion and his enemies used every means to undermine his influence. Had his foes been of the contemptible sort he might the more easily have risen superior to their assaults. But the great University of Oxford was arrayed against him, looking upon his utterances respecting traditional views with the feeling of King Lear.

"How sharper than a serpent's tooth it is to have a thankless child."

It would have been a relief to Arnold to have fought even singlehanded, but to stand silent and serene until every weapon of malignity had been expended and the storm had entirely passed was an exhibition of heroism almost without a parallel. How like Abdiel, true to his convictions, leaving the host of rebel angels gathered around Satan's standard,

> "Nor number nor example with him wrought
> To swerve from truth his constant mind,
> Though single. From amidst them forth he passed
> Long way through hostile scorn which he sustained
> Superior, nor of violence feared aught."

The Tempest Cleared

When the tempest cleared away Arnold was seen like some lofty mountain whose brow was bathed in the sunlight while the storm

159

had raged below. The voice which had sustained him in the night of storm spake again and it was the voice which Abdiel heard:

> "Servant of God, well done; well hast thou fought
> The better fight, who single hast maintained
> Against revolted multitudes the cause
> Of truth, in word mightier than they in arms;
> And for the testimony of the truth hast borne
> Universal reproach, far worse to bear
> Than violence; for this was all thy care
> To stand approved in sight of God, though worlds
> Judge thee perverse."

Then the remarkable reaction set in. The tide of popular feeling which for years had been so strongly against him now turned in his favor, and he was borne on the crest of this wave to some of the highest places in the kingdom.

His theory of education for which he had contended so bravely in his loneliness was now generally received. Pupils flocked around him at Rugby in unprecedented numbers.

His theological views which had raised such an outcry were now enthusiastically adopted. The solitary star had become the center of a system and multitudes were rejoicing in its light. Even Oxford University would do him homage, and through Lord Melbourne he received one of her most important professorships. When he came up to Oxford to deliver his inaugural lecture it would seem that too much honor could not be shown him.

No hall in the University was large enough for the multitudes which gathered to hear a man who had dared to think for himself and to prove true to his convictions. The audiences which crowded Oxford Theater at every lecture, listening with rapt interest to every sentence from his manly lips, paid the highest tribute to that exalted character whose homage is that of the human mind for the mightiest of all forces.

His Hour of Triumph

But that was not Arnold's hour of triumph when he saw the gathering and lauding crowds. There was nothing heroic in that, because men were acting in masses, moved by the popular current. Arnold's triumph was when he felt that he could stand alone, or when he saw kindled in the breast of his Rugby pupils the same heroic spirit which would have led them to die for their leader and the truth.

> "The self-approving hour whole worlds outweighs
> Of stupid starers and of loud huzzas;
> And more true joy Marcellus exiled feels
> Than Caesar with a Senate at his heels."

One more element in Arnold's character remains to be noticed and that is his manly piety. Piety was the hem and border of his character that kept its great web from unraveling. Piety interwove those golden purposes which shine in every utterance and act as it held him faithful at his post, however obscure. His decision of character was due in no small measure to that intense desire which marked him from the hour he came to Rugby, "to try whether the public school system did not have in it some noble elements which might produce fruit unto life eternal."

His love and practice of truth were such that his pupils knowing that their word was confided in so long as they were continued in school used to say, "It is a shame to tell Dr. Arnold a lie—he always believes one."

He considered that all the relations of human life were in a healthy state only when subordinate to their common relation to God. His ideal state was the kingdom of God on earth. Such a life is a caravan of spices which, going through the desert, distills its sweetness through all the air to cheer the weary pilgrims who follow in the way."

Chapter XII

The Man

IN ANY group Eugene Russell Hendrix stood out. He had a commanding presence and the story was often told of the negro porter on a Pullman car who kept addressing him as "Colonel" until the Bishop said to him, "I am not a colonel." Then the porter called him "Judge" until the Bishop said, "I am not a judge either; I am a bishop in the Methodist Church." The porter quickly said, "Well, I knew you were the head of whatever you are in." Above the average height and weight he carried himself with dignity and a bearing that indicated leadership. His head was large and well shaped; his eyes were keen and sparkling when he was interested; and the neatly trimmed Van Dyke beard gave him an impressiveness of countenance no one could ever forget. One recognized him as a man of intelligence, and his wide experience, added to his intelligence, made him a delightful conversationalist. His table talk in the dining room, or his conversation in the drawing room made him a welcome guest in any home. Many times have I heard people say, "I remember that Bishop Hendrix was once in our home. He is my ideal of what a bishop should be." Even children in a home would remember his visit after they grew to maturity, because he knew how to talk with them. A son of a minister recalls his words to him, "I was only ten years old when he was a guest in our home, but I remember the words he spoke to me as he put his hand on my head when he was leaving." No one who had known any close contact with him ever forgot him, and I wish it were possible for me to make him live for those people who never knew him.

The casual contact would give the impression of austerity or at least of hauteur. Many thought him distant or difficult to know because they hesitated to approach him, but those who came close enough for personal conversation were delighted with his affable manner. One was conscious always that he was in the presence of a

Bishop Ivan Lee Holt and Mary Matilda Hagerty, great granddaughter of Bishop Eugene Russell Hendrix. The occasion was the dedication of Hendrix Hall and the unveiling of a tablet in honor of the Bishop's mother, Isabel Hendrix, at National College of Christian Workers, Kansas City, Missouri.

great man; one would not with familiarity slap him on the back; but one went away after a conversation with him to say, "He has a keen mind and a very warm heart." Even one who was sure he could not get close to the Bishop might well come to have for him a deep affection when he had sat and talked with him a few times. He gave the impression of disinterestedness to some because he had little time for small talk when he was busy with so many great tasks.

The criticism which one heard most frequently was a comment on his consciousness of his importance. There were those who spoke of him as an egotist. Often an address would begin with, "In China Li Hung Chang once said to me," or "When in Washington last the President said to me," or "Mr. Gladstone and I were in conversation one day." Egotism is an irritating thing when a man makes for himself unwarranted claims, but when a man has numbered among his acquaintances many of earth's great, and has been all over the world, such introductions to addresses are not really egotism. They record the world in which he lived just as another might introduce a message by a story from the farm or by a reference to his home town. A listener who might not like the introductory sentences would be so impressed with the thoughtfulness of the address that long before the end of it he would be saying, "This man has really been places and known people of consequence. Any leader in any land would be glad to call him friend." Then would come some revelation of a deep human emotion which makes all people kin, and the listener would be thankful that one like him had brought him into the presence of the great ones of earth. When he talked about God and about Jesus Christ in equally familiar terms, one understood that he knew them also; and sooner or later there came into his voice a tenderness and into his words a reverence which led one to recognize a genuine humility. The great man was also a humble man in the presence of his Lord, and when he prayed he was a child of God, a sinner saved by grace.

My own contacts with him lead me to thank God for every remembrance of him. The first time I heard him preach was forty years ago at the dedication of the Grand Avenue Methodist Church at Grand and Connecticut Avenues in St. Louis. His sermon was a message on John the Baptist as a fore-runner of Christ. "There was a man sent from God whose name was John. What went ye out for to see, a reed shaken by the wind?" It was a compelling plea for a worthy witness. In 1912, when I was minister at Centenary Church in Cape Girardeau, Missouri, I went to New York in October in order to hear the giants in the pulpit, J. H. Jowett and Charles E. Jefferson and S. Parkes Cadman. Hoping to shake hands with these great leaders I had a feeling that the man whose letters of introduction would gain me entree to their presence was Eugene R. Hendrix. The Bishop sent me the letters and they did for me what I sought. At the Fifth Avenue Presbyterian Church I heard Jowett preach and was given during the week every opportunity to learn of the program of that church. I sat in the study of Charles E. Jefferson high up in the tower of Broadway Tabernacle. I spent an afternoon with S. Parkes Cadman; though I had asked for ten minutes of his time he kept me for three hours and, with his genius for friendship and understanding, he made the young minister feel that they were comrades in a common task. That was one of the memorable experiences of my life and it was possible through an introduction by Bishop Hendrix.

Then there was the Sunday when he preached in the Chapel of Southern Methodist University in the fall of 1915. I was Chaplain of the University and President Hyer had agreed with me that we should have a Sunday afternoon service at the University since we were so far out of the city of Dallas, and since it was so impossible for our boarding students to go in numbers to the city churches for worship on the small street car that made trips from the campus. I had the idea that the service should be a University Service such as I had seen at the University of Chicago. The members of the choir wore academic gowns, we had a processional and recessional, and I was anxious for the preacher to wear a gown. Such services were unknown in Texas at that time and I consulted the Senior Bishop of my Church, Eugene R. Hendrix. He not only approved my plans but agreed to come and preach on the first

Sunday. He wore the gown that Sunday, as did Bishop Edwin D. Mouzon on the following Sunday. Bishop Mouzon was the Presiding Bishop of the North Texas Conference and lived on the campus. The criticisms came when the bishops had come and gone, and I continued the practice they had begun. There was a condemnation of the "introduction of popery" on the campus and we had to discontinue the services. It looked for a time as though we might not be able to use caps and gowns at Commencement. In my concern and worry came a message from Bishop Hendrix, "Do not be discouraged. You were right and the time will come when such services will be held." Of course the cap and gown have been in use at the University at all Commencements since, and when I went to Texas as bishop twenty years later the choirs of many churches, large and small, came into the services with vestments.

Bishop Hendrix was the Presiding Bishop in Missouri from 1914 to 1918 during the war years, and during the concluding year of my pastorate at Cape Girardeau, as well as during the years of my service at Southern Methodist University. I remember so well the first session of the St. Louis Conference at which he presided in Caruthersville. I was concluding my third year at Cape Girardeau and was bringing to completion the building of a new church after a disastrous fire had destroyed the former church. Dr. John A. Rice was concluding a four-year pastorate at First Church in Fort Worth, and at his suggestion a committee from that church came to Cape Girardeau to interview me about going as his successor. Bishop Hendrix assured me that he would support my decision. It was a very difficult decision to make. The church at Fort Worth paid a salary more than twice as large as the salary I was receiving; as a matter of fact the salary was the same as that paid at that time by St. John's Church in St. Louis, the largest salary in the denomination. The committee was most insistent on my going and after three weeks of consideration I decided to go. The bishop presiding at the Central Texas Conference, James H. McCoy, asked Bishop Hendrix for my transfer and all was arranged. Then before the St. Louis Conference met Bishop McCoy had a meeting with his Cabinet in Central Texas. The Cabinet insisted on the appointment of a Texas man, and Bishop Hendrix was advised of the embarrassment of Bishop McCoy. On his way to Caruthersville to Conference he passed through Cape Girardeau, and I boarded the same train. I had three hours with him, and I can never forget that conversation or his concern for my welfare. He said to me, "I know what difficulties a young man can face in the leading church of a Conference when the Presiding Elders oppose his coming, and I advise you not to go." When I told him that I would be perfectly happy to go back to Cape Girardeau for my fourth year he went on to say, "You made up your mind to leave your Church and I would like to take you to my home church in Kansas City. My family has long attended Melrose Church and my only son is Superintendent of the Sunday School. We want you there as pastor." It was my conviction that I ought not to leave my church at Cape Girardeau to go anywhere else in Missouri, but the Bishop had asked me to go to his church. When I hesitantly voiced my conviction he understood, and was most sympathetic in his further conversation. Then at Conference the representatives of two churches in St. Louis asked the Bishop to appoint me, and I had another conversation with the Bishop, pleading to return to my Church and finish the building. That was clearly my duty. Then finally on Saturday came a telegram from Bishop McCoy in Birmingham saying that the committee from First Church in Fort Worth was with him and was insisting on my appointment; therefore he was overriding his Cabinet and asking earnestly for my transfer. I went away to preach in Kennett on Sunday, and left the decision entirely with the Bishop. On Saturday night the Bishop sent for me to come to the Cabinet, and I was out of town. He said to the Cabinet, "I must decide this matter and I am not going to send a young minister into a situation where the Presiding Elders oppose his coming. He returns to Cape Girardeau." With that he tore up the telegram asking for my transfer. Rarely has a minister faced in one week so many important decisions with his bishop, and I can never forget his courtesy, his kindness and his understanding. When I would hear someone refer to the Bishop's autocratic or authoritarian attitude, I would recall those days of an important week in my life and ministry, to bear my testimony to his brotherly consideration. No bishop could have been more anxious to enter into the life of one of his preachers. I knew him more than once to make decisions of a very positive character, and his determined firmness in such decisions would easily lead some affected to speak of his autocratic methods. As over against such an interpretation I remember a very dramatic hour in the General Conference of 1918 at Atlanta to which I have previously referred in this book. The bishops were being vigorously criticized by one of the able delegates from the North Texas Conference for their failure to visit their churches, their appearance only at Annual Conferences while living in other states, and their superior attitudes. The speaker then turned to Bishop Eugene R. Hendrix, who was in the Chair, and used some such words as these, "I am sorry, Sir, to voice these criticisms when you are in the Chair. We honor you and if all the bishops had served the church with the ability and spirit you have shown there would be no criticism of the episcopacy." It was a great tribute and apparently represented the feeling of the Conference.

After his retirement it was my privilege to visit Bishop Hendrix several times in his home. It was not easy for him to accept retirement after more than a generation of activity in the Episcopacy. He missed his associations with ministers and laymen at the Annual Conferences, and was anxious to serve his church in every way possible. A bit impatient and restless he was kindlier through the experiences of the years. With a heart mellowed through years of human contact he seemed gentler than I had ever known him. He was wishing that he could talk with anyone who had a feeling of being hurt and wronged, and often said as I left, "Tell my brethren of my love for them and my interest in all their work." He was pleased to be with the family again because there had been long periods of absence through the years. Loving his home and his family he had come back to spend his last years with them. They realized his happiness to be among them but they knew too well that he had too long been a part of the great world outside to be perfectly content. He was where he wanted to be, but sometimes he would sit and would look through the windows of his home, watching go by a world of which he had long been an important part. It seemed to me in those last visits with him as if he could not live long in retirement, and I often saw the tears in his eyes as he talked of his church and his long years of service. I could look into the windows of his soul as I had many times looked into the windows of his mind. One of the regrets of my life is that an automobile in which I was riding from St. Louis to Kansas City for his funeral broke down, and it was impossible for me to be with his family and pay my tribute to a great bishop whose ability I admired and whose friendship I treasured. Such is the record of some of the revealing contacts I had with him, contacts through which I came to know the man. One of the tragedies of high office in the church, as in the state, is that it makes it impossible for all who work with a leader to know him as a human being and a man. I thank God I came to know this leader.

There are many letters among his papers which he had kept through the years, and so many of them speak of his personal characteristics. His friend, Dr. E. B. Sanford, a fellow-student at Wesleyan University, wrote to a member of the Hendrix family in 1912: "I have been thinking over the Bishop's life work with care, and while friendship may strengthen the verdict, I would not hesitate to say that he has won the highest place among Wesleyan University's living alumni. His relation to all the Protestant Churches through his activities and leadership in connection with the Federal Council has given him a national recognition of which both you and your children may well be proud." Another fellow-student of the Wesleyan days wrote a bit more intimately to the Bishop at the time of his election. It was C. C. W. Nullord of Yonkers, New York, and he wrote: "You were, even in the old college days, just such a serious, truthful soul, loyal with uncompromising fidelity to every noble conviction, transparently clear and clean, utilizing every faculty, energy and moment so fully and conscientiously that every one of us in the class of 1867 knew you were destined for grand service. Don't you recall some of the old Band Meetings?

Don't you remember how we used to wait on the Lord? From the old Band will ascend many a prayer for you now." From these letters one selects such adjectives as "truthful, loyal, conscientious, clear and clean" and is aware of the impression he made on the campus. But from these letters also one knows how strong were the ties of affection binding him and his associates of student days. There is a note of rejoicing in another's success, and no word of envy or jealousy. There is an expression of appreciation which indicates how close were the human contacts, and how friendly was the relationship. He was the kind of student other students liked.

Among his colleagues in the Episcopacy none knew him better than Bishop Charles B. Galloway. It is difficult to select the letter which ought to be quoted from the numerous ones written by the eloquent Mississippi bishop to his friend, but here is a paragraph in one letter: "But for you there is a place apart in my heart. More and more during twenty years I have enthroned you in my affections as one of the dearest and truest friends of my life. We seem to be near to each other in our tastes and views and life purposes."

There are several letters among his papers from the able leader of Southern Methodist women, Miss Belle Bennett, and I quote from two of them. The first is dated in 1906: "You have done more to encourage and develop the growth of the Woman's Society than all of the other members of the College of Bishops. The women know and appreciate this. Personally, your Christian attitude as well as your sympathy, advice and brotherly kindness have meant more to me than I can tell you." The other letter from Miss Bennett is dated in 1909: "Out of the years of acquaintance and friendship with you I have learned to prize your Christian judgment, wise counsel, and ever enlarging vision of the world's need, and how to get it."

These words were written by two of the ablest and most beloved leaders Southern Methodism ever produced. They pay tribute to wise counsel and advice, but they speak also of brotherly kindness, sympathy and enthronement in affections. To inspire such friendships and create such emotional responses a man must know how to be a friend. A cold and distant, an indifferent and haughty person could not warm the heart and kindle the affections of others as did Eugene R. Hendrix.

Tributes to his personal influence came again and again from the great churchmen of his day. Dr. Robert E. Speer wrote in a personal letter: "It is always a pleasure to think of you and of your satisfactory influence on the right side of the great problems of the church and society which we are facing at this time." Though there are many such evaluations of his religious leadership nearly every letter is written in such an intimate and personal way as only real heart-felt friendship can inspire. He came to such recognition on the national and international level as no bishop of his church had known, but he never lost the personal touch and nearly every tribute to his leadership carries with it an appreciation of the man.

He was very liberal in his attitudes and in his theology, but he was never shallow in his thinking. That is the reason why he was so rarely criticized for his opinions or accused of heresy. It is only fair to acknowledge that many preachers of his church raised questions about his theological positions, as expressed in his books or in articles printed in theological reviews, but there were very rarely any attacks on his liberalism. The reason obviously was that there was no question about the depth of his religious experience or of the fundamental soundness of his faith. He was a generation ahead of most ministers of his church in his interpretations, but no one was inclined to question him because it was felt that he was one who had come to his convictions after study and thought, and after years of intimate fellowship with his Lord. It has always been surprising to me that, while he was criticized because of his position in the Vanderbilt controversy or because of his interest in unification or because of some progressive policy in church administration, he was so rarely challenged for his theological views. In addition to the reasons given above I wonder sometimes if there was not a compelling influence of his own personality which gave to his words the impressiveness of authority. He was too formidable an opponent to challenge.

He was too human to claim perfection and he never anticipated canonization as a saint. After listening one night to a very earnest preacher who made claims to the attainment of perfection in this life a very wise old superannuate said to me: "I have known and heard many preachers in my time. It is my experience that a real desire for perfection frequently makes a man a saint, but a profession of having attained it usually makes him a Pharisee." Lord Tweedsmuir, formerly Governor-General of Canada, once wrote: "We are condemned to fumble in these times, for the mist is too thick to see far down the road. But in all our uncertainty we can have Cromwell's hope. To be a Seeker is to be of the best sect next to a Finder, and such an one shall every faithful, humble Seeker be at the end." So I would transcribe a sentence of Henry Adams: "After all, man knows mighty little, and may some day learn enough of his own ignorance to fall down and pray! Dogmatism gives place to questioning, and questioning in the end to prayer." These words perfectly express the intellectual and spiritual outlook of Bishop Hendrix. He knew too much to be dogmatic in any insistent way; his questioning led to prayer. He belonged to the group of the Seekers, of those called to be saints. Deeply spiritual he was ever conscious of his own failures, and hoped in God's good time to attain perfection, to pass from the ranks of the Seekers and join the ranks of the Finders.

He was possessed of social graces, brought up in an atmosphere of culture and refinement. His father was the banker of the community and the son did not experience the hardships many young men of his day had to face. He was privileged in war days to attend college and seminary, and to know social contacts in the homes of his professors. His wife was the daughter of Nathan Scarritt and inherited from her father some of the wealth he was enabled to create. Consequently Bishop and Mrs. Hendrix were able to build a home and to establish a standard of living beyond those which his salary as a bishop would have provided. He was often referred to in the church as "a rich bishop." The property he and his wife had would never have justified such classification, but their income enabled them to live more comfortably than most of their colleagues in the episcopacy. They were generous in their gifts; they were able to give their children the best of education and training; they could afford to travel widely. The Bishop knew how to dress well, and in any social gathering of wealth or refinement he was always at home. The social graces he knew, however, came from another source than his background of experience in homes of comfort and modest luxury. They came out of a deep regard for man his brother and out of fellowship with God the Father. He could not be other than courteous because he loved mankind so much and because he was so deeply Christian. The Great Teacher was at home at the table of a wealthy citizen of Bethany because he was so deeply human, and at the same time so conscious of an abiding fellowship with his Father in Heaven.

A biographer seeks to be objective in his appraisal but he is aware of the fact that he is setting forth his picture of the man about whom he writes. Great as is my admiration of the man and the bishop I am aware of the fact that he was not at home on every platform and with all types of people. He could speak to a group on a college campus and few ministers of his day did more of that. He was urged to take the presidency of a state university and the chancellorship of another, and among his honorary degrees were two from two of the largest of state universities; he knew the language of the campus and not simply that of the church school campus. He could not so easily preach to a mass meeting of humbler or less informed people. He was impressive as a preacher in a church and was a master of pulpit eloquence in the pulpit of a cathedral. He could not so easily preach to a crowd on a street corner or in a public park; he had the consecration and zeal for going to those who were down and out and he used to go to missions for prayer services during his college days; but neither his langauge nor his presence would make him a popular preacher for the masses. There were preachers of his day who could speak to the masses and who were not at home in the college chapel or in the cathedral pulpit. It is the desire of every true minister of the gospel to be "all things to all men," but most preachers have the ability to reach some classes more effectively than they reach others— perhaps that is true of all of them. At any rate it is the glory of our

Methodist pulpit that it is not typed. We have many types to reach many groups, and Eugene R. Hendrix was one type. There is no question in the world but that many Methodists of his day would have found it quite impossible to understand him; for them he was of a different class and "belonged to the purple" with little understanding of the masses. In that they were partly mistaken. While he could not speak to them so convincingly as some, his deep concern for the masses of people in his own land, in mission lands and around the world, is apparent in many of his appeals to the more privileged classes, and in his emphasis on social salvation. He had a passion for humanity and wanted to spend himself for its salvation. He loved to quote Watts's great hymn as the basis of that passion—

> Were the whole realm of nature mine,
> That were an offering far too small;
> Love so amazing, so divine
> Demands my soul, my life, my all.

The masses of humanity were those for whom Christ died and every man among them might find that Savior whom in the early years of his life the Bishop had found. His language might not be the convincing and compelling medium through which the average man would see glimpses of his need and of his Savior, but in the preacher's heart was all the deep yearning any man could feel for the salvation of his brother man.

The Bishop was a man of very great courage. He was in the group of churchmen from around the world which assembled at Constance in Germany on the eve of the outbreak of the First World War. The men who journeyed there hoped they might do something to stop the threatening war as spokesmen for the Protestant Churches. They knew they faced danger and they had to endure many hardships before they returned home, because war came as the Conference was being organized. The same courage that led him to take risks in that effort characterized him when he took a conscientious stand on some issues in his own church with the majority against him. Sometimes he stood almost alone, and it would have been so much easier to yield or to compromise. It would not be true to say that he was always right, or that subsequent events proved that he was always right, but when after thoughtful and prayerful consideration he came to a position, he was prepared to stand by it, whatever the consequences to himself. In resigning the Chairmanship of the Board of Trustees of Vanderbilt University he did so because his position as bishop in a church that had severed its relationship with the university made it impossible to continue, but as he resigned he took occasion to say that he did not endorse the course his church and its bishops had taken. I knew him to take a stand on an issue before conferences in his administrative area which could make him very unpopular with some preachers and many members, but he believed he was right and he held to that course which he was convinced he should take. To make use of a phrase which has long been current in traditions of leadership, "he had the courage of his convictions." He could never be cruel but he could be strong and determined.

In any democracy it is always difficult to determine whether the individual creates the environment or whether he is the product of his environment. Dr. James W. Lee, one of the really able preachers of my day, wrote a book on "The Geography of Genius" calling attention to the fact that climate and the physical configuration of a continent or land can have a great influence on the kind of people who grow up in certain areas. So it is, and I suppose Eugene R. Hendrix was definitely a product of the Reconstruction Era in the United States, as he was a product of a Methodist home and a Methodist movement. But it was given to him to assume constructive leadership and to leave the mark of his own organizing genius as well as his strength of character and flights of prophetic imagination when he seemed to escape from his native valleys and explore the regions of the world that lay beyond the summits of the loftiest of American mountains. Matthew Arnold used to be critical of certain American traits because they seemed to him out of tune with the European tradition of which he felt himself the guardian. An American critic can be no less intolerant of England and things British. Then sometimes appears a man who can see the values in both national traditions, however truly he is a child of one. In spite of the vastness of the American Continent a community nestled in its mountains or lonesomely placed on its prairies may be isolated and apart. A native of such a community may always be placed as belonging to it, no matter where he lives, but again a native of such a community can take its contributions to his life beyond the mountains and the prairies and transform them into the characteristics of a larger citizenship. Eugene Russell Hendrix was a Missourian who became an American and an American who became a world citizen. So with his religious environment. He was cradled in Methodism, and to the end of his days he loved his church, but he moved beyond the mountains and across the prairies in his ecclesiastical contacts until he sensed the meaning of fellowship in the larger church of our Lord, Jesus Christ.

Within a generation have come such changes in our life and world as no other generation has known; some of these changes were under way before the death of Bishop Hendrix and they have continued to transform our world. During two world wars we thought that our system of Christian ethics was being challenged, that these wars were revealing conflicts between barbarism and civilization. Today Faith is being attacked, Faith as we have known it. Of course Blake is right: "Man must and will have some religion; if he has not the religion of Jesus he will have the religion of Satan, and will erect a synagogue of Satan." The struggle today is between two philosophies of life, only one of which is Christian. We need trained minds and thoughtful attitudes, but we need also a devotion that refuses to yield to indifference or nonchalance. We will find the struggle exhausting, and our own strength only weakness. We must turn to God in our weakness. He will doubtless remind us of the great cloud of witnesses, the communion of saints, whose leadership and strength in their day may be much more than an inspiration. They may be our valiant comrades in the fight, and among us who are called Methodists no leader of the yesterdays can wield a more valiant sword in this present conflict than Eugene Russell Hendrix.

"Almighty and Everlasting God, whose mercies our fathers have experienced in every generation as they have borne witness to Thy power to save, grant us the might of Thy Spirit, that, following in the steps of thy faithful servants, we may turn to Thee and meet the needs of our generation." Amen!

An Appendix

The Episcopal Address

(Prepared and delivered by Bishop Eugene R. Hendrix at the General Conference of the Methodist Episcopal Church, South, at Asheville, North Carolina, in May, 1910.)

BELOVED brethren of the ministry and laity, elect of the Church for your sacred responsibilities as counsellors and legislators, grace and peace be unto you from God our Father, and from the Lord Jesus Christ by whom we know the Father. We give unto you our Christian salutations and rejoice with you in our common inheritance that God has given unto the Gentiles repentance unto faith and has taken us also into his covenant of life and peace. "For this is the record that God hath given unto us eternal life, and this life is in His Son." We worship the eternal Father of the eternal Son for without sonship there is no fatherhood. It is the eternal Son in the bosom of the Father by whom is made known unto us the godhead of both Father and Son through the Holy Spirit proceeding from the Father and the Son. Called to be saints our daily prayer for the whole church is that she may manifest the power of sons of God, and so realize her high calling of God in Christ Jesus. We are as yet the potential Church, but we devoutly thank our Lord who condescends to be head over all things to His church for the ceaseless honor which He puts upon the church which is His body and which is complete only in Him. We are grateful to Him for that great religious movement called Methodism which has leavened and quickened the life of Christendom during the 18th, 19th and part of the 20th centuries, and has become the leading force of Protestant Christianity throughout the world. As we meet for the third time in this eventful century, when our divine Lord is seen leading His hosts to their greatest victories, we dare utter our doxology: "Now unto Him that is able to do exceeding abundantly above all that we ask or think, according to the power that worketh in us, unto Him be glory in the church and in Christ Jesus unto all generations, for ever and ever. Amen."

Lutheranism is the least part of the work of the Reformation led by Martin Luther in the 16th century, although numerically the largest Protestant force. So Methodism is the least part of the great religious movement of the 18th century under the Wesleys and Whitefield. Both movements were unspeakably great in the moral and religious freedom which became the inheritance of all Protestant churches. Yet Methodism must stand as the peculiar expression of that last great religious movement and so the object of deepest interest to all students of Christianity. Harnack, the foremost religious thinker in Germany, declares, "No type of believers has interested me more than the Methodists. If I read Church History correctly that denomination is richest in experimental religion, most active in Christian work, most fertile in results of all since the time of the Reformation." We are familiar with what the best English historians like Lecky and Green have said as to the influence of Methodism in saving England in the 18th century, but we are concerned to know what may be expected of Methodism in the 20th century. In one of the great Quarterlies in a notable article on our "Representative Religions," occurs this tribute: "On the whole, the Methodist Church will be seen to be a great organization moving on the world for definite and powerful results, striking where there is most to be done. It converts for all the churches, but it still keeps itself larger than any of the rest and increases at a faster rate." A Unitarian organ frankly says: "Methodism has had a grand mission to fulfil in modern Christendom; a mission of mediation between different sects on the one hand, and between an exclusive Church and a neglected world on the other. And there is a moral majesty in the firm and sure tread with which it has marched to the accomplishment of its work."

It is such tributes to modern Methodism that make us serious as we contemplate the responsibilities of leadership. Not only do leading Protestant thinkers declare, "Methodism holds the future; if Methodism fails, America fails"; but a foremost prelate of the Roman Catholic Church, the late Archbishop Spalding, said, "The only sect that Roman Catholicism fears is organized Methodism, and this fear is based upon its aggressive zeal and its hearty presentation of truth to the common people without making any preposterous claim to apostolic successorship or offensive assertion of being 'the' church. I greatly fear the influence of Methodism upon the second and third generation of imported Romanists." If we have such influence with other churches it is largely because our converts are from the world and not from other churches and our fidelity to the faith of the fathers has won for us the title given by the most influential preacher of the Congregationalist Church as "the mightiest Protestant force in the modern world." Speaking of the scanty supply of preachers in other churches the foremost minister in another Church recently remarked in public, "What would the rest of the churches do but for the preachers that Methodism furnished?" Is this to be one of the ways God will use in giving a preachable theology to some other churches? Our rapid growth has not been due to immigration, as in both the Roman and Lutheran churches, but, as in all lands, from the preaching of a gospel of spiritual power. We are now laboring on all the continents, and in not less than one hundred and fifty of the babbling tongues of earth ecumenical Methodism is at once the John the Baptist and the apostle Paul of modern Christendom, seeking alike to prepare the way of the Lord and to build up the faith as we spread scriptural holiness over all these lands. Our threatened pietism has become world-wide evangelism. Nor has there ever appeared a more signal proof of the vitality of our American Methodism in all her history than when the combined Methodist laymen of the United States and Canada during the past year pledged themselves to become responsible for the evangelizing of more than 200,000,000 souls, or more than one fifth of the remaining unevangelized billion of the pagan and Mohammedan world.

The Church as a Force of Nearly Two Millions

Now, as the second largest Methodist Church in the world and the third largest Protestant Church in America, we assemble in our sixteenth General Conference at the close of the most peaceful and prosperous quadrennium in the history of the Methodist Episcopal Church, South. Every year of the quadrennium has been marked by a net increase of members larger than the increase in the whole quadrennium when we met in Dallas eight years ago. Our net increase during the past four years in members alone is 207,754, an increase larger than the whole membership of all save a very few churches in the United States. This net increase is more than half of our entire gain during the last decade. Our present membership, not including our 11,570 traveling and local preachers, is 1,822,402, which is nearly 500,000 more than all the Methodists on the continents of Europe and Australasia. To increase our census to more than 2,056,000 we need only add, and justly, the 233,911 members of the Colored Methodist Church in whose behalf we legislate and give, as in the forty years of their separate history since we set them apart. Their steadfast friends and counsellors, charged in no small measure with the responsibility of their success, we rejoice no less in their prosperity than in our own, and our constant prayer and hope is to see them increasingly effective as a great missionary force both in this country and in Africa.

Our nearly two million laymen are led and taught by 7,618 traveling preachers who have the cooperation of 4,952 local preachers, many of whom serve as supplies and are doing efficient work. Four years ago we reported a decrease of 2,006 in our local preachers as having taken place during the previous decade, but we are now happy to report an increase of 297 during the quadrennium. As the increase comes at a time when the Church has set a higher standard alike for the equipment and work of the local ministry, it is a sign of progress and encourages the hope that our lay preachers may become a growing force alike in numbers and usefulness. Doubtless the present law requiring the district conference both to license and to renew the license of local preachers, as well as to receive a report of their work and to pass their characters, is having a wholesome influence wherever properly endorsed. We have greater need than ever of the right kind of local preachers (not simply exhorters) who study to show themselves approved of God and of men, rightly dividing the word of truth. What makes British Methodism the largest religious force in England next to the Established Church is the skilled labor of some 20,000 lay preachers added to the faithful work done by the 2,500 trained and well-educated itinerant ministers.

INCREASE IN OUR MINISTRY

It is gratifying to report that during the past year we admitted the largest number of ministers on trial in our history. These 331 new preachers will greatly reduce the number of charges left to be supplied, while the noteworthy revival of lay activity promises yet larger accessions to our itinerant ranks in the near future. During the past year forty-six preachers were admitted to our traveling ministry from fourteen other churches. The largest number, fifteen in all, came from the ministry of the Methodist Episcopal Church, and ten came from the ministry of the Methodist Protestant Church. The question is sometimes asked, "Why do our preachers leave us?" In view of a much larger number seeking a place in our ministry it might be asked, "Why do other preachers come?" In response to that question one from the Protestant Episcopal ministry frankly answered, "I want to have the privilege of calling mourners." Another from the Congregationalist ministry, well and favorably known among us, sought "a witnessing church where people told their religious experience, and had one to tell." So we pray that our church may ever remain a witness of the living Christ and of the power of His resurrection. This it will do despite even a General Conference which, as usual, is held in two sections and by two sets of representatives, one in the church papers declaring what the church should do and the other set here and now to do what they deem best. During the last General Conference not less than 500 memorials and petitions were before the Committee on Revisals alone. During the last Congress there were forty thousand bills introduced as against less than 200 in the first Congress. Alike in Church and State we are "a government by discussion." Happily our legislation is not for the whole of American Methodism with the great diversity of local conditions and needs.

Our Increasing Material Resources

It is interesting to note that in the sixty-six years of our separate existence as an integral part of American Methodism, although much of our territory was the scene of the greatest civil war in history at whose beginning the South was accredited with thirty per cent of the wealth of the country and at its close with only eight per cent, the Methodist Episcopal Church, South, after deducting all indebtedness, has now not less than $75,000,000 in property, including churches, parsonages, schools, orphanages, hospitals, Publishing Houses, endowments and loan funds. There is annually a notable increase in the amount given for the support of the ministry and for conference claimants, amounting during the last year to $4,778,897, an increase over the previous year of $371,782. There was paid last year some $4,000,000 for churches and parsonages alone, until now we have 16,239 churches and 4,925 parsonages, for many of which latter we are indebted to the women of the Woman's Home Mission Society. Now after giving $9,000,000 annually for church equipment at home and for ministerial support, it is fitting that we should give in millions for education and church extension and missions.

During the quadrennium we have given for education, including plants, equipment and endowment, the sum of $3,075,000. For Church Extension there was donated by both Parent and Conference Boards and loaned by the Parent Board a total during the quadrennium of $834,734, aiding a total of 2,356 churches, including those aided by both Boards. There has been an increase in amount raised on the assessment during the quadrennium of $165,384 and an increase in the Loan Fund Capital of $109,612. During the like period there has been a notable increase in our resources in our foreign missions under the six different flags other than our own where we labor for the Lord of the harvest. In these fields we now have 25,210 members who during the past year have given $52,-880. There has been an increase of 181 churches and chapels in our missions until now we have 348 and 149 parsonages, many of which have been built by the natives themselves and at their own charges, especially in Korea, where also has been our largest numerical growth. There has been an increase in the value of our property in our mission fields of $789,323 during the quadrennium, until now our property of all kinds there is estimated at $1,783,454. If to this be added the $644,000 in property held by the Woman's Foreign Missionary Society we have a total valuation of $2,427,454. Much of this value comes from the great appreciation in the property due to Christianity in these fields. Thus a piece of land bought in Korea fifteen years ago for some $3,000 was within ten years sold for $30,000, the proceeds going for grounds and buildings in another part of the city of Seoul, the capital. Alone in our mission fields does the number of our Sunday School scholars exceed the number of our members. Thus while we had an increase there during the quadrennium of 7,677 members there was an increase of 8,663 in Sunday School scholars. We have now 460 Sunday Schools and 26,478 scholars, officers and teachers. We have 70 schools and colleges with 4,586 students. We have five hospitals and dispensaries, three of these in Korea, and during the past year alone there were treated 64,448 patients. We now have 217 missionaries under Parent Board, an increase of 25 during the quadrennium. But as the wives of missionaries are included in this number the total force is not representative of a great Church of nearly two million communicants. Many of these missionaries are now being supported by individuals or churches while the noble Laymen's Movement has led to the erection of some churches and hospitals as well as the support of schools as specials. The total sum subject to appropriation has been limited by the collection of the preceding year. Were it possible to regard the assessment as simply the minimum which must be reached, a sum for the guidance of the pastor but to be far exceeded by the church, the needed income could be had from year to year under the worthy purpose of the laymen to bring up our total to not less than $3,000,000. Detailed reports of our great mission fields, together with statements concerning the Home and Educational departments of the Parent Board including the flourishing Training School, will be made by the Secretaries.

The healthy progress of the work done by the Woman's Foreign

Missionary Society is most encouraging. During the quadrennium our missionary women have raised $941,898, an increase of $395,-194. They report also an increase in the value of their property of $247,000. Their greatest asset, next to their valuable school property in all their fields, is their 90 missionaries, the 88 native helpers and their 4,975 pupils. Most worthy of mention is their Scarritt Bible and Training School with its 257 graduates, 99 of whom are in the foreign field, 39 are deaconesses and 31 home missionaries and 58 trained nurses.

The Woman's Home Mission Society is enjoying great prosperity having raised for connectional work during the quadrennium $622,279, being nearly twice the amount raised the previous four years. They still liberally aid in parsonage building, building or repairing during the quadrennium 747 by the gift of $87,470 and making loans of $32,700 to 61 others. They now have 12 schools, 29 industrial schools and 58 deaconesses. They have 28 organized City Mission Boards and employ 63 trained workers and 318 volunteers. During the quadrennium they have expended for this latter work $136,345. They have long set us the example of great diligence and success and have greatly aided in local work as well. The good women have long exercised most of the rights of the laity that have been exercised by anybody. They memorialize the General Conference on the subject of what they want as well as what they do not want, and you will of course give their memorials due attention without discouraging the laymen who are just finding out what rights have long been unused or forgotten.

Our Publishing Houses

We now have three Publishing Houses, the one at Nashville, the one in Dallas and the one in Shanghai, China, in which we have a half interest. Detailed reports of the work of each will come before you. Through the publication of works translated into the Spanish language the Nashville House has greatly aided our Cuban and Mexican work, and other churches have gladly availed themselves of our excellent translations which are used among Spanish-speaking peoples alike in South America and even in Spain. The weekly journals in Spanish, Portuguese and Chinese are invaluable in our mission fields. It is to be hoped that wise measures may be taken to distribute more widely our various periodical and book publications, so as to justify the name of a Publishing rather than a Printing House.

Our Hospitals

The great Robert A. Barnes Hospital promises to be one of the notable institutions of the world. Its superb site fronting on Forest Park, St. Louis, Missouri, awaits the speedy erection of the group of buildings whose plans have already been approved by the leading hospital experts in the world embracing necessary laboratories for original investigation. Delay has made possible the accumulation of a million for endowment in addition to the cost of grounds, buildings and equipment for a like sum. Under the will of the late Robert A. Barnes, whose mother was a devout member of our Church, this hospital is bound forever to the Methodist Episcopal Church, South, and its funds are administered by three able Trustees who are members of our Church. Most commendable are the Wesley Memorial Enterprises of Georgia which included an excellent hospital. Hospitals enterprised alike in this country and in Mexico, China and Korea are doing important service in ministering to both the bodies and souls of men, women and children, and are invaluable aids in extending the Kingdom of God.

Our Home Base

Methodism has found friendly soil in the new world and its development here most fully realizes the conception of its providential founder, who believed in a strong organization and in large freedom of action inspired by a constraining love on the part of all who belonged to it. The growth of our nation in numbers and resources has been the marvel of history, excelled only by the growth of Methodism in the United States. Thus with her 64,701 organizations Methodism not only ranks first, by the last religious census just published, but she has 30.5 per cent of the whole number of Protestant organizations in the United States. Of the increase in the

13,212 Methodist organizations during the last sixteen years covered by the census, while 15.8 were in the Methodist Episcopal Church 18.7 per cent were in the Methodist Episcopal Church, South. Fully four fifths of all the American Methodists are contained in these two denominations. The proportion of increase during these sixteen years has been 33.3 per cent in the Methodist Episcopal Church and 35.4 per cent in the Methodist Episcopal Church, South. The rate of increase in the population of the Continental United States during this period was 32 per cent while the rate of increase in the membership of the Methodist Episcopal Church, South, was 37 per cent, or 5 per cent greater than the rate of increase of the whole nation.

METHODISM A WORLD-FORCE

We are wont to speak of our nation as a world power, especially now that our flag floats in two hemispheres and our voice has become most influential, whether at the Hague Peace Conference or in securing a Treaty of Peace between warring nations on the other side of the globe. But is not the Church now become a world-force since it is her influence that has helped to make the nation a world power? She has planted the cross and builded churches and schools and hospitals and religious publishing houses and possesses lands far beyond where our national banner can ever float as a symbol of sovereignty. The aim of American Methodism is not to be established by the state but to establish the state. Like her Lord she can say, "My kingdom is not of this world." If her danger once was to aspire to a controlling voice in our national government by virtue of her growing numbers God has strangely saved her from such an entangling alliance. Since our first two bishops, Coke and Asbury, called on the newly-elected President Washington to assure him of the prayers of the people called Methodists in administering the affairs of the new nation, Methodism has ever sought the things which make for civic righteousness and so establish the nation. Men converted and trained at our altars have served the nation in the highest offices of the land, alike in the executive, legislative and judicial departments of the state. McKendree, our first American bishop, was an officer with Washington at the surrender of Cornwallis at Yorktown, and a wise and devout Methodist president was in the White House when Spain surrendered and relinquished her last holdings in the Western Hemisphere. Another of our Presidents, although not himself a Methodist frequently declared his judgment that "Methodism best expresses the religious consciousness of the American people." As pioneers no less than as defenders of the faith we have given our gospel alike to frontiersman and immigrant, and safeguarded our cities, which are our modern frontiers, with wise and righteous laws for the proper observance of the Sabbath and the protection of our homes against the criminal evils of the liquor traffic. No question has ever been raised as to where Methodists would be found on any and all moral questions which affect civil and religious liberty. We gladly point to those states where our influence is confessedly greatest to show the moral and religious character stamped upon the commonwealth. In all this we are but true to our Methodist traditions throughout the world until alike in the mother country, in Canada, in South Africa and in Australasia, Methodism has become a world-force because its citizenship is in Heaven. It has helped to secure and establish religious freedom because its gospel has been the wisdom of God and the power of God wherever preached in all the world. Only an anathema awaits any other gospel.

METHODISM STRONGEST IN THE SOUTH

Now Methodism has always been strongest in the South from the days of Asbury and McKendree, and here was the field of their great labors. More densely populated then Virginia and Maryland gave Jesse Lee to be the apostle of Methodism to New England, and Freeborn Garretson for like service in Halifax and New York. We have been richly repaid with such fruits as Wilbur Fisk and Stephen Olin and Elijah Hedding of Vermont and Joshua Soule of Maine and Henry B. Bascomb and Linus Parker of New York. Considering the relative density of population for more than a century the largest returns of Methodist preaching have always been in the South. Thus in 1860 each church had increased some 300,000

187

in membership since the division sixteen years before, despite the then denser population of the North. In 1864 the General Conference of the Methodist Episcopal Church faced a loss during the quadrennium of five per cent of their membership, while at the close of the Civil War we had 300,000 less members than we had twenty years before. Despite our loss of 130,000 colored members in two years, mostly to the Methodist Episcopal Church and to the African Methodist Episcopal Church, our gain in membership was over 137 per cent while the gain of the Methodist Episcopal Church was 81 per cent, or 56 per cent less. In the meantime we deducted all our colored members which had numbered 207,766 when the war began. It will be remembered that nearly 300,000 of the membership of the Methodist Episcopal Church are colored and from the South, which has ever been such a fruitful field while 305,000 are from foreign mission fields. Reckoning on the basis of white membership alone in the continental United States the disparity is not so great in the comparative number of members, and reckoning on the basis of present density of population the growth of the Methodist Episcopal Church, South, is the larger. In fact, our growth last year showed a net increase of 64,051 while that of the Methodist Episcopal Church was 63,047. Now that we are preaching the gospel in German, French, Italian, Bohemian and Spanish, on our own soil, we may well learn from the enterprise of our sister church which has followed up her religious work begun among the immigrants until she has not less than 66,000 members in Scandinavia, Germany and Italy. To her we rejoice is given the privilege, that Paul longed for, to preach the gospel to them that are in Rome also. Paul after he stopped persecuting them of this Way or Method became himself rather fond of the early Methodists and all later Methodists claim Paul as their apostle, despite some things in his writings hard to be understood as Peter found them. Men have long since found out that with a proper base line, and one or two angles, they have been able to search the whole face of the heavens. Happily our instruments of search are now turned to the great unevangelized world and we are triangulating the field of vision in harmony. Ten years ago our sister church turned over to us, at first cost of equipment, because ours was the far larger work, all her missionary work in Brazil, so that we alone are now working among the Portuguese-speaking people. At the same time by common consent we refrained from entering Porto Rico and the Philippines and they refrained from entering Cuba, where God has so signally blessed our work. In the meantime we are working side by side and in great harmony in Mexico, in Japan, in Korea and in China. Through our wise Joint Commission on Federation may like harmony prevail along the base line in America, lest our field of vision become confused.

METHODISM UNDER THE CONSTITUTION

This being the completion of a century of Methodist history under the Constitution, which our fathers so wisely adopted in 1808, the same year that they gave us our first American bishop McKendree, we are reminded that for a hundred years the bishops have been following the examples set by him of presenting a formal address at the opening session of each delegated General Conference. We may fitly pause to consider to what extent we owe to organized Methodism the strength and efficiency of our system. Our very growth has determined largely our history and our government and polity. The most democratic of all churches, recognizing chiefly the paternal oversight of John Wesley and Thomas Coke and Francis Asbury, who were chosen Superintendents by the whole body of preachers, the Superintendents or bishops were at first members of the General Conferences, with all the rights and privileges of members, making motions and voting. This continued even after the actual membership in the General Conference was limited to ministers of four years' standing. When the rapid growth of the Church, now so widely extended, made necessary a delegated General Conference in 1808, they delegated to it all their power and authority under given restrictions, which restrictive rules could be changed only by the vote of the body of preachers in the Annual Conferences. Membership in this delegated General Conference was determined either by seniority or election, as each Annual Conference might determine for itself, but for a hundred years it has been invariably by election. This became the legislative department of the Church restrained only by the restrictive rules. In doubtful legislation Bishop McKendree sought the judgment of the Annual Conferences, and so held in check what seemed unconstitutional acts. Bishop Soule who drew up the Constitution took the same view as Bishop McKendree as to what powers were delegated to the General Conference, and these views of the two great framers and interpreters of the Constitution ultimately prevailed in that part of American Methodism which for two generations has been known by the legal style of the Methodist Episcopal Church, South.

THE SO-CALLED VETO POWER OF THE BISHOPS

In 1854 a majority vote of the General Conference of the Methodist Episcopal Church, South, gave the bishops authority to interpose their objections to any legislation that was deemed by them unconstitutional, until finally passed upon by the whole body of traveling preachers. This majority action appeared in the Discipline from 1854 to 1870, but without the authority of law, until it was finally adopted by the necessary two-thirds vote of the General Conference of 1870 (there being only four negative votes) followed by the necessary three-fourths vote of the Annual Conferences (there being only nine negative votes) and thus for forty years has been the recognized law of our church. On nothing have our preachers and laymen been more unanimous for it was adopted by the first General Conference where laymen were members. While this law has been invoked only once, and that twenty-four years after its adoption, and in the same city where it was adopted by the General Conference of 1870, it has given dignity and stability to our ecclesiastical legislation which has called forth the just admiration of other churches. Some of the strongest commendations have come from some of the bishops of the Methodist Episcopal Church, living and dead. The supreme and unlimited General Conference ceased to exist after a Delegated General Conference had been provided for under the Six Restrictive Rules, and any assertion of the power of a General Conference as unlimited provides a legislative body which is at the same time judge of the legality and constitutionality of its own acts, "an intolerable state of affairs," as Bishop Merrill strongly declared in print. Before his lamented death Bishop Merrill, the ablest legal mind of the Methodist Episcopal Church, writing of the well-defined differences between the two churches said:

"The most serious difference between the two churches, the one which will be hardest to overcome, has respect not to the episcopacy or its power, but to the General Conference itself. With us the General Conference is supreme in that it is the judge of the constitutionality of its own acts. We have no supreme court, no tribunal of any sort, aside from the General Conference, to which can be referred questions of the legality of the legislation of that body. This is the lame point in our system, and it is a serious defect. In state, national or municipal affairs, such condition would be intolerable. The Southern Church has provided a check upon hasty or inconsiderate legislation, by requiring that when the constitutionality of a measure is questioned, the bishops pass upon it, and submit it to the judgment of the members of the Annual Conferences, according to the plan of amending the Constitution. Without allowing the bishops the right to veto General Conference action, they are empowered to suspend a challenged action till it can be passed upon by the Church in her Constitution-making power and form. That may not be the best possible way of meeting the necessity of judicial opinion of the legislation by the General Conference, but is better than none, and, of course, better than anything we have, as we have absolutely nothing. Some of the leading ministers of the Southern Church have remarked that they never could submit to belong to a church governed by a body made up as is our General Conference, without some sort of judicial body to pass upon the constitutionality of its acts. It is not an easy thing to answer the objection, or to justify the position in this regard which we are forced to occupy. Of course in the negotiations we could confess our weakness and accept their regulation in the absence of any better provision."

OURS A GOVERNMENT OF LAW

Our Church stands for the government of law rather than the government of men, as in the days before the Constitution of the

Church was formed and adopted. Bishop McKendree put himself in accord with the spirit of American institutions by his statesmanlike views in this General Conference of 1808 which gave us at once our Constitution and our great American bishop, who was also justly recognized as our great Chief Justice, our John Marshall in interpreting the Constitution. Our Church was also alike fortunate in being the chosen field of labor of Bishop Joshua Soule, the author of the Constitution, the Senior Bishop of American Methodism in 1844, who cast in his lot with us because we stood for the Constitution of the Church as interpreted by Bishop McKendree and himself. These two great legal minds held that the General Superintendents as elected by the General Conference are repositories of executive power, and are held responsible as overseers of the whole Church, being accountable to the General Conference for their administration. The several Annual Conferences are not independent bodies, as in churches with a congregational form of government simply, but are under the control of general rules and even an order of business in the form of questions adopted by the General Conference, to be enforced by responsible Superintendents. Thus should a preacher depart from the doctrine or discipline of the Church it is the bishop's duty to correct, remove from office or bring him to trial according to the discipline. Should even an Annual Conference dissent from the doctrine or discipline of the Church the bishop should enter his protest and bring the case before the ensuing General Conference, as well as give an account of his own administration.

Thus the better to carry out the ends of legislation the bishops are held responsible as the executive officers of the Church for the faithful administration of the government of the Church according to the provisions of its discipline, as well as for their moral conduct, the doctrines that they preach and for all decisions which they make on questions of ecclesiastical law. As executive officers they safeguard the Annual Conferences against any attacks on their constitutional rights by the legislative department of the Church, and the General Conference against departures either in doctrine or discipline on the part of an Annual Conference. Our Church has been greatly indebted to such legal minds as Bishops Paine and McTyeire in following up the interpretations of Bishops McKendree and Soule who gave us our Constitution. The episcopacy existed before the General Conference, and the Delegated Conference was brought into being under certain restrictive rules, one of which was that they shall not change or alter any part or rule of our government, so as to do away episcopacy, or destroy the plan of our itinerant general superintendency. It was made both general and itinerant that it might the better serve as the executive department of our government, as the General Conference afterwards became the legislative department of the Church. Its creation was that of the whole body of preachers before they created the General Conference with its delegated power and authority. For this view of our government the Methodist Episcopal Church, South, has uniformly stood, as it stands today. Bishops exist for something else than merely to register appointments already prearranged. They are sent out to administer vows and to see that they are observed, to appoint preachers who are in good standing, to form legal districts according to their judgment, and to over-see the spiritual and temporal interests of the Church. Thus have they helped to make the Church increasingly effective for the conversion of the world and in building up believers in their most holy faith.

By virtue of so well defined a system of Church government all ministers at their ordination promise reverently to obey them to whom is given the charge and government over them, and any failure to keep his own ordination vows to exercise justly his authority would be regard as a grave offense on the part of the bishop representing the Church. What is called a strong central government is based upon the fullest confidence in the representative of the Delegated General Conference in serving the highest interests of the whole Church. As moderators of the General Conference, under rules adopted by that body, the bishops, while not obtruding their views in shaping the legislation of the Church, are at times courteously invited to give any information or even judgment, from their supposed wider outlook and disinterested devotion to the best interests of the kingdom of God. It is on them that comes daily the care of all the churches. Our bishops do not discount themselves by foolish and baseless claims as successors of the apostles, nor are they discounted by distrust and discourtesy on the part of their brethren in the ministry, many of whom are their spiritual children to whom they can say, "If to others I am not an apostle, yet at least I am to you; for the seal of mine apostleship are ye in the Lord."

Doctrinal Fidelity

Happily Methodism has never had a doctrinal schism however wide the differences on lay representation and other questions of polity which have led to divisions. All Methodists can heartily agree to the common faith so clearly and admirably stated a decade ago in the Address of the Bishops of the Methodist Episcopal Church, written by the wise and devout Bishop Andrews, honored by universal Methodism, and quoted afresh by Bishop Goodsell in the Episcopal Address at the last General Conference of that Church:

"We believe in one living and personal God, the Father Almighty, who in perfect wisdom, holiness and love pervades, sustains and rules the worlds which he made. We believe in Jesus Christ, His only Son our Lord, in whom dwelt all the fullness of the Godhead bodily, who was in glory with the Father before all worlds, who became flesh and dwelt among us the brightness of the glory of God and the express image of His person, who died for sins, the just for the unjust, that He might bring man to God, who rose from the dead, who ascended on high, having received all power in heaven and on earth, for the completion by grace and judgment of the kingdom of God. We believe in the Holy Ghost, very and eternal God, the Lord and Giver of life, by whose operation on men dead in trespasses and sins they are quickened to repentance, faith and loving obedience, are made aware of their sonship and are empowered to rise into the full stature of men in Christ Jesus. We believe in the impartial love of God to the whole human family, so that none are excluded from the benefits thereof except as they exclude themselves by willful unbelief and sin. We believe that faith in Christ, the self-surrender of the soul to His government and grace, is the one condition upon which man is reconciled to God,

194

is born again, becomes partaker of the divine nature and attains sanctification through the Spirit. We accept the moral law confirmed and perfected by the divine Teacher and set forth authoritatively in the Holy Scriptures; and we believe in eternal consequences of good and evil, inherent in the constitution of the human soul and declared with utmost solemnity by Him, the final Judge of human life."

DIVERSITIES OF GIFTS AND MINISTRATIONS

Having so much in common with our fellow-Methodists throughout the world we rejoice in the honorable part which each has to bear in maintaining at its best the great religious movement of three centuries. Any undue laxity as regards either teaching or discipline on the part of any sister Methodism should make the other representatives the more careful to maintain the standards of life and teaching that God has so signally blessed. If "God made man men that they might help one another" perhaps the priceless heritage of our fathers is thus being the more sacredly guarded. It needed the varied gifts of the Wesleys and Whitefield alike to inaugurate and to perpetuate Methodism, although preaching substantially the same doctrines. Had either Whitefield or Charles Wesley survived John Wesley in the sole leadership it is doubtful whether Methodism would have survived its first century. "Who knoweth whether thou art come to the kingdom for such a time as this?" Now there are diversities of gifts, but the same Spirit. And there are diversities of ministrations but the same Lord.

GOD HAS HONORED OUR LEADERSHIP

As a distinct Methodism, while prayerful observers of what other Churches are enterprising and doing, we have never been content to be mere imitators or followers. The power of initiative has led us to make important changes in our polity when it seemed wise. The Methodist Episcopal Church, South, thus far is the only Methodism that has corrected the confessed weakness of making a General Conference the sole judge of the constitutionality of its own acts, thus leaving unlimited authority unchecked by responsibility. We first dispensed with a fixed probation of six months, an example followed forty years afterward by the Methodist Episcopal Church. The most complete example of lay representation, alike in the Annual and General Conference, was set by us both to the British Wesleyans and to the Methodist Episcopal Church which they have followed only in part even after many years. Our General Conference was first to establish Training Schools for Missionaries, one under the Woman's Foreign Board and the other under the Parent Board of Foreign Missions. The work of women as promoters of parsonage building early recognized by our General Conference as a distinct society has since become The Woman's Home Mission Society with its scores of deaconesses and missionaries. We were the first, through our Board of Missions, to recognize and welcome the Laymen's Missionary Movement which has given new inspiration to all the Churches. Our last General Conference by a large vote showed that we were ready to unite with the other Churches of ecumenical Methodism in such a statement of our fundamental doctrines as might be most adapted to present conditions, especially in our great mission fields, and which three great Methodisms actually have done for the Methodist Church in Japan. We are seeking to adapt our work in congested sections of our large cities by the aid of Institutional Churches and Religious Settlements. Hospitals under the auspices of our Church have been established or are being erected in several of our larger centers. We are studying the confessed mistakes of other churches in the adjustment of their several Home and Foreign Boards of Missions so as to secure for ourselves what is best adapted to our peculiar needs. But while seeking to make full proof of our ministry as a Church we are not unmindful that our very growth in numbers brings the responsibility of an increasingly efficient ministry. Our work needs not to be less evangelistic but more *intensive* to develop our new converts and to make them workmen that shall not be ashamed, alike as students and teachers of the Word of God. Alike by higher standards of admission and by more thorough preparation of our preachers and their deeper consecration, we are seeking the greater efficiency of our preachers who must minister to our growing and devout laymen that are asking to be led to do better and greater things for the Lord.

Our Church and the Negro

No Church has better understood or been more successful in its work for the negro than has ours, until now the more thoughtful men of the nation are turning to us for counsel, and the negro himself for leadership. We have maintained the most cordial relations with our contingent of Negro Methodists so long organically connected with us, and who since their separation have grown from less than 20,000 in 1870 to 233,000 in 1910, with more than $3,000,000 in church property, aside from their schools and colleges. Their growth during the sixteen years covered by the last census was 33.7 per cent, while the growth of the African Methodist Episcopal Church, the largest body of Negro Methodists, was 9.3 per cent. For twenty-five years their oldest colleges which we helped to found and maintain have done much toward recruiting their ministry with worthy leaders. They lack what is all important to their best development as a church—the missionary passion. They are ever being moved with a deepening desire to obey the great Commission. How shall we their spiritual fathers and trusted leaders help them to find themselves in this new age? Under the leadership of men like Bishops Andrew and Capers and Paine a single Annual Conference was known to raise each year as much as $25,000 for missionary work among the negroes. Robert Paine as early as in 1823 offered himself as a missionary to Africa, asking to be accompanied by selected companions from among the negro preachers of the South. That spirit gave us more than 200,000 converts among the negroes in this country before the Civil War, the largest returns from missionary work then known in history. Their songs and prayers safeguarded many a plantation home in the darkest days of fratricidal strife. We owe them no less a debt of gratitude than they owe us, for we were "companions in the sorrowful way." Methodism has never fairly faced Mohammedanism, the most formidable foe of Christianity. Africa is now becoming the great field of the propagandists of the religion of the false prophet. The battle field of the twentieth century is the Dark Continent. Shall Ethiopia in vain stretch out her hands unto God and our great Methodism, more in sympathy with the negro than any other, and better capable of inspiring and directing his labors, have no part in the conquest of the Dark Continent for our Lord? Is not the force actually preparing for our leadership as when young Paine longed to go out to battle? May we not hope and pray that the greatest chapter in the history of missions shall be this yet unwritten chapter which the hand of God shall write in Africa, as he leads our awakened ministers and laymen to their gracious and glorious open door of opportunity?

The Church under the Dominion of the Future

The future of Methodism will depend on how fully she faces the future. Churches like nations may be judged by whether they draw their inspiration and ideals mostly from the past, and so become the slaves of precedent, or from the present and are controlled mostly by questions of present advantage and popularity, or from the principles of right and progress which underlie future achievement. Our Lord sought to make his church the church of the future as He looked steadfastly at the conquest of future generations, alike putting aside the traditions of what had been said by them of the old time and the Jewish crown of his own time, as he went alone to the mountain of vision and of God. True Methodism, like John Wesley in Epworth Church yard preaching to the people from his father's tomb stone, is gratefully reverent toward the past as it seeks to become a part of the kingdom that is yet to come in its fullness. It does not cling to old weapons, however useful in their day, when rifled cannon and weapons of precision are available for its great battles. It adopts nothing because it is the fashion of the hour, whether it be a doctrine or a form. Its strength has been largely in its essential continuity of its teaching and method, while it faces the future because our Lord, in His great commission, has put it under the dominion of the future. She has kept her Lord in the midst by being with Him on the outposts where new conquests are to be made.

When Rome refused the laity any part in the public worship sturdy John Knox, who made the Reformation real in the British Isles, saw how important it was to make congregational worship possible in contrast with mere priestly celebration of the mass in a foreign tongue, so he introduced responsive reading of the Word of God. Mr. Wesley was careful to continue it in all settled congregations and so sought to introduce it in America, despite the more primitive conditions of society here. Our two great Methodisms, after more than a century, determined on a uniform order of worship as well as on uniform catechisms and a joint Hymnal prepared by able Joint Commissions for the use of both Churches. We regret that larger use is not made of them. Our Methodist worship should be uniform as intended by our General Conference, and our people led by our preachers should be encouraged to use it, especially in the towns and cities, and as far as possible in the rural districts. We are in danger of a mongrel worship, when the minister departing from our own form seeks out novelties, such as "silences," "invocations," "blessing the alms bason," "chanting the Lord's prayer," and whatever else he hears some other church is using. Whatever else this is, if in fact anybody dare try to name it, it is not Methodist worship. Our people deserve a more substantial diet than that which the wise men of Methodism have given us. A crude extemporized worship does not belong to the church of the future any more than an undrilled and badly-armed militia can be counted the army of the future.

A Flexible Time Limit

Methodism follows the genius of its founder in seeking to adapt itself to changed conditions, especially on the frontiers and in the great cities. In the more primitive days the interchanges of preachers often took place every six months so as to give the people the most aggressive work in men. Our early fathers did not have many sermons but they were on the great doctrines and they were mighty to the pulling down the strongholds of sin and Satan. The need of more pastoral supervision and the carrying out of larger plans for city church extension work under experienced leaders led to the extension of the limit ultimately with us to four years. Petitions for the further extension of the limit or even its removal will come before you. Our last General Conference made it lawful for the bishops to appoint for a longer period than four years those preachers who were working under the auspices of the Board of Missions, having been accepted by the Committee of Candidates of the Parent Board, "on the basis of candidates for foreign work as to fitness and tenure of office, provided that such city missionary work be subject to the approval of the Annual Conference Board of Missions; and candidates, when accepted, shall be nominated for appointment to the bishop in charge of the conference in which they are to work: provided further that this law shall not be construed to forbid Annual Conference Boards of Missions employing other than such candidates." You will doubtless give careful consideration to the memorials for greater flexibility in the time limit, both as to the wisdom and practicability of such change, and how best safe-guarded. Doubtless the average length of the pastoral term in the event of a change in the law will be less than it is now, the exceptional pastor being the beneficiary of the longer term of service. You will consider equally and primarily the needs of the city population who may seek a greater flexibility in the pastoral term.

MORE ATTENTION TO THE PASTORAL OFFICE

Doubtless more attention among us should be given to the pastoral office if our church realizes to the full the ascension gifts of our Lord, "who when he went up on high gave some to be apostles; and some, prophets; and some, evangelists; and some, pastors and teachers; for the perfecting of the saints, unto the work of ministering unto the building up of the body of Christ." The wise pastor is one who looks upon his church not only as his field but his force, and seeks to develop personal power in each worker. Great pastors make possible great laymen, as great leaders make possible great armies as they follow great plans of battle to mighty victories. Restlessness in the pastoral office is always to be deprecated and disturbs and weakens the flock of Christ. There is no more important, more delightful or more fruitful field of work in all the

Church than the work of the pastorate. It is not length of service always that makes a great influential pastor. Maltbie D. Babcock was found to be such after less than two years of service, even in New York City, because he had magnified the pastoral office in other fields. Let our preachers covet earnestly the best gifts that we may have such pastors as Baxter and Rutherford and Spurgeon and Chalmers and Cuyler, as well as Fletcher of Madeley.

Fraternity and Federation

It is pleasant to report the kindliest relations with other churches. A philanthropist belonging to another communion once directed a considerable sum of money to be used by our church and when asked why he had given it to us rather than to his own church, his reply was, "Because there are more of the Methodists and they get along better with other churches." Our relations with the great Methodist bodies in Canada and in Great Britain and Ireland, as well as with our twin sister, the Methodist Episcopal Church, have been cemented with the usual fraternal visits by chosen messengers who will make their reports. During the present session we will have with us honored representatives from these three great branches of Methodism with which we have so much in common and whose notable successes in all the continents add much to the history of the religious movement called Methodism. It is a part of the unfinished book of Acts—the Acts less of the Apostles than of the Holy Spirit, whose presence in the church is always attended by the emergence of great personalities, men full of faith and the Holy Ghost.

The two General Conferences of American Methodism have long since acted favorably on plans of Federation whereby each Church agrees to respect the work of the other in this country, as is done in foreign fields, and thus avoid both waste and friction. To make operative this wise general plan there will be laid before you additional action taken by the Joint Commission on Federation. Happy and harmonious results have followed where the new plan has had a fair trial, and some communities now have a united Methodism in place of two weak and rival ones. There remains too

201

much unoccupied territory confronting each of these great churches, alike in rural districts and in the cities, to waste men and money in useless and un-Christian competition. Our wise laymen in both churches, now taking so much interest in missionary work, are properly asking how wisely we are using the missionary money in erecting altar against altar in given sections of our common territory and country. Especially worthy of consideration of the Joint Commission on Federation is some wise and statesmanlike scheme for administering under a Joint-Board the educational work being done for the negro by both churches, looking to preparation for missionary work both at home and in the Dark Continent.

The Ecumenical Methodist Conference

The Fourth Ecumenical Methodist Conference meets in 1911 in the city of Toronto. We have already appointed representatives on the Executive Committee. Our Church is entitled to representatives which you will arrange to appoint. These great Pan-Methodist gatherings not only register the numerical and material progress of Methodism but of world-wide Christianity, and they call out the deliverances of our most thoughtful men on the spiritual and practical questions which profoundly interest and concern all Christendom. Other great religious bodies are also much interested in our proceedings.

The Federal Council of the Churches of Christ in America

A Christian philosopher with power of vision said, "The nineteenth century has made the world a neighborhood; shall not the twentieth century make it a brotherhood?" The same churches that have stirred the nation by their great laymen's meetings, whose success has been greatest because they were interdenominational were federated four years ago through the action of the highest ecclesiastical judicatories. Thus thirty-two churches having more than 100,000 preachers and some 17,000,000 communicants, all acknowledging the deity and lordship of Jesus Christ, have unanimously adopted a Plan of Federation which brings to public realization that they are constitutionally federated and so express their Christian fellowship and unity. They believe that the Lord's work can better be done in cooperation than in separation. They thus encourage devotional fellowship and mutual counsel concerning the spiritual life and religious activities of the Churches, better observance of the Sabbath and of the sacredness of the marital bond, deeper and wiser interest in religious education and a higher type of civic righteousness, a better understanding between the Church and the laboring classes who were being separated, the safe-guarding of child labor, the seeking alike the moral and physical welfare of women who are bread-winners, and the fullest cooperation in the work of missions at home and abroad. This wonderful spirit of Christian unity which now marks nine-tenths of all the Protestants in America has inspired all cooperating churches and constitutes a vital condition of all forward movements in Christendom. The deity of our Lord, our mighty Leader in the faith, has been given powerful emphasis, and His followers have never had such faith in the gospel as the power of God unto salvation to every one that believeth.

Our own Church, true to her catholicity and religious spirit, has had no small part in this great Federation of Churches, our General Conference being the first of all the chief judicatories to endorse it. Our influence went far in helping to frame and to adopt by a unamimous vote the original basis of federation, acknowledging the deity of our Lord, and in shaping the Plan of cooperation which has been unanimously adopted by the great churches of Christ in America! The Spirit of Christ so manifestly present in all the meetings and work of the Federal Council of Churches leads to the hope and belief that our Lord will mightily use this great movement in the furtherance of His kingdom in all the world, that men might know that the Father has sent Him and that there is one flock and one shepherd. The once lonely watchmen are now seeing eye to eye and together are they lifting up the voice to sing. The great movement is even more an inspiration than an organization and is bringing a Christian atmosphere and climate into all the world-field. Even Rome is studying a voluntary unity in contrast with a compulsory unity to which all else is sacrificed.

Change of Name

The tendency is always to give the shorter name whether to a church or to a railroad. Thus our nearest neighbors all through our common territory, though their legal style is The Presbyterian Church in the United States, are usually, almost invariably called "The Southern Presbyterian Church." So the same tendency is observed with regard to our Church which in 1844 was known as "The Southern General Conference of the Methodist Episcopal Church," while the twin sister was called "The Northern General Conference of the Methodist Episcopal Church." We shortened it a year later to The Methodist Episcopal Church in the South, and then our present name The Methodist Episcopal Church, South, on the theory of Carlyle that "the nation that shortens its weapons extends its boundaries." Whatever our legal style we will always be called Southern Methodists as in our great federal and fraternal gatherings our brethren are called Northern Methodists. In all the mission fields and great Councils our fellow-Christians are given to recognizing each other by what they are doing for Christ rather than by what name they bear or what section they hail from. No greater calamity can come to a church than to aspire to be the American or national church, with its natural tendency to claim all that is in sight. We are too world-wide to seek to be simply national. Sympathizing with our Northwestern brethren, whose fathers welcomed us because of our name, and because we preached Christ and Him only, we see no sufficient reason for any change. Moreover the sense of the whole church was taken comparatively a few years ago on the change of our name to the Methodist Episcopal Church in America, the same to be reported to the General Conference of 1886. The bishops reported that only 91 had voted for the change and 3,415 had voted against it. The Episcopal Address reporting the result of the vote added, "It is to be hoped that a corporate name which was first introduced by Bishop Paine and adopted by the Committee of Nine into their report to the General Conference of 1844, which was further recognized at Louisville in 1845 and in the formation of our first General Conference in 1846, which is the title by which all our lawsuits for the recovery of property was known and in favor of which the Supreme Court made its decree, the title and name by which we were known through the ample and deep experiences of the Civil War, the name which was reaffirmed by a constitutional vote of the Church in 1866 and 1867, and by which the status of our Church was recognized by the Cape May Commission in 1876, and about which our whole domestic and foreign missionary work has clustered, will be accepted fully and forever as the primal and final designation of our beloved Methodism." Since our greatest prosperity has been given us since 1886, about doubling our membership and resources, we dare think we hear an added testimony in the "Yea," saith the Spirit, "for their works do follow them."

The Endowment Fund for Superannuates

Ours is the first Church to inaugurate on a large and worthy scale an Endowment Fund for Superannuates. This was done on the recommendation of the bishops eight years ago when the General Conference resolved to establish a connectional fund of not less than $5,000,000 for that purpose. Already encouraging progress has been made and the present assets of the Fund are estimated at $251,873. The Board of Trustees having the matter in hand are much encouraged by some liberal legacies known to have been made for this Fund. While many Annual Conferences have endowment funds for their own superannuates and conference claimants, this connectional fund is shared by all and takes care of worthy men in smaller and frontier conferences. Some modification in plan of collections and disbursements will be asked by the Board of Trustees which will be indicated in their memorial.

Other Methodisms Lead Us in Sunday Schools

It is a notable fact that we are behind other Methodisms in the relative number of Sunday-School scholars compared with church members, while the present opportunity of the Church in reaching the young was never greater. Thus the Wesleyan Methodists of England, our only true "mother church," report their members and probationers as 520,868 and their Sunday-School enrollment as 987,953. The Primitive Methodists of England report 212,168 members and probationers and 465,531 scholars. The United Methodist Church reports 186,905 members and 323,675 scholars. The Australasian Methodist Church reports 150,751 members and 231,553 scholars. The Methodist Episcopal Church reports 3,442,631 members and probationers and 3,368,162 scholars. We report 1,822,402 members and 1,270,995 Sunday-School scholars. That our shortage is not due to lack of children is manifest from the fact that in the sixteen states most occupied by us there are 4,663,193 of school age who are not in the Sunday School, or 400,000 more than there are now in the Sunday Schools of all the Churches. Here is our field of untold riches. Here are the reserves on which the Methodism of today must draw to make the aggressive forces of the Methodism of the future, if we maintain anything like our primacy among the churches.

THE TWO PROCESSIONS

Bishop Keener startled the whole Church twenty years ago by pointing to the two processions to be seen on any Sunday morning, a procession of adults going to Church and a procession of children coming from the church at the hour of preaching service. Nor has that latter procession ceased to move from the preaching service to the church's great loss, often hopeless loss. While 80 per cent of our church membership comes from the Sunday School there are 60 per cent of the Sunday School that are not reached. The churches that have the most dependable growth are those that pay most attention to gathering and retaining their youth under competent instruction, and that have the largest number of Sunday-School scholars as compared with church members. Under wise pastors and capable laymen much stress is being properly put upon what is called "The Bible School," where efforts are being successfully made to gather and retain those of all ages in intelligent study of the Word of God, and so to create a passion for it. With the work properly graded and under teachers truly equipped the whole church develops a hunger for the Word. The pastor thus finds an increased demand for expository preaching and often the problem of the second service is solved, as one service is given to this helpful and instructive form of preaching where old and young are held and fed.

Despite the fact that so much of our territory is rural and with a nearly 85 per cent of our population living in the country, yet several of our Annual Conferences, like the Western Virginia and Holston, under these conditions report as many Sunday-School scholars as church members. The Los Angeles and Montana Conferences and the Asiatic and South Brazil fields report like favorable returns. Were all the conferences equally diligent and enterprising we would have some 600,000 more youth under our religious instruction, and that many more reserves to draw on in building up the kingdom of Christ. Nor does this include the added families who may be reached through their youth. In view of our approaching change in the water front of the country and the great increase in the numbers dwelling in cities and towns, with greater accessibility to the churches, we should have a Sunday School census larger than that of church members, in place of a ratio of 68 per cent as now, and with slight change for many years. The friendly disposition toward religion, even in the public schools and state institutions of higher grade, with the situation uncomplicated by the presence of a large foreign population of an alien religion, makes the outlook encouraging throughout our bounds.

The Epworth Leaguers

Our pastors have not always rightly appraised the work and worth of the Epworth League and have shown a consequent lack of zeal in its behalf despite its distinct place in the life of youth. During the last twenty years it is estimated that a million of our youth have been passing under its influence. They have thus acquired a richer knowledge of the history of the Church and of Missions and a new sense of responsibility for the church of the future. Through the faithful efforts of the Leaguers it was made possible to open our mission in Korea besides the valuable help that has been given in other fields. The quadrennium closes with some 100,000 Leaguers whose contributions for the past year reach $75,000. During its history some 700 young ministers have shared the privileges and inspiration of the Epworth League. Like the Sunday School, its ranks need constant recruiting, and all the more as there is not an adequate substitute for it in our economy. Properly used it becomes a veritable training school for Christian workers. Thus may our young people learn the expulsive power of a new affection in place of the love of pleasure which from the days of Tertullian has always been a stronger motive than even fear of martyrdom.

Our Vanderbilt University

We call it "our Vanderbilt" because it should find a place in the heart of the whole Church to which it belongs. Our Church has from the beginning of its existence greatly rejoiced in the liberal gifts from without that made possible the Vanderbilt University, when our plans for a Central University proved abortive for lack of both interest and means, as already different parts of the Church had weak and struggling colleges which prevented any united effort on a large scale for a great central institution. The General Conference in 1874 recorded its appreciation of the first notable gift from the Vanderbilt family "to build and endow a university under the control of the Methodist Episcopal Church, South." For twenty years the new university was the central institution of eight patronizing conferences which confirmed the Trustees chosen by the Board of Trust, who under the charter were vested with power to fill any vacancies subject to such confirmation. In the language of the Board of Trust and under its authority "to make the University entirely connectional and to relate it to the whole Church" a committee consisting of A. W. Wilson, C. B. Galloway and E. R. Hendrix drew up and presented a memorial asking the General Conference of 1898 "to accept the relation and control of the Vanderbilt University hitherto held by the eight patronizing conferences." The General Conference accepted that responsibility to take effect as soon as the consent of all the patronizing conferences was obtained, full legal steps and all the preliminary steps were taken. The action cited the fact that the title of the property was vested in the Board of Trust for the said patronizing conferences of our Church. Some of the bishops questioned from the beginning their legal right under the charter to act as Trustees without being chosen and wishing that no legal question be raised as to the effect of their votes on the sale of bonds and other changes in the vested funds necessary from time to time, favored election by the Board and confirmation by the Board of Education to which the General Conference had given the authority of confirmation. Accordingly on recommendation of a committee composed largely of the bishops in attendance the Board chose five of the bishops in order of seniority, and they were duly confirmed as Trustees by the Board of Education.

The last General Conference appointed an able Commission of jurists who were instructed: "1. To inquire into and determine the relations of the Vanderbilt University to the Methodist Episcopal Church, South. 2. To take legal steps, if necessary, to perfect the transfer of the University from the patronizing conferences to the General Conference of said Church. 3. To define the charter rights of the bishops of said Church." This Commission duly reported their findings and, as instructed, made their report to the College of Bishops, to the Board of Education, and to the Vanderbilt Board of Trust, giving it as their judgment that no clause in the charter conferred any authority in law upon the bishops to act as members of the Board of Trust. They concluded also that the ownership of the University by the Methodist Episcopal Church, South, had to be through the Board of Trust who hold the title. They also gave as their opinion that under the charter of the University and the laws of Tennessee the bishops of the Methodist Episcopal Church, South, sustain the relation of visitors to the Vanderbilt University, defining the office of visitor to be judicial, not executive or legislative. The visitors are to judge whether the acts of the Trustees are within the laws of the institution, and whether the by-laws are in the spirit of the trust. The bishops on receiving the report of the Commission accepted accordingly the responsibility as authorized by the action of the General Conference in appointing the Commission, and will continue to exercise it when deemed necessary. The Commission while declaring a formal transfer of rights and authority by the eight patronizing conferences to the General Conference not absolutely necessary, nevertheless advised such a transfer, which accordingly has been made by most of the interested conferences in the very form and language suggested by the Commission.

The action of the Commission being certified to the Vanderbilt Board of Trust the following action in the handwriting of Bishop Galloway was unanimously taken: "1. We cordially receive the action of the Commission and direct that it be filed with the records of the Board. 2. We hereby express our appreciation of the ability and fidelity with which the members of the Commission have discharged their important duties. 3. Recognizing and rejoicing in the ownership of the Church in Vanderbilt University, and all the responsibilities arising therefrom, we welcome any supervision by the College of Bishops that may aid us in executing the great trust committed to our hands, 'so as to insure the observance of the charter, the conditions of specific gifts, and the statutes of the states.'"

The high standing of the Vanderbilt University, its able faculty and with more than 1,000 students in all its departments, despite its inadequate although growing resources, is a matter of satisfaction and a cause for gratitude to the whole Church. The able Board of Peabody Trustees in closing up their great trust under the will of Mr. George Peabody, determined to donate $1,000,000 as endowment to the "George Peabody Teachers College," on the condition that it be located near the Vanderbilt University so that there might be suitable exchange of work to the mutual advantage of both institutions. This will secure for the South a genuine Teachers College of the highest grade. The two institutions are under entirely separate Boards of Control and will remain so, seeking only effective cooperation, making not a single but a double star in the educational firmament, and the creation of a great educational center where its influence will be most wide-reaching and beneficent. In view of this enlarged opportunity of Vanderbilt for reaching the future teachers of the South all the more important is the speedy completion of the endowment of the Chair of Religious Pedagogy, for whose establishment the last General Conference authorized the use, to the extent of $50,000, of the undirected Children's Day funds. In order to complete that endowment this year, if possible, the Sunday School Board has postponed Children's Day to June 12th.

THEOLOGICAL EDUCATION

Deeply impressed by Paul's frequent injunction that the preacher "be apt to teach," our founders, themselves the sons of a great University were wont to meet in the Holy Club at Oxford, the better to know and interpret the Holy Scriptures. The pains-taking exegetical studies of the Greek New Testament used in those meetings are to be seen in the Bodleian Library. John Wesley translated and published a revised New Testament ninety years before our modern Revised New Testament was published, and the foremost New Testament scholars who gave us the latter gratefully acknowledged their debt to Mr. Wesley's translation of the previous century. Our Church cannot be true to her traditions and ignore the best results of consecrated learning, and we are unwilling to be classed with those provincial Churches which are unfriendly to sacred learning. The Preachers' Institutes, being held annually at Vanderbilt and other educational centers, are a sort of University Extension Course where some of the leading and most reverent biblical scholars from both sides of the Atlantic have awakened a deeper passion for the study of the revealed Word. Unless our young preachers follow safe and reverent guides they may follow blind leaders into the ditch of confusion and doubt. The great need of all of our centers of learning is the evangelistic spirit and the testifying to the things we know, proclaiming our beliefs, not our doubts. Genuine revivals of religion which clarify the brain and warm the heart as well, should be sought and expected annually in each of our institutions of learning under the leadership of our wisest preachers who are specially adapted to such evangelistic work. Ideals of life formed in a Christian college have always wielded large and permanent influence alike upon ministers and laymen.

A study of local conditions in that section of the country where our Church is naturally expected to do its best work shows that we have been too indifferent to the theological education of our ministers, even being mostly dependent on outsiders for the endowment of our sole department of theological training. Single institutions for the theological education of the negro have larger endowments and a larger attendance than ours. The Baptists who labor everywhere side by side with and constitute with us so large a share of the Protestants in the United States have a theological seminary with over 300 students and an investment in plant and endowment of some $2,000,000. We rejoice in their wise example and in their increasing interest in an efficient ministry to which they owe so much. Our twin sister, the Methodist Episcopal Church, has ten theological seminaries in this country, with 840 students and an investment of over $4,000,000 in separate buildings and endowment. Our brethren of the Northern Presbyterian Church have twelve separate theological seminaries, representing an investment of $10,000,000, with over 700 students for the ministry. It is conceded by those best acquainted with the conditions that the most successful theological seminaries are those which make the strongest appeal as resting on their own foundations and with their own distinct endowments. Our largest givers to Church beneficences have their local colleges to which they are attached and where the demand for financial aid is great, but they might become interested in a theological seminary resting on a foundation of its own and not a mere department in some other institution where it must share with other departments alike in the attention and income of an institution under a common Board.

The demand of the laity for better equipped and more efficient preachers must be met in part by themselves in providing greater facilities for ministerial education. The educated man has the ear of the educated and no loss can be more damaging, next to losing the ear of the poor to whom the gospel must be preached, if the credentials of our Lord be claimed, than to have no longer the ear of the educated and influential in a community. It was this neglect in France that made possible the French Revolution, and the loss of the influence of the Church. The growing interest in education for our children means an increased interest in the education of our preachers if our children be satisfied with their ministry. Better facilities for the education of our young preachers are necessary if we would not expose them to the allurements of better equipped theological seminaries all over the land, and to the ministry of other Churches. It becomes the Church to concern herself about her ministers, alike as regards their reenforcement in numbers and in quality of leadership. Why should there not be the earnest intercession in every home, as in Scotland, that at least one noble son be called to the ministry of the word. It is ascertained that sixty-seven per cent of our ministerial candidates come from homes of family prayer. Above all should the devout and watchful pastor seek to impress upon promising young men the supreme claims of the Lord of the harvest, so that every charge might have some worthy representative in the Christian ministry. Only from the bosom of a living Church can God win a living ministry. One command of the Lord is as enduring as the great commission itself, "Pray ye the Lord of the harvest that He will thrust out laborers into His harvest." The very perpetuation of the ministry is conditioned on prayer.

Our Board of Education

After too long delay in creating a Board of Education we owe much to it for standardizing our institutions of learning, for valuable aid to some struggling but promising institutions, and for seeking to foster the spirit of education in its best sense and with its worthiest ends. Especially helpful has it been to the educational work of the Colored Methodist Episcopal Church in America, five of whose institutions are aided by our Board of Education and have been the better brought to a warm place in the hearts of our colored brethren whose giving for Christian education has been notable. The Correspondence School under the auspices of the Board has now an enrollment of more than a thousand preachers and is doing a worthy and commendable work alike for the undergraduates and those who are taking a post-graduate course. It prepares the way for as well as supplements the work of our Theological Department for those who would make full proof of their ministry. The literature issued by the Board of Education helps to extend the influence of the able educational addresses given under its auspices.

213

LOYALTY OF OUR COLLEGES

While rejoicing in the large and helpful gifts which have come to some of our colleges like Randolph-Macon, Wofford, Millsaps and Hendrix from noble philanthropists who are using their large wealth in the interest of education, preferably for established institutions with a recognized mission, we express both the hope and conviction that no gift from any source be received by way of our institution that means the weakening of its recognized obligation to the Church which fosters it or loosens the bonds which unite it to the heart and confidence of the Church which founded it. By the Christian college is not meant among us one under narrow and close ecclesiastical control as in the Church of Rome, but one whose Board and Faculty are composed of Christian men who love and exalt our divine Lord and Saviour. It is Christianity that has made man a thinker, and only under Christian auspices can there be the broadest and fullest investigation, and so the completest education which trains the mind and heart and will to loftiest worship and to noblest character. While we cannot blame philanthropists for insisting that we make provision for our own theological education, as every self-respecting Church should do, we deem that no money could be less acceptable to our Lord than that which is obtained by compromise on the part of the receiver that would make Christ less than supreme in his own Church. Let no indifference to the work of Christian education on the part of preachers or laymen be used as an excuse for seeking help outside the Church under conditions that would lead us to deny the Lord that bought us, or to renounce His bride. Our Lord lays upon his Church the responsibility of both looking unto and hastening the coming of His kingdom. The noble instances, mostly of Christian liberality, amounting during the past year to nearly $150,000,000, show that the good seed are the children of the kingdom who believe in Christ and are willing to entrust their millions to men who love and follow Him. True Christian education must ultimately rest on Christian giving. The Church administers these great trusts not as a mob but through chosen and trusted representatives and thus the better safe-guards them.

214

A Creative Religious Epoch

It was the remark of a philosopher that "there are certain epochs in the world's history that may be called creative epochs, when intense feelings elevate all the powers supernaturally. Such for example was the close of the eighteenth century when the revolutionary spirit of the age manifested itself in the creation of an almost preternatural abundance of military talent." How can we account, in the first age of Christianity, for the emergence of great personalities, men brought to their best, save under the Holy Spirit who brought them to the highest state of efficiency? They were good men and full of the Holy Ghost and of faith, and much people were added unto the Lord. The mighty tides of the Spirit lifted men above the commonplaces of an unheroic age like the 18th century and developed great leaders capable of planning great campaigns on two continents. The missionary era of the Church began under such impulses a century ago for Methodism has always been a missionary movement with a mission to spread scriptural holiness over these lands. It was not individualism run mad with the new wine of liberation from a great state Church. It caught the true spirit of the Church militant and became a militant Church, with elements of true leadership. It has been the spiritual cavalry of modern Christianity ready to reconnoiter or to lead the charge. Nowhere is a minister of a secular spirit more out of place than in the spiritual atmosphere of self-surrender where men are willing to spend and be spent as true soldiers of the Lord Jesus. Its itinerancy has been most exacting of its leaders whose circuits have taken in the circumference of the planet, some never to return from their distant outposts of service. Other churches are studying its economy and are begging for a better supervision of their frontiers and of their foreign missions. With its experience, its doctrines, its practice and its discipline, it is not strange that Methodism added more converts among the heathen last year than any other form of religious activity. It used to be said, "Only France can destroy France." Only Methodism can destroy Methodism. Our foes like the foes of the early Church come from within—self-indulgence, pride, ambition, worldliness, contentions, these alone can stay our triumphant march and progress until the Lord's own kingdom come. Spiritual elevation is absolutely essential to lift us over the bar and out into the open sea of largest success for Christ in these latter days when the total membership of the mission churches has more than doubled in fifteen years. But while a million souls have been won for Christ in heathen lands in that time the spiritual quickening of one land expects a million added this year in Korea alone. The harvest is now a hundred-fold where we had been content with five-fold. The 2,097,963 native Christians last year gave $4,859,906, a sum far exceeding all that Christian America was doing not many years ago.

The rejuvenescence of the American Bible Society for its indispensable work by large gifts of some $2,000,000 last year, the present gathering of 5,000 laymen in Chicago who have caught the vision during the most wonderful campaign reaching from sea to sea that any land ever knew, the assembling of the World Missionary Conference in the land of Livingstone and Duff, as ships are now weighing anchor in nearly every port, with our own representatives sharing in the responsibilities and successes of all these movements, tell of a new religious era when the kingdom of heaven suffereth violence and all men begin to press into it. There must be no surcease in that war. The forces of Christendom are being mobilized "The Son of God goes forth to war, Who follows in His train?"

With a work so vast and the field so ripe and the battle not half-won we sorely miss not a few of our tried and valiant leaders who as delegates or bishops we were wont to meet in our great quadrennial gathering—Paul Whitehead, Young J. Allen, John M. Mason and John W. Heidt, honored and loved members of more than one General Conference, until it seemed that we could not do without them at the secretary's table, or guarding the legislation on the floor of the house, or sending out the clarion call for laborers for the ripening harvest. Never in a single quadrennium have we been called to bury so many of our General Superintendents. Fourteen names, less one, representing all the living bishops who presided at Birmingham, were signed to the Journal of the last General Conference, and the Church rejoiced in the hope that most would be permitted to report for renewed service at this session. Two had asked relief from their exacting duties, and two had been commended by the General Conference to the consideration of their colleagues for lighter work, until their health became more vigorous. The remaining ten little thought that not less than three of their number would be called to join the three taken from the confessedly feeble to whom had been assigned lighter work or none. Within six months after adjournment occurred the almost tragic death of Bishop John J. Tigert, just as he reached his fiftieth year, and after holding but one Annual Conference. Strong in intellect as in body, with a love for all that was good in philosophy and theology which he had made his life study, this able Review editor, blessing the church with his valuable service as guide in the vast field of literature, this efficient Secretary of several General Conferences, this specialist in the constitutional history of Methodism, this diligent student and fervid and clear expositor of the Holy Scriptures, this growing scholar and Christian, like the eloquent Bascomb from his same native Kentucky, gave the Church only a few months of episcopal service where she fondly expected many fruitful years.

The sweet-spirited, genial Alexander Coke Smith soon followed his younger colleague. Those who knew his feeble frame rejoiced with misgivings in his sanguine hopes of restored health as he longed to live and give the Church a score of years of faithful service. A beloved pastor in village and city, an esteemed professor in more than one of our church colleges, a tender preacher because a sympathizing friend, delighting to tell on the house-tops what he heard in the ear in his enforced retirement, he passed from us after a little more than a quadrennium of episcopal service but leaving a lasting memory of his gifts and graces.

The Church still deemed herself happy so long as the St. John of the College of Bishops was left, John Cowper Granbery with his modest but ripe Christian character, a life-long sufferer from pain of which he never complained, brave on the battle-field as he was searching and tender in the pulpit, a model preacher in his homiletical and spiritual treatment whether of a topic or a text, a wise and inspiring teacher of preachers young and old, whether in the Vanderbilt Wesley Hall or in the busy general pastorate, living to

serve the Church as a bishop for nearly a quarter of a century, as a
thinker favorably known outside of his own communion, a just man,
honored and loved by great and humble, "the beloved disciple" has
left us the legacy of an unsullied name and of a fragrant piety like
that of Tholuck who said, "The heart makes the theologian." No
wonder the wise McTyeire said of him before his election, "Granbery is not much talked of now for one of our new bishops but
when the Church gets to praying they will think of him." How glad
the angels must have been to see him who was so long a time-
exposure of his ascended Lord.

William Wallace Duncan soon followed his Virginia colleague.
Of noble presence and genial nature, there was no more tireless
worker among us, knowing no period of rest or recreation, which
he so much needed in order to do his best work and to still his
anxious spirit ever concerned for the kingdom of God, a lover of
books and of men, a teacher in the pulpit and in the chair, a welcome and radiant guest, loved of little children as was his Lord,
working in many fields and never deeming his work complete,
whole-souled and generous to every worthy cause, blessing all with
what he was even more than with what he did, a grateful Church
will never cease to cherish his memory and to love him.

Chosen to his high office at the same time and on the same ballot
with Bishop Duncan was the Chrysostom of the Church, Charles
Betts Galloway. With native oratorical gifts of a high order he
consecrated to the pulpit what would have won lasting fame in
the Senate or at the bar, for he had known in early manhood the
meaning of a surrendered life. With capacity for leadership that
made him the foremost citizen, because the most useful, in his native state, progressive but not radical, committed to all that made for
civic righteousness and wise in knowing just what was fitted to the
hour, the eloquent advocate of temperance because the friend of
humanity, beloved of the negro as of the white, and ever addressing the largest congregations of both, sensitive to criticism but
heroic in action whether in the black belt or in the university or the
capital, he commanded the eager ears of all good men and led them
to victory. Incapable of envy his genial soul rejoiced in the success

of his brethren and true as Jonathan, he prized a friend more than a throne, wise in planning and faithful and tireless in execution he had all the elements of a great bishop. Charles B. Galloway was chosen to preach the opening sermon at the last Ecumenical Methodist Conference as Matthew Simpson and William Arthur had been chosen for like service at the other two Pan-Methodist gatherings, and he ranks with these and other great masters of assemblies. No man among us so fully responded to the demands of a great occasion and none was more worthy of the epitaph of John the Baptist—"a burning and a shining light." Alas! he shone because he burned, and in twenty years of episcopal service he gave the Church forty years of his strength. He made our name known to all Methodism and to the saints of all the Churches. Stricken in the midst of the battle he died, like Paul, still planning great things for his Lord. What a meeting between apostle and bishop in the presence of their Lord, as each bore on his person the marks of the Lord Jesus.

When lonely Eve bereft of her children welcomed to her arms a third son she called his name Seth, for she said, "God hath set me another son in place of Abel." He was to be the setting that should produce a forest of noble trees for the garden of the Lord. Once our Church had an Enoch who walked with God and was not for God took him, but his going made heaven nearer. A generation later many who knew Enoch Mather Marvin were reminded of him in Seth Ward, a true itinerant, of native, homely strength, simple in tastes, waxing stronger in intellect and in grasp of truth, presenting the great doctrines with clearness and unction, sympathetic and unselfish, wise and just in counsel and tireless in service. He became a revelation to the whole Church as wisely selected by the Board of Missions as Assistant Missionary Secretary, not being sufficiently known to be the choice of the General Conference, he went abroad from his native Texas to preach a gospel mighty enough to save a world. The qualities that made him great as a pastor in Houston and Galveston, in time of disaster, were even more fruitful of good in the foreign fields where he wrought as Secretary and bishop. The Church was fast learning to appraise him at his true worth as a

219

bishop when he went abroad to die in Asia, for which he had so often pleaded at the bar of the Christian conscience. Domestic love claimed his body to rest in American soil but his great soul goes marching on to find its truest and satisfying rest in the glorious vision of a saved world.

Only in the case of Bishop Ward's conferences in Eastern Asia did any conference lack the presidency of one of our number. By exchanging work we have been able without inconvenience or delay to meet all the conferences throughout the quadrennium, even during this last year when so greatly bereft. With the growing demands of our work alike in Eastern Asia and in South America it is deemed important that we make an annual visit to each of those fields as to the conferences in North America. In view of the depletion of our ranks we recommend the election of additional bishops, praying that God may make good His promise made to His church through Jeremiah, "I will give you pastors according to mine heart, which shall feed you with knowledge and understanding." They will not be perfect men, else they would be the only perfect men in a Church full of imperfect men. If ever perfect, they will be made perfect through suffering, as there shall come upon them daily the care of all the churches, as upon those who are the servants to all.

HALF OF OUR STRENGTH UNUSED

Great as have been the successes of the Church, we lament that they have not been greater. We have not put forth half our strength. It is harvest-time, and requires toil by day and night to gather in the harvest which has come from the sowing of our fathers, as they sought to serve their generation by the will of God. Other men have labored, and we have entered into their labors. Great as have been our achievements, they ought to have been greater, and they do not equal our opportunities for which we are responsible. After we have done what we have rather than what we might, we confess ourselves unprofitable servants, and pray for wisdom and grace to do better work for our Lord to hasten his kingdom. We dare not boast even while we rejoice in our Lord's leadership and blessing.

THE EPISCOPAL ADDRESS

"Lord God of hosts, be with us yet,
Lest we forget, lest we forget."

"For of him, and through him, and to him are all things: to whom be glory forever."

New Yor ██████ **eehan** has had
over thi ██████ legions of fans
with he ██████ pathian tales. She has received
numerou ██████ throughout her career, including being a
nominee for the Romance Writers of America RITA and
receiving a Career Achievement Award from *Romantic Times*,
and has been published in multiple languages and in many
formats, including audio book, ebook and large print.

Visit Christine Feehan online:

www.christinefeehan.com
www.facebook.com/christinefeehanauthor
https://twitter.com/AuthorCFeehan

Praise for Christine Feehan:

'After Bram Stoker, Anne Rice and Joss Whedon,
Feehan is the person most credited with
popularizing the neck gripper'
Time magazine

'The queen of paranormal romance'
USA Today

'Feehan has a knack for bringing vampiric Carpathians
to vivid, virile life in her Dark Carpathian novels'
Publishers Weekly

'The amazingly prolific author's ability to create
captivating and adrenaline-raising worlds is unsurpassed'
Romantic Times

915 00000099853